A Nutritional Approach to
Restoring Health and Wellness

Dairy-Free KETO COOKING

with 160 Squeaky-Clean
Low-Carb, High-Fat Recipes

Kyndra D. Holley

Victory Belt Publishing Inc.
Las Vegas

First published in 2019 by Victory Belt Publishing Inc.

ISBN-13: 978-1-628603-69-9

The author is not a licensed practitioner, physician, or medical professional and offers no medical diagnoses, treatments, suggestions, or counseling. The information presented herein has not been evaluated by the U.S. Food and Drug Administration, and it is not intended to diagnose, treat, cure, or prevent any disease. Full medical clearance from a licensed physician should be obtained before beginning or modifying any diet, exercise, or lifestyle program, and physicians should be informed of all nutritional changes.

The author claims no responsibility to any person or entity for any liability, loss, or damage caused or alleged to be caused directly or indirectly as a result of the use, application, or interpretation of the information presented herein.

Front and back cover photography by Hayley Mason and Bill Staley

Cover design by Justin-Aaron Velasco

Interior design and illustrations by Yordan Terziev, Boryana Yordanova, Charisse Reyes, and Elita San Juan

Printed in Canada

TC 0119

Dedication

My husband pointed out to me that I have dedicated every book I have ever written to him. I guess I never really thought about it, but it makes sense because he is the single biggest source of light, joy, and love that I've ever known. So I will leave it at that. I dedicate this book to my one and only, Guacamole Jon.

You didn't think I could stop there, did you? I'm way too verbose for that…

I also dedicate this book to all of you out there who are looking for something better—a better way to live, a better way to feel, and a better way to be. It's never too late to embrace change and design the life of your dreams. It is through our struggles that we find strength and by way of resiliency that we experience growth. Just know that you are not alone and that you are capable of far more than you give yourself credit for.

> "What if you were assigned this mountain to show others that it can be moved?"
>
> —**Unknown**

In memory of Jack and Bella Little. *I hope you are running wild and free over the Rainbow Bridge.*

Table of Contents

LETTER TO THE READER

Hey, friends! First, let me start by thanking you for supporting this book. It means the world to me. I am truly honored and humbled by the fact that I get to do something day in and day out that I am passionate about and that sets my soul on fire. None of it would be possible without all of you. So THANK YOU from the bottom of my keto-loving heart.

As you hold this book in your hands and flip through its pages, I hope that you can feel the love and passion that I poured into it. My goal with this book was to pick up where *Craveable Keto* left off and to provide a resource for anyone trying to navigate their way through a dairy-free ketogenic lifestyle, whether it be due to food allergies, autoimmunity, gut health, or just personal preference. Whatever your reason, finding delicious keto recipes that are free of dairy can be a challenge. My mission in creating this book was to offer you a dairy-free keto road map that does not require unfamiliar specialty ingredients or a gourmet kitchen. The recipes in this book are rooted in simplicity and call only for ingredients that you can find at your local grocery store. As a person who is not a fan of coconut and feels that it really has no place in savory dishes, I also wanted to provide dairy-free substitutions that go far beyond coconut.

In addition to showing you that a dairy-free approach to keto is anything but bland and boring, I hope to help guide you down the path to restoring health and wellness while living a lifestyle that nourishes you in mind, body, and spirit. Whether your goal is to lose weight, heal your body, or simply find your own personal version of food freedom, this book is designed to help you achieve it.

If you suffer from dairy intolerances or food allergies, then this book is for you. If you are someone who just loves easy-to-make, delicious food, then this book is also for you. I've covered all the bases to make sure that this book includes a little something for everyone, even including suggestions for adding or reintroducing dairy for all my fellow quesophiles.

In addition to the recipes, you will find five different seven-day meal plans—egg-free, nightshade-free, nut-free, sweetener-free, and 30-minute meals—as well as a ton of valuable resources to help you find the version of keto that suits your body's unique nutritional needs. There is no one-size-fits-all approach to life, and there is certainly more than one way to successfully live a ketogenic lifestyle.

My hope for this book is that it becomes a well-loved, tattered-up, spilled-on fixture in your kitchen for many years to come.

From my heart to your kitchen,

Introduction

MY STORY

When I look back on where it all started—you know, all this weight and food business—I see that while my issues with weight developed a little later than I realized, my poor relationship with food began far earlier than I realized. Many of the years I spent thinking I was fat were in fact just years spent standing out from my peers. Being different. Looking different. Not fat, just different. I was taller, and I developed earlier. This made me stand out as larger than the other kids, because I was. But the thing I didn't recognize was that it didn't make me fat or even overweight; it just made me different. Unfortunately, as many of us know all too well, being different is not something that is typically celebrated, especially among children. What I learned from all these experiences is that even from a young age, the people who surround you provide the lens through which you view yourself. It shouldn't be that way, but it is.

I didn't get to a place of self-loathing on my own. I can thank my peers during the most impressionable and formative years of my life for that. Because, let's face it, without the opinions and actions of others along with mass-marketed societal beauty standards, how would we come to believe that we are anything but uniquely beautiful in our own right? I think very few people reach a place of shame and unworthiness without outside influences. Whether it is watching your mother continually diet and berate her own body or hearing a classmate audibly whisper that you clearly don't have the body of a cheerleader, there are always those not-so-subtle nudges into the mindset of "less than." Even if you don't feel it at the time, you wake up one day, and all of a sudden you can pinpoint every single moment that compounded and led you to start thinking you weren't good enough or worthy of love, happiness, and opportunity. Where "no" became your standard RSVP without giving the invitation one second of thought. Where you began to meet every compliment with uncertainty as to whether the other person might be mocking you. Where you truly began to wonder if you have even one redeeming quality.

When you have a weight problem, you are constantly aware of and even obsessing about things that a person of average weight and health doesn't even have on the radar. For example, I cannot tell you how many times I dined out and felt like I should order a salad so that other people wouldn't judge my food choices. God forbid that a big hearty salad was just what sounded good to me at the time. Then my mind would quickly write a script of judgmental thoughts that everyone around me was surely thinking: "Of course the fat girl ordered a salad. Isn't it cute that she is trying to diet?" On the flip side, if I'd had a busy day, missed lunch, got a workout in, and was ravaged by dinnertime and I ordered a large entrée with a side salad and even asked if people wanted to split an appetizer, then the internal script would read something along the lines of, "Of course the fat girl is going to order everything under the sun. No wonder she's fat. Why can't she get it together?" And the sickest part of it all is that I typically dined with the people who cared about me the most. I know that I am not alone in this and that many of you reading this book have likely experienced the same inner dialogue and feelings of shame and mental anguish. Until someone has felt this amount of anxiety over simply looking at a restaurant menu, they couldn't possibly begin to understand or even sympathize.

For decades I let my weight define me. I let it become this beacon of darkness that dictated every decision I made and nearly every thought I had. I put on a good face, and honestly I don't think most of the people in my life had any idea of how badly I was struggling. But internally I agonized over everything. I had turned worrying about my weight into a full-time job, and it was exhausting.

I spent years thinking that if only my outside could match my insides, people would come to know that they had been missing out on a loyal and wonderful human being. As if merely losing the weight and shedding the armor could undo all the psychological damage that had been done and lessen the load of the emotional baggage that I was carrying. Little did I know that losing the weight was not going to fix everything that was broken. It was only a small piece of the puzzle.

My poor relationship with food began pretty much as soon as I started eating solid foods. I didn't realize until I was well into adulthood that although I had the free will to make healthier choices, I was almost programmed by my upbringing not to. I didn't know any better.

I know my mom did the best she could with the meals she prepared as I was growing up, and I don't fault her for it. She was simply doing the best she could with the knowledge and the resources that she had at the time. But when I look back on the food of my upbringing, I see how devoid of nutrients it was. Other than bagged salad mix, I'm not sure there was ever a fresh vegetable in our house—unless of course you count the steady rotation of a big ol' bag of russets. All our vegetables came from cans or were frozen. The three in constant rotation were canned corn, canned green beans, and frozen Brussels sprouts. We regularly ate TV dinners and dined out at places like Skippers, Kings Table, and Taco Time. We always had soda and chips in the house, and I frequently ate things like canned ravioli and Top Ramen for lunch. Dinner would be chipped beef gravy on white bread, spaghetti with garlic bread, or meatloaf and mashed potatoes. Now, don't get me wrong, I still love a lot of those foods. I'm not saying I didn't like them. I'm just saying that I see where it all began, my unhealthy relationship with food and my overeating. Sugar and carbs were my main food groups growing up. After leaving home and moving out on my own, this trend continued because it was all I knew.

Fast-forward to all the years I spent working in restaurants, where things really spiraled out of control. For many of those years I was working in Italian restaurants, and most of my meals consisted of pasta and bread. After work I would go out to the bars with my coworkers and drink and eat fried foods. This is when I really began to pack on the pounds. Unfortunately, this is also when I fully grasped just how cruel people can be. Being judged so harshly and ridiculed for one single trait when there are a million other things that people should want to know about you is devastating. It causes a ripple effect over your entire life.

I began defining my self-worth in a series of moments, spread out over the years, but all strung together. Each one chipped away at me, a little at a time, until I got to a point where I didn't really love myself at all. I tried every diet gimmick on the market. If there was a lotion, potion, pill, or wrap, I was all over it. I knowingly engaged in disordered eating on a regular basis: I would binge and then tell myself that I just wouldn't eat at all for a couple of days to make up for it. This cycle went on for years. I was in a spiral of self-sabotage. I would lose a little bit of weight only to gain it back and

> The world breaks everyone, and afterward, some are strong at the broken places.
>
> —Ernest Hemingway

put on even more. Each failed attempt just added to my insecurity and self-loathing. I was wasting all my time and energy looking for a quick fix. If I had spent even a fraction of that time actually putting in the hard work, I would have found lasting change a decade earlier.

It wasn't until I was in my mid- to late twenties, when a coworker introduced me to the Atkins diet, that I found something that didn't seem too hard or restrictive and that I thought I might be able to stick with long term. While I still knew very little about nutrition and was focusing solely on counting carbs, regardless of the food source they came from, I lost about 50 pounds relatively quickly. It really gave me a false sense of what health and wellness was. I thought that I had arrived at some imaginary finish line. I thought I was fixed. I had lost the weight, and I thought everything else in my life was going to magically get better. I truly believed that my weight was at the heart of every single issue I had. I also hadn't learned that low-carb is a lifestyle and not a diet. I simply thought I was done. I had finally put in the work, and now I could go back to living life the way I used to.

Well, I think you can guess where this story is leading. Yes, I gained all that weight back and then some. I didn't realize that in order to maintain the results I had achieved, I had to continue showing up and putting in the hard work every day.

Until that point, I thought the only thing wrong with me was that I was fat. I had assumed that once the weight was gone, everything would be right in the world again. So much goes into weight gain—especially when you have regained weight. In a lot of ways, I wished I never would have lost it at all. I felt like everyone who had ever mocked me, doubted me, or bullied me had been right about me all along. Not only was I going to be fat forever, but I had no willpower or follow-through. I felt like I was fooling myself to think that I could ever be different. Be better.

By the time I had lost all the weight again, I had come to see low-carb as a lifestyle. I knew that I would find success if I stuck with it long term. I had fixed that part of the equation. I thought that was the only missing piece that had led me to gain all the weight back the first time. After I put the weight off for the second time, I still felt this profound sense of emptiness and loneliness. Again, nothing in my world had changed except for my waistline. How was it possible that I looked so different, but nothing about the world around me looked different? I just couldn't understand it. Why wasn't I happy? After all, losing the weight was all I had ever wanted.

After a series of hard life events, I regained the weight a third time. It wasn't until this final relapse that I realized it was never about the weight. I mean, obviously it was a little bit about the weight, but I came to realize that my weight was only one small piece of the puzzle and that the emotional baggage I was carrying far outweighed the physical baggage I was carrying. I wasn't fixing everything that was broken. Weight becomes a shield. It puts blinders over your eyes—something you can hide behind. It steals your joy and literally feeds your insecurities. The first time, I thought it was all about changing the food I ate and reaching a destination. The second time, I thought the missing piece was simply sticking with the food that had helped me reach the finish line. But this last time, I finally realized that the reasons you put that food in your mouth hold far more weight (pun intended) than the food itself does. I was consistently eating daddy issues, ridicule, loneliness, unworthiness, fear of failure, insecurity, and self-loathing. I ate them in the form of anything that tickled my taste buds. I was so emotionally broken that I couldn't even see what I was doing, let alone tell where it all was coming from.

I had no idea about the amount of emotional healing that I needed to do to put myself on a true path to lasting change. I had to learn to go beyond food and dig deep into the darkest parts of myself to find and attempt to fix all the reasons that made me turn to food for comfort. Through a lot of work, therapy, self-exploration, and purging of toxic relationships, I learned that there is light on the other side. I also came to see that all the cracks and brokenness were just ways for the light to get in. I became less attached to the outcome, traced things back to where it all began, and started rebuilding myself piece by piece, and only then was I able to fall more in love with myself. The scale alone was never going to give me the wholeness that I had spent years desperately seeking.

This analogy is going to seem out of left field, but bear with me. My husband, Jon, and I have a peace lily plant that we bought when we first moved into our home. It was always in the front room. It got frequent care and adequate water, but it never bloomed. The foliage was green and beautiful, but the plant remained the same. It didn't die, but it didn't grow, either. It just existed. Then one day I thought to bring it into the kitchen and put it in the bay window with our fresh herbs. Within less than a week, I noticed the first signs of a tightly wrapped white flower bud waiting to bloom. A couple of days later, up popped another bud. Who would have thought that all that plant needed was a little more light to thrive? It instantly struck me that there was a beautiful analogy for my own life here. This peace lily had everything it needed to survive, but it didn't have the missing piece that it needed to *thrive*. I couldn't help but think of all the times in my life when I had given myself only the bare minimum that I needed to survive and offered myself none of the things that I needed to thrive.

Fixing what was broken with my emotional wellness was the missing piece that I needed to go from merely surviving to abundantly thriving. To a place of loving myself and accepting myself at all shapes and sizes.

Someone asked me recently how I came to a place of acceptance with my body and with who I am as a person. I replied that one day I simply realized that the decades of hating myself had never gotten me anywhere and that perhaps a new approach was in order. This awakening didn't come without an acknowledgment that there was a lot of work that still needed to be done. I consistently work at it every single day. Every day I have to choose to love myself, accept myself, and give myself grace. It is definitely a practice. It is not something that comes easily to me, and some days I do better than others. The biggest changes were realizing that other people's opinions of me are none of my business and that sometimes you have to teach people how to treat you by setting clear and concise boundaries for what you will and will not accept. I wish I could have gotten to this place years, if not decades, ago. All that time I spent hating myself and wanting to change myself robbed me of precious moments that I can never get back. It stole all the memories that I never had the chance to make because of fear, insecurity, and embarrassment. It took me almost forty years to fully grasp it, but little by little I finally came to realize that you can't hate yourself to health.

> "Owning our story can be hard but not nearly as difficult as spending our lives running from it. Embracing our vulnerabilities is risky but not nearly as dangerous as giving up on love and belonging and joy—the experiences that make us the most vulnerable. Only when we are brave enough to explore the darkness will we discover the infinite power of our light."
>
> —Brené Brown

Why dairy-free?

My foray into a dairy-free ketogenic lifestyle began out of necessity rather than desire. Because, let's face it, cheese is delicious, and few people give it up simply because they don't like it. For me, it started with some health challenges. At the end of 2016, I got whooping cough. I was very sick for nearly seven months. During that time, I was put through several courses of antibiotics. You see, whooping cough isn't nearly as common as the flu or even bronchitis, so for my first two trips to the emergency room, the doctors were operating under the "when you hear hoofbeats, think of horses, not zebras" approach to treatment. Because the classic "whoop" had not presented itself yet, they treated me for bronchitis, and both times they sent me home with antibiotics, an inhaler, and some cough syrup. For my third trip to the ER, however, it was clear that what I was being treated for was not what I had. By this time, I had the classic, unmistakable whoop that gives pertussis its nickname. The doctors also swabbed me for the flu to make sure I didn't have both going on at the same time. They told me that unless whooping cough is caught immediately, it can only be treated symptomatically, and I had to just wait it out. It went on for so long and was so violent that I remember turning to Jon at one point and telling him that for the first time in my life, I actually thought I might be dying.

Toward the end of this period of sickness, which was now far surpassing the length of time even whooping cough should last, my doctor began to wonder if I might have some sort of secondary infection, so she put me on another round of steroids and antibiotics. By this point, I had been on three rounds of antibiotics in six months' time. Little by little, the cough finally subsided in June 2017 after plaguing me for seven months. I was left with some breathing challenges and exercise-induced asthma, but overall I began to feel like myself again. I spent the next month wrapping up my book *Craveable Keto* (yes, I wrote that book while I had whooping cough). When I got that book finished and off my plate, life was starting to return to normal.

Just four months later, in November 2017, Jon and I traveled to mainland Ecuador and the Galapagos Islands. It was truly the trip of a lifetime. But on the flights home, I started to feel really sick. My stomach was churning, and I was in a lot of pain. By the time I got home, I was in a world of hurt. I couldn't keep anything in my body, not even water. On about the fourth day after arriving home, when nothing had changed, I decided it was time to go to the ER. They must have thought that I was drug seeking or something, because they treated me really poorly, even after I explained that I had just traveled to South America. They gave me anti-nausea medication and painkillers and sent me on my way. I went home, but I didn't get any better. On about day ten, I went to the ER again. I was doubled over in pain and still couldn't keep anything down or in. I knew something was really wrong, and much to their chagrin, I brought a stool sample with me. I was severely dehydrated, and it turned out that I had intestinal parasites—giardia, to be exact. The doctors put me on two antibiotics—Cipro and Flagyl—to be taken simultaneously. I don't know if you are familiar with these drugs, but included in the list of things they treat are black plague and anthrax exposure. They are very strong antibiotics. This made for five rounds of antibiotics in a twelve-month period. That is more than I should have had in my whole lifetime. Needless to say, it ravaged my gut.

Unfortunately, antibiotics cannot differentiate between helpful and harmful bacteria. So, along with the bad bacteria in my gut, they took with it all the good bacteria, which play crucial roles in immunity, digestion, metabolism, mental health, and so much more. This happened not just once, but five times in one year. My gut barely had time to repopulate the healthy bacteria before it was wiped out again. My body had gone through war, five times over.

This delicate balancing act of gut bacteria is critical for overall health and wellness. In an otherwise healthy person who is not already immunocompromised, one course of antibiotics might cause a couple of days of digestive distress, and then things will return to normal. But in my case, the prolonged illnesses and repeated courses of antibiotic treatments resulted in post-infectious colitis (inflammation of the digestive tract) and a series of strange symptoms that I would later learn were the result of new food intolerances. I always knew that gluten was an issue for me, and I had been living a gluten-free lifestyle for a number of years, but I started reacting very strongly to dairy and eggs as well. Have you ever heard the phrase "Everything starts in the gut"? The truth of that statement was never more evident to me than it was during this time. I felt as if my body was rebelling against me. In addition to digestive distress, I was suffering from brain fog, rashes, joint pain, hormonal imbalances, food intolerances, and sinus issues, among other symptoms. I just felt generally unwell. I also felt powerless because I was living my life, eating all the same healthy low-carb foods as before, but my body was raging, and I didn't know how to fix it.

I started doing a lot of research, and I ended up having my naturopath run an IgE/IgA/IgG antibody assessment on me. This simple blood test measures your reactions to about 150 common foods, spices, and herbs. Antibodies are proteins made by the immune system to fight antigens, such as bacteria, viruses, and toxins. The body makes different antibodies to combat different antigens. The role of an antibody assessment test is to see which foods your body is creating an abundance of antibodies for. In the simplest terms, it determines which foods are being treated as foreign invaders by your body and are potentially causing reactive symptoms like gas, bloating, sinus issues, joint pain, rashes, and headaches.

My test results provided confirmation of what I already knew to be true just by what I felt happening in my body: I was highly reactive to eggs of all types, as well as dairy. The test also confirmed that I was still highly reactive to gluten.

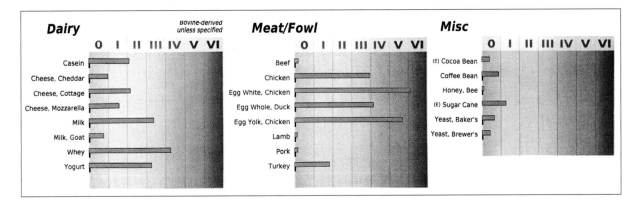

Report Summary

The following classifications correspond to the Reaction Class noted on your Food Antibody Assessment report. The classification of 0 to VI identifies the level of food-specific-antibodies measured from your blood sample via US BioTek's proprietary semi-quantitative ELISA (Enzyme-linked Immunosorbent Assay). Not all antibody tests (i.e.: IgA, IgE and IgG) may have been ordered by your practitioner.

IgE: Class I and greater
(none)

If IgE was tested along with IgA and/or IgG, any food that scored Class I and greater for IgE is *listed above* irrespective of IgA or IgG antibody levels.

Class IV and greater	(High to Extremely High antibody levels)	
IgA:	**IgA & IgG:**	**IgG:**
(not tested)	(none)	Chicken Egg White, Chicken Egg Yolk, Duck Egg Whole, Rye, Wheat Gliadin, Wheat Gluten, Whey

Class III	(Moderate antibody levels)	
IgA:	**IgA & IgG:**	**IgG:**
(not tested)	(none)	Chicken, Milk, Radish, Yogurt

Class I/II	(Low antibody levels)	
IgA:	**IgA & IgG:**	**IgG:**
(not tested)	(none)	Casein, Cheddar Cheese, Cottage Cheese, Garlic, Mozzarella Cheese, Pineapple, Sesame Seed, Spelt, String Bean, Sugar Cane, Turkey, Whole Wheat

This report does not identify anaphylaxis. Avoid all foods to which you have had an anaphylactic reaction (consult your practitioner).

I decided it was time to conduct a strict elimination protocol. I took it even further than omitting eggs, dairy, and gluten; I also cut out alcohol, all sugars and sweeteners, nuts, and carbonation. My goal was to avoid all common gut irritants in an attempt to heal my gut from the year it had just been through, and honestly all the years of poor lifestyle and dietary choices that came before that. In addition to omitting those foods, I added in everything under the sun that was proven to have a positive impact on gut health. I ate fermented foods, took glutamine and probiotics, increased my intake of collagen, drank bone both, you name it—if it was proven to be effective and not a weird gimmick, I did it. I really wanted to heal myself from the inside out. And if I'm honest, the effort may have been largely fueled by the fact that I have a major love affair with eggs and refused to believe that I would never be able to eat them again.

After a lot of trial and error and multiple elimination protocols, I was finally able to reintroduce eggs and dairy. However, I learned that I have a threshold I cannot cross or I will start to see symptoms again. The changes in my health took these foods from everyday items to just occasional items, and I have learned to be okay with that. The human body is an amazing thing. If you are willing to listen to it, it will always tell you what it does and does not want.

I have found that a ketogenic lifestyle with little to no dairy is what helps me personally feel my best and thrive. As my own story took this turn, so did my business. My first thought was that if I was going through this, countless other people were dealing with it as well, and a dairy-free cookbook might be a much needed resource. I have made it my mission throughout this book to show you just how delicious keto can be, even without dairy. I hope you enjoy using it as much as I enjoyed writing it.

TEN SIGNS THAT IT MIGHT BE TIME TO DITCH THE DAIRY

The path to a dairy-free ketogenic diet looks different for everyone. While some people opt in simply as a matter of personal preference, others are forced to eliminate dairy due to food intolerances, autoimmune issues, or other diseases and illnesses.

Then there is a whole other group of people who may have no idea that dairy is the cause of many of their mysterious symptoms or the reason they feel "off" or generally unwell. I can't tell you how many people I know who have tried essentially everything (except omitting dairy) in an attempt to chase down the root of their symptoms only to find out later that dairy was the one thing causing all their issues.

If you are curious whether you might fall into the latter category, I have compiled a list of ten signs that you might not be tolerating dairy as well as you thought. Please note that many of these are crossover symptoms with a variety of diseases and illnesses. This list is not meant to replace medical advice, but rather to aid you in opening a dialogue with your healthcare practitioners about whether switching to a dairy-free ketogenic lifestyle might be beneficial to your overall health and wellness.

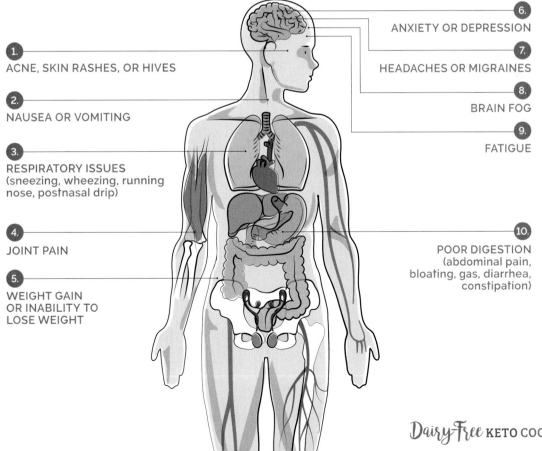

1. ACNE, SKIN RASHES, OR HIVES

2. NAUSEA OR VOMITING

3. RESPIRATORY ISSUES (sneezing, wheezing, running nose, postnasal drip)

4. JOINT PAIN

5. WEIGHT GAIN OR INABILITY TO LOSE WEIGHT

6. ANXIETY OR DEPRESSION

7. HEADACHES OR MIGRAINES

8. BRAIN FOG

9. FATIGUE

10. POOR DIGESTION (abdominal pain, bloating, gas, diarrhea, constipation)

FAQ

Do you track macros?

I no longer track my macros (macronutrients are carbohydrates, fat, and protein), but I did when I was just getting started on keto. I was diligent about tracking every last bite of food that went into my mouth. It helped me to stay on track with my goals, but even more than that, it helped me to truly get a feel for the nutritional values of the foods I was eating. It was also a great opportunity to pinpoint exactly where something might have gone wrong if I plateaued, stopped reaching my goals, or let old habits creep back in.

I am at a point now where I can ramble off the total and net carbs in almost any food I eat. Why? Because I eat real, whole, nutrient-dense foods, and while I eat a wide variety of dishes, I eat a lot of the same foods. I have transitioned into a more intuitive approach to eating. I will discuss this more throughout the book, but I have learned to listen to the cues my body sends about hunger and cravings and fuel it accordingly. While I certainly don't discourage strict tracking, as it can be an immensely helpful tool, I just reached a place where it was no longer serving me and began to feel like a second job. The key to sustainability in just about anything is ease. If your healthy lifestyle starts to feel like a chore, it may be time to rethink your approach. I hope you pick up some pointers throughout this book to help you do exactly that.

Do calories count?

The short answer is, While I believe that keto makes calories less of a concern, they should in no way be disregarded altogether. Check out the section "Breaking through the dreaded weight-loss plateau" (pages 31 to 33) for a more in-depth take on this topic.

How is keto different from Paleo?

Keto and Paleo, while different, share a lot of similarities, especially if you take a real-food approach to your ketogenic lifestyle. If you are already living a real-food keto lifestyle, then the main difference between Paleo and keto is likely the inclusion of dairy. While the Paleo template strictly calls for no dairy, whether or not to consume dairy under a ketogenic template is a personal choice. My hope is that this book will help bridge the gap between the two for those of you looking to utilize a Paleo-style template to guide your low-carb, high-fat diet. The Paleo diet is based on the idea that to promote optimal health and wellness, we should eat only those foods that were available to early humans during the Paleolithic era, because those are the foods that our bodies are designed to digest and absorb. They include meat, seafood, eggs, nuts, seeds, fruits, vegetables, herbs, spices, and healthy fats.

While Paleo is somewhat rigid by design, there is more room for customization with keto. Keto is a high-fat, low-carb, moderate-protein diet that transitions your body from burning sugar for energy into a fat-burning machine. While some people may argue that there is only one true way to live a ketogenic lifestyle, I would argue the case for bioindividuality. We are all unique, and we have different nutritional requirements to thrive. Throughout this book, I will cover some of the many approaches to keto and help you determine which one is right for you.

Yes, it is entirely possible to complete a round of Whole30 under a ketogenic template, although it definitely takes some planning. While I am not able to add information about Whole30 compliance to the recipes in this book, many of them would be suitable for Whole30. Once you know what you can and can't eat during the Whole30 program, finding recipes that fit into the program is actually quite easy. For help, check out the Whole30 section in my recipe index on peaceloveandlowcarb.com.

Can you do a keto Whole30?

What are net carbs? Do you count total or net carbs?

Net carbs are the total carbs per serving minus fiber and sugar alcohols (not to be confused with sugar). Personally, I split the difference here: I count net carbs in fruits and vegetables and total carbs in everything else. For more information on why I do it this way, check out the section "Fruits and vegetables" on pages 56 and 57. If you are counting net carbs and you aren't achieving your health and wellness goals, I would recommend switching to total carbs and seeking to identify areas that might need tweaking. Many keto convenience foods have a lot of added fiber as well as sugar alcohols, so a snack bar with 2 grams of net carbs may have between 20 and 30 grams of total carbs, and that can throw things off track for a lot of people. I think the safest bet is to count total carbs and stay away from too many convenience foods, no matter how clean the ingredients are.

Cheat is not a word in my keto vocabulary. It is a word that is deeply rooted in diet culture. Keto is a lifestyle for me, not a diet. I wouldn't cheat on my husband, and I'm not going to "cheat" on my healthy lifestyle. Food should not be used as a punishment or a reward, and it shouldn't be something we hold over our own heads with feelings of guilt and shame tied to it. Viewing food in this light paves the way for disordered eating and an unhealthy relationship with food. Food is meant to nourish our bodies and sustain life. As Ann Wigmore said, "The food you eat can be either the safest and most powerful form of medicine or the slowest form of poison." Food should be enjoyed and celebrated.

What is your take on cheat meals/days?

When I eat foods that aren't low in carbohydrates and don't necessarily fit my everyday nutritional template, I usually have planned to do it, and then I go right back to the way I normally eat. For example, my husband and I love sushi. Rice is far from low-carb, but we still enjoy sushi on occasion. I never come home from that meal feeling the need to beat myself up.

That being said, if instead I dove face-first into an emotional eating binge full of sugar, carbs, and gluten, then I would take a step back and seek the root cause of the emotions that led me to choose foods I know are unhealthy. Food can be the first thing we turn to in an act of self-sabotage. Sometimes the greatest gift we can give ourselves is grace and acceptance. There is no shame in starting over. It's all about getting up more times than you fall down.

Do you work out? Do you have to work out to lose weight on keto?

I do work out, and I really enjoy it. I like CrossFit, hiking, yoga, walking—you name it. Variety is key for me. I'm also an avid fan of research and education. I have my Level 1 CrossFit coaching certificate, yet I have never coached a single session outside of leading Saturday morning workouts with friends in our garage gym. But even then, I am probably more of a cheerleader than anything. I got the certification because I wanted to learn more about proper technique and body mechanics to avoid injury in my own workouts.

I don't work out because I hate my body; I work out because I love my body and want to honor it. I work out now so that I can enjoy this body in my golden years. Fitness is part of my retirement plan. If the food I eat is my pension, then fitness is my 401(k). I'm investing now in my future health. Not to mention that movement is crucial to my overall mental health and well-being.

I've worked out at 280 pounds, at 180 pounds, and at every stage in between. Mobility is freedom, and I don't take that freedom lightly. A sedentary lifestyle is a major contributor to chronic illness and deadly disease. If weight loss is your goal, then you can certainly achieve it with a ketogenic diet alone, but I recommend incorporating as much movement into your life as possible. For more about the importance of movement, check out pages 43 and 44.

Can I drink alcohol on the keto diet?

I cover this topic in greater depth in the section "Breaking through the dreaded weight-loss plateau" (pages 31 to 33), but I don't believe there is one right answer here. The decision whether to include the occasional alcoholic beverage in your keto lifestyle is entirely up to you. It is all about assessing your goals and then making decisions based on the things that either help you attain those goals or take you further away from them.

Why no dairy?

My journey into a dairy-free ketogenic lifestyle began when I was facing serious gut health issues and developed food intolerances as a result (see pages 14 to 16). The perfect storm of events ultimately led to some health challenges that forced me to critically examine the foods I was eating and to cut out some of the foods I knew and loved as part of my daily routine, namely dairy and eggs. After a strict elimination period and a careful reintroduction, I have been able to work dairy and eggs back into my diet in smaller, less frequent quantities.

To help determine if dairy might be moving you further away from your health and wellness goals, review the section "Ten Signs That It Might Be Time to Ditch the Dairy" on page 17.

To properly address this question, I feel it is important to start with what intermittent fasting is not. Intermittent fasting is not starvation. It is the practice of alternating between cycles of eating and cycles of fasting, with specific time frames in mind. It is not so much about what you eat as about when you eat. Many people who practice intermittent fasting typically eat all their meals in a six- to eight-hour window and then fast for the remaining sixteen to eighteen hours in a twenty-four-hour period. This is why you commonly see 16/8 or 18/6 in reference to fasting schedules. Many people report feeling less hunger and increased energy while practicing IF. While the weight-loss benefits are what bring a lot of people to intermittent fasting, there are many other benefits—fasting increases fat burning, lowers insulin and blood sugar levels, and reduces inflammation, just to name a few.

What is intermittent fasting, and do you practice it?

I do practice intermittent fasting. I typically don't eat between the hours of 8 p.m. and noon. All my eating happens within an eight-hour window. This was not a routine that I forced myself into, nor was it something I ever set out to do intentionally. I simply began listening to my body's true hunger cues and eating only when I was hungry. It took a lot of critical examination and honesty with myself. Was I truly hungry, or was I just bored or feeling emotional? I don't follow any rigid guidelines or time frames. If I am truly hungry outside of that noon-to-8 p.m. window, then I eat. Conversely, if noontime rolls around and I am still not hungry, then I don't eat. I never force myself to eat to meet macros or a fasting schedule. I let my body be the boss. That being said, I cannot eat within a few hours of bedtime, even if I am hungry. When I do, I don't sleep as well, and I wake up with a savage feeling of hunger and a hint of nausea. Sounds fun, right?

While I am happy to share with you the supplements that I personally take, this should not be considered a prescription for your supplementation regimen. To determine your own nutrition and supplement needs, I recommend working closely with your medical practitioner. With that disclaimer out of the way, I take magnesium, zinc, turmeric, vitamin D with K2, methyl B-12, and resveratrol. The two supplement companies that I trust the most are Thorne Research and Pure Encapsulations.

What supplements do you take?

Is kombucha keto-friendly?

I get asked this question A LOT. My answer is a lot like my answer to the question about drinking alcohol on a ketogenic lifestyle: it is entirely up to you and depends on your specific health and wellness goals. I incorporate kombucha into my daily routine because it does wonders for gut health and tastes amazing. So, for me, the benefit outweighs the cost (the extra carbs). I adjust what I eat throughout the day to accommodate the carbs in the kombucha.

But what about the sugar in kombucha, you might ask? While kombucha is made with sugar, the SCOBY (symbiotic culture of bacteria and yeast) eats that sugar during the fermentation process, and very little, if any, residual sugar remains in the final product. That is why many kombucha brands don't even include sugar in the ingredient list. Kombucha, like many things in life, is all about figuring out what works for you and what doesn't.

1.

WHAT IS KETO?

> While weight loss is important, what's more important is the quality of food you put in your body—food is information that quickly changes your metabolism and genes.
>
> —Mark Hyman

What is keto? Well, how about we start with what keto *is not?* Keto is not just an approved list of foods to eat. Keto is not a fad diet. Keto is not a one-size-fits-all template.

Keto—short for *ketosis*—is a metabolic state. Keto is a framework that can help you cater your own low-carb nutritional approach. Keto is low-carb and high-fat. Keto is a lifestyle.

KETO 101

What is keto, and how does it work?

Keto is a high-fat, moderate-protein, low-carb diet. Please note that when I use the word *diet* throughout this book, I do not mean it in an "I'm going on a diet to lose weight" sort of way; rather, I am using the word *diet* in reference to the specific types of foods that a person eats. The primary goal of a ketogenic diet is to switch your body over from burning glucose (sugar and carbs) to burning ketones (fat) for fuel. This is known as the metabolic state of ketosis.

What are the benefits of a ketogenic diet?

While many people turn to a ketogenic lifestyle for the weight-loss benefits, there are so many other amazing benefits. They include:

increased mental clarity and focus

balanced hormones

better sleep quality

more energy

less inflammation

fewer cravings

balanced emotional wellness

lower blood pressure

How do I become a fat-burning machine?

When you decrease the amount of carbohydrates in your diet and increase your intake of healthy fats, the amount of glucose in your body begins to decrease. As your glucose stores are depleted, the amount of insulin, the hormone that helps regulate blood sugar, secreted from your pancreas also decreases. This allows your liver to begin breaking down your body's fat stores into ketones and start burning ketones for fuel. This is especially great if you are trying to lose weight, but the benefits go so far beyond weight loss alone. Once you become fat-adapted, you will also experience fewer cravings, less hunger, increased energy levels, and greater mental clarity.

How is burning fat for energy different from burning sugar for energy?

Now that you know what happens in your body once you start to decrease your intake of carbohydrates while increasing your intake of healthy fats, let's take a look at how this process differs from what happens in your body while you are using sugar for fuel, as you would on a standard American diet.

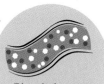

Eat a high-carb diet

S.A.D. (Standard American Diet)
High in refined sugar and carbs

Blood glucose levels rise

Blood glucose levels crash, resulting in cravings and fatigue

Rush of energy

Insulin shuttles glucose out of the bloodstream and into the body's cells

Pancreas releases insulin into the bloodstream

Eat a low-carb, ketogenic diet

KETOGENIC DIET
Low in carbs, high in fat

Blood glucose and insulin levels remain stable and fat is burned for energy

Liver converts fatty acids to ketones

Fatty acids travel through the bloodstream to the liver, heart, and muscles

Blood glucose levels fall

Fat cells begin to release stored fatty acids

But isn't ketosis dangerous? How is ketosis different from ketoacidosis?

There has been a lot of confusion in this area, even among medical professionals and nutritionists. Ketosis and ketoacidosis are two completely different metabolic states. As I covered above, being in a state of ketosis means that your body is burning fat instead of glucose for energy. Simply put, as your reserves of glucose begin to run out and your insulin levels drop, your body begins breaking down its own fat stores for energy.

Ketoacidosis, on the other hand, refers to diabetic ketoacidosis, and it is a complication of type 1 diabetes. It results from dangerously high levels of ketones and blood sugar at the same time. This combination makes the blood too acidic and can affect the function of critical organs such as the liver and kidneys. It is a medical emergency that requires prompt treatment.

How will I know if I am in ketosis?
Do I have to be in ketosis to succeed on a ketogenic diet?

While it is my personal opinion that you do not have to track nutritional ketosis to have a great deal of success on a low-carb, high-fat diet, many people like to have verified results. If reaching a state of ketosis is your goal, there are several ways to measure and track your ketone levels.

Blood ketone meter: Testing your blood is considered to be the most accurate method of measuring ketone levels, but it is also the most expensive. If nutritional ketosis is your goal and you are serious about tracking it, this is the way to go.

Ketone breathalyzer: A breathalyzer measures ketones through the acetone levels in your breath. This method is not as accurate as blood testing because it cannot provide you with a specific ketone level, but it can give you a good idea of whether or not you are in ketosis.

Urine ketone strips: The least expensive option, urine test strips are also the least reliable form of testing for ketones. Over time, as you become fat-adapted, your body will excrete fewer ketones in your urine, and this can lead to false readings showing that you are not in ketosis when in fact you are.

What are macros?

The word *macros* is short for *macronutrients*, which are the nutrients that you need in larger quantities to sustain energy, growth, and bodily functions. There are three macronutrients: fat, protein, and carbohydrates.

When people in the keto community throw around the word *macros*, they are usually referring to the breakdown of the three macronutrients into percentages and how those percentages make up a person's total caloric intake after a full day of eating. For a standard approach to the ketogenic diet, the breakdown is as follows:

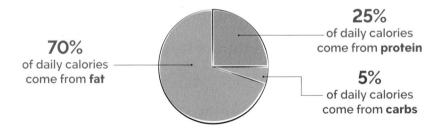

70% of daily calories come from **fat**

25% of daily calories come from **protein**

5% of daily calories come from **carbs**

This is just a basic guideline and not a hard-and-fast rule for everyone. A lot goes into determining the right macros—and the right approach to keto, for that matter. The nutritional needs of someone who is suffering from an autoimmune condition are going to differ from those of an otherwise healthy individual. Even two people with the exact same health conditions will have different nutritional needs. It is important to figure out exactly what works for your body and not try to force yourself into a nutritional template that doesn't suit you.

THE MANY FACES OF KETO

As if I didn't just throw enough information at you, I think it is important to drive home the fact that while what I just outlined is a general breakdown of how a ketogenic diet works and how it's different from a high-carb standard American diet, I do not believe that there is a one-size-fits-all approach to keto.

If you were to pop the question "What is keto?" into Google or even just start asking around on social media, there is a solid chance that you would get about twenty different answers. Why is that? Well, it's because of bioindividuality.

So what is bioindividuality, anyway? In the simplest terms, it means that differences in genetic background, sex, age, lifestyle, anatomy, metabolism, body composition, activity level, stress level, disease, illness, insulin sensitivity, gut health, and so on all play a part in determining our individualized nutritional requirements. Given that, how could there be one version of keto (or any lifestyle, for that matter) that worked for everyone?

I could sit here and tell you every single thing I did to lose weight, heal my gut, reverse my food sensitivities, and restore myself to a place of vitality, and you could go and do every single one of those things and not see the same results. Why? Because we are all unique individuals with vastly different nutritional and lifestyle requirements.

All that being said, my goal here is not to cause confusion, but rather to clear it up in order to help you find the approach to keto that is right for you. First I'd like to cover some of the terminology that you will hear in reference to different variations of the keto diet and address what those terms mean as they pertain to a ketogenic lifestyle. Then I will provide you with tips to tailor an approach to your specific needs.

STANDARD KETO This is what most people are referring to when they say that they live a ketogenic lifestyle. Standard keto focuses on specific macronutrient goals, with the ultimate goal of entering ketosis. This is a low-carb, moderate-protein, high-fat approach, with 70 percent of calories coming from fat, 25 percent from protein, and 5 percent from carbs.

LAZY KETO As with any less-than-scientific term, the meaning of "lazy keto" can vary significantly depending on whom you ask. However, the underlying theme is focusing on a daily carb intake goal, usually under 20 grams, rather than tracking calories or overall macros. It may also include eating any foods that fit within that carb allotment, without regard for food quality or nutrient density.

DIRTY KETO This is more of an "if it fits your macros" approach with no real regard for nutrition. Dirty keto follows the same nutritional breakdown as standard keto, except that there is no emphasis on where those macronutrients come from. Instead of a healthy option like one of the recipes in this book, a meal might consist of the lowest-carb offering from a fast food restaurant. Many "dirty" options lack micronutrients (vitamins and minerals) and are full of chemical additives and preservatives.

AIP KETO This approach is similar to clean keto (see page 30) except that it also omits the foods necessary for following an autoimmune protocol diet: alcohol, caffeine, eggs, nuts and seeds, legumes, yeast, natural sweeteners, and nightshades.

CARNIVORE KETO Carnivore came out of the gate strong and has the support of some big influencers in the keto community. The premise behind it is that you eat a keto diet that consists of animal foods alone. There are no rules regarding macronutrient breakdowns or portion sizes; you simply eat until you are full. This approach consists primarily of meat, seafood, eggs, dairy, and bone broth. Because no vegetables are included in this way of eating, carbs are negligible; you would just get trace amounts of carbs from dairy products and/or shellfish.

 CLEAN KETO This is exactly what the name implies: a clean way of low-carb, high-fat eating. It focuses on whole foods from quality sources, like grass-fed and grass-finished beef, pastured pork and eggs, wild-caught seafood, and organic vegetables, herbs, and spices. It is free of dairy and processed foods. Most of the recipes in this book fall into this category, with the exception of the sweet treats.

 CYCLICAL KETO A cyclical approach to keto involves adhering to a standard keto approach five or six days per week, followed by one to two days of increased carb intake. The higher-carb days are meant to replenish the body's depleted glucose stores from high-intensity workouts and are often referred to as "refeeds." This approach is popular among ketogenic athletes who keep to a rigorous training schedule.

TARGETED KETO A targeted keto approach combines elements of standard keto and cyclical keto. This is another favorite among athletes. The goal is to become fat-adapted and remain in a state of ketosis. Once you have been doing that for a minimum of thirty to sixty days, you begin incorporating more carbs into your diet thirty minutes before a workout. The idea is that your body knows how to use the glucose effectively and quickly and then return to producing ketones right away, which allows you to remain in ketosis despite the increases in carbs.

I am not here to promote or condemn any of these approaches. I know what works for me, and my job isn't to judge anyone else's plate, but rather to help you figure out what you want to have on your plate. My goal is to help you determine the nutritional approach that works best for you where you are now, at this stage of your life.

While I believe that locally sourced, minimally processed, grass-fed, pastured, and organic foods are the way to go, it took me many years to get here. I continually worked within the framework of what I had, cleaning up my fridge and pantry as my finances allowed and working toward the ultimate goal of eating a diet rich in real, whole, nutrient-dense foods.

If there is one thing I absolutely cannot stand, it is watching someone be berated for doing the very best they can. I see it daily on social media, and it makes me sad that we live in a world where you can be judged so critically for what is on your plate, especially when you are giving it your all and working to make better choices.

I certainly ate my share of processed low-carb frankenfoods back in the day. I was doing the best I could with the information and budget I had at the time. I don't know a single person who went from a diet high in processed foods and refined sugar and carbs to the perfect picture of whole-food nutrition overnight. But I know plenty of people who simply did their best and continually worked to learn more about food and how it affects the body, and to clean up their diet over time.

There is nothing wrong with starting with the approach that best suits your current lifestyle and then working to make gradual improvements. After all, isn't the very slowest runner still lapping everyone on the couch? Perfectionism is the enemy of progress, so ignore the keto police and live your best keto life!

TROUBLESHOOTING KETO

Breaking through the dreaded weight-loss plateau

So you are cruising along on your ketogenic lifestyle and doing everything right (or so you think), and almost as if out of nowhere, your progress completely stalls. Sound familiar? Trust me, we have all been there.

Before I cover some of the things that might be hindering your progress, let's talk about what actually constitutes a weight-loss plateau. I can't tell you how many times people have reached out to me telling me that things have stalled and they haven't lost any weight for three days. I know immediately that part of the problem is weighing every day. To me, the definition of a true weight-loss plateau is not losing any weight in three weeks, even when you can unequivocally say that you are doing all the right things (see below). If that isn't the case, maybe what you're experiencing isn't a stall at all; perhaps your body composition is changing and you are building muscle. How do you look? How do your clothes fit? How do you feel? Maybe it's time to ditch the scale for a while and start utilizing other benchmarks to gauge your success.

With that out of the way, let's look at why stalls happen. They happen because your body is a master adapter. It craves to be in a constant state of homeostasis, which simply means that it wants to maintain a consistent state of internal balance, regardless of the changes happening within and around it.

Let's go over some of the major culprits and what to do about them.

Consuming too many carbs: For anyone encountering a true weight-loss plateau, my first questions are always "How many carbs are you eating per day?" "What are the sources of those carbs?" and "Are those total or net carbs?" I am usually met with ballpark figures or "I'm not really sure." This is the first area I recommend addressing. It is easy to lose track of your carbs by having a second helping of dinner or mindlessly snacking your way over your goal. I recommend keeping a food journal and writing down everything you eat for at least two weeks to get a better feel for the true number of carbs you are consuming daily. There are a lot of tracking apps that you can use, but for me, putting pen to paper always works best.

If you are consistently meeting, and not exceeding, your desired carb allowance each day and you are tracking net carbs, my next piece of advice would be to spend a couple of weeks tracking total carbs instead. Leave the fiber and sugar alcohols in your totals to get a truer picture of what might be causing your weight loss to stall.

Lastly, identify hidden sources of carbs in your diet. They are likely hiding in plain sight in foods and products like these:

- cough syrup and medicines
- imitation crab meat
- liquid eggs
- low-fat and fat-free versions of foods
- milk alternatives
- powdered bouillon
- prepared condiments, dressings, and sauces
- preshredded cheese
- processed meats
- protein shakes
- shellfish (see page 55)
- store-bought seasoning blends and spice packets
- sugar-free foods
- vitamins and supplements

Eating too much dairy: While I realize that this is a dairy-free book, I wanted to include a note about dairy for the people who will use this book but do sometimes include dairy as part of their healthy ketogenic lifestyle. Dairy is a major culprit in weight-loss plateaus. Dairy products contain varying amounts of lactose (the sugar that is naturally present in milk), which is known to slow or even halt weight loss. Additionally, you may have a dairy allergy without being aware of it. This was the case for me, and it was one of the things that led me to transition to a dairy-free keto way of eating (see pages 14 to 16). If you aren't ready to give up dairy completely, try cutting back on dairy and make sure to eat only full-fat dairy products.

Eating too many nuts: Nuts are another major contributor to weight-loss stalls, largely due to the fact that it is easy to overindulge. For snacking, I recommend portioning nuts into single-serving packs and writing the carb count on the pack. That way, you always know exactly how many nuts you are eating and how many carbs one serving of a particular type of nut contains. It is a good idea to cut out low-carb baked goods that contain nut flours as well. As much as we all love a good keto-friendly sweet treat or bread replacement, they are often the very foods that are moving us further away from our goals.

Consuming too much artificial or natural sweetener: Some artificial sweeteners, and even some natural sweeteners, have been shown to increase appetite and cravings for sweet foods. It is best to use sweeteners in moderation. Plus, if you cut them out altogether, I think you will be amazed at how much sweetness there is in everyday whole foods. When you have truly detoxed from sugar and sweeteners, it is surprising how sweet something like a yellow bell pepper begins to taste.

Drinking too much alcohol: The body has five different fuel sources—alcohol, exogenous ketones, protein, carbohydrate, and fat. This is the order in which your body will process these fuel sources, known as oxidative priority. Because alcohol has the number one position, your body will process alcohol before anything else. Alcohol is converted to acetate in the body. Acetate is a quick-burning fuel source that cannot be stored. So what does this have to do with weight-loss stalls? Well, because the body can't store alcohol, it must burn it off before it can move on to burning the next fuel source in priority. That means that while your body is busy processing the alcohol you are drinking, the other fuel sources—protein, carbohydrate, and fat from the foods you eat—are stored instead of burned. Excessive alcohol consumption can also lead to poor food choices, which contribute to weight-loss stalls and even weight gain.

Eating too many calories: While many people believe that calories don't matter on a ketogenic diet, I have to disagree. While I think that keto makes calories less of a concern, they should not be disregarded altogether. Keto is by definition a low-carb, high-fat diet. On this I think we can all agree. One gram of protein contains 4 calories, as does one gram of carbohydrates. One gram of fat contains 9 calories. Since we eat so much fat on a ketogenic diet, calories are vastly increased. The restriction of carbohydrates is what keeps us from gaining weight with a high caloric intake and a high fat intake. But what happens if you eat strict keto all day and then at dinner you dive face-first into a plate of pasta and garlic bread? (I hope you aren't doing this!) Or maybe you simply overindulge in healthy keto foods and greatly surpass your typical carb allotment? Now you have just had a high-calorie, high-fat, *and* high-carb day. That is the perfect recipe for massive weight gain.

Stress: I can't stress this one enough. (See what I did there?) Excessive stress can bring weight loss to a screeching halt. Not only can stress lead to massive cravings and binge eating, but it also increases the body's production of the stress hormone known as cortisol. While cortisol helps your body respond to stress, when the body creates an abundance of cortisol due to prolonged stress, excess belly fat can develop. While I realize that the stressors in life are sometimes beyond your control, there are some practices you can incorporate into your daily routine to help counteract the negative effects of stress—yoga, meditation, calming essential oils, and less screen time, just to name a few.

Banishing the keto flu

So you decided that you were ready to jump in and start living a ketogenic lifestyle. You stocked your kitchen with all the right foods and you are doing everything right, but BAM—all of a sudden you feel like you were hit by a truck. You may be experiencing the phenomenon known as the "keto flu."

> **Here are a few more reasons that you may be encountering a weight-loss stall:**
> • Your body is adapting to a new set point.
> • You are letting old habits creep back in.
> • You are not eating enough real food or are eating too many frankenfoods.
> • You are exercising too much or not enough.
> • Time of the month/fluid retention/hormones.

When you are transitioning from a standard American diet to a low-carb, ketogenic diet, you may go through a short adjustment period. While some people can adopt a ketogenic diet without any side effects, within the first week others experience one or more of the following symptoms as their bodies switch from burning glucose to burning fat for energy:

- constipation
- diarrhea
- difficulty sleeping
- dizziness
- fatigue
- headaches
- irritability
- muscle cramps/ soreness
- nausea
- poor concentration
- stomach pain
- sugar cravings
- vomiting
- weakness

When the "flu" isn't really the flu

Although you may feel like you are experiencing flu symptoms, you are not actually suffering from the flu. How long you will experience these symptoms depends on how metabolically flexible your body is. The symptoms typically ease and then go away completely within a few days to a week, sometimes longer.

These symptoms are often brought on by an imbalance of electrolytes, which regulate the flow of water in and out of your cells. Common electrolytes include sodium, potassium, magnesium, and calcium. Restricting carbs lowers insulin levels, which triggers the liver to begin converting fat into ketones. Most of the cells in the human body can use ketones for energy instead of glucose. Once your body starts using ketones and fat for energy, you enter a state of ketosis.

So what does ketosis have to do with electrolytes? Well, when your insulin levels drop, your kidneys begin to release more sodium in your urine, along with water. If you have ever found yourself urinating a lot when starting or returning to keto, this is why.

While this transition can bring with it a welcome amount of weight loss in the first couple of weeks, the loss of sodium and water can also bring on the symptoms of keto flu. But not to worry; once you banish the keto flu, increased energy, mental clarity, and weight loss (if that is your goal) are right around the corner.

Easing the symptoms of keto flu

So how do you ease the symptoms of keto flu? The first step is to work on replenishing electrolytes. Most of what you need can be obtained from real, whole-food sources. Add foods that are high in potassium (fish, clams, meat, leafy greens, tomatoes, avocados, coconut water) and foods that are high in magnesium (leafy greens, raspberries, avocados, broccoli, cabbage, seafood, dark chocolate), and work to replenish sodium. You can add ½ teaspoon of Real Salt or Himalayan pink salt to a glass of water to help replenish your sodium levels. In addition to eating healthy, nutrient-dense foods, the following tips should have you feeling better in no time:

- **Hydrate:** Drink plenty of water. A good rule of thumb is to drink half of your body weight in ounces per day. For example, if you weigh 180 pounds, you would drink 90 ounces of water. If you struggle to get enough water every day, you can add a flavored electrolyte replacement powder to give your water a more appealing taste.

- **Rest and restore:** Give your body some time to rest as it transitions to fat-burning mode. Shoot for eight hours of sleep each night, and try to keep stress at a minimum in order to keep your cortisol levels down. Meditation and yoga are good practices during this time. Limit screen time to reduce your exposure to blue light, which suppresses the release of melatonin in the brain, leading to poor sleep quality.

- **Drink bone broth:** Drinking bone broth (page 370) will help you not only rehydrate, but also replenish sodium and potassium. Plus, it is just really delicious and comforting.

- **Take activated charcoal:** As you become fat-adapted, you will start losing excess body fat. Toxins are stored in these fat cells. Activated charcoal binds to those toxins and transports them out of the body.

- **Increase fat intake:** Increasing your fat intake will help reduce cravings and speed up the rate at which you become fat-adapted, lessening the duration of keto flu. Starting your morning with a Boosted Keto Coffee (page 340) is a great way to get in some added healthy fats.

- **Supplement electrolytes:** If you are struggling to get electrolytes from foods (as noted above), you can use an electrolyte replacement powder. My favorite brand is Ultima Replenisher. One scoop mixed with water provides vitamins A and C, calcium, phosphorus, magnesium, zinc, selenium, copper, manganese, chromium, and sodium. It has no artificial flavors or colors, no sugar, and zero carbs. It tastes really good, too. My favorite flavors are cherry pomegranate and grape.

tip: To avoid keto flu altogether, I recommend easing into keto and gradually tapering your carb intake by 10 grams per day. Focus on eating real, whole, nutrient-dense foods and increasing your consumption of fat as you slowly lower your carb intake. This approach will be less shocking to your body, and you should have no problem transitioning into your new healthy way of eating.

Cracking the code on cravings

Have you ever had a craving so strong that you were almost incapable of thinking about or doing anything else until the craving was satisfied? Me too! I think we have all been there. But what do these cravings actually mean? What are our bodies trying to communicate to us?

While cravings can strike for a number of reasons, the most common cause of a strong food craving is usually a vitamin, nutrient, or mineral deficiency. Those French fries you are craving are not your body's way of telling you that it wants fries. Rather, you may have an essential fatty acid deficiency and could benefit from increasing the amount of healthy fats in your diet.

Modern foods are created to be hyperpalatable, which leaves you craving more, more, more. It also leads to an overconsumption of less nutrient-dense foods, which results in weight gain. There is a reason why it seems nearly impossible to stop eating chips once you start: they are designed to have exactly that effect. Humans have evolved to seek out foods that contain high amounts of fat, sugar, and salt, and processed foods are filled with these ingredients. These foods stimulate the dopamine centers of the brain and leave you craving more, which can lead to food addiction, obesity, and chronic health conditions.

A meal that is well balanced and just right for your body's current nutritional needs will:

- leave you feeling satiated but not stuffed
- provide steady energy that lasts until the next mealtime
- cause no digestive discomfort
- leave you feeling mentally and emotionally stable
- not cause cravings

The chemicals in modern-day packaged and processed foods disrupt our normal hormonal cues for hunger and satiety and create a disconnect with the innate wisdom of our bodies. When we aren't overloading our bodies with hyperpalatable processed foods filled with synthetic chemicals and instead eat real, whole, nutrient-dense foods, we are able to realign with the body's natural intelligence. Over time, your cravings will begin to tell you exactly which vitamins, minerals, and nutrients your body needs at any given time because you will crave whole, nutrient-dense foods. Until then, I have created a chart to help you get to the bottom of what your body is really asking for when those strong cravings strike.

What Those Cravings Really Mean

CRAVING	REASON	WHAT TO EAT INSTEAD
Acidic foods	Magnesium deficiency	Raw cacao nibs, nuts, dark leafy greens, salmon, halibut
Carbonation/Soda	Calcium deficiency	Broccoli, kale, mustard greens, almonds, chia seeds, tahini
Cheese	Essential fatty acid deficiency	Salmon, ground flax seeds, walnuts, avocado, olive oil, coconut oil
Chocolate/Sweets	Magnesium deficiency	Raw cacao nibs, nuts, dark leafy greens, salmon, halibut
Coffee	Phosphorus deficiency	Chicken, beef, liver, eggs, garlic, mushrooms, almonds, sesame seeds, pumpkin seeds, Brazil nuts
Fried foods	Essential fatty acid deficiency	Salmon, ground flax seeds, walnuts, avocado, olive oil, coconut oil
Pasta/Bread/Pastries (carbs)	Chromium deficiency	Onion, romaine lettuce, tomato, cinnamon, peppers, avocado, broccoli, celery, chard
Potato chips/ French fries	Essential fatty acid deficiency	Salmon, ground flax seeds, walnuts, avocado, olive oil, coconut oil
Red meat	Iron deficiency	Spinach, dark leafy greens, seaweed, red meat
Salty foods	Chloride deficiency	Fish, celery, olives, tomato, sea salt, lettuce, seaweed

TIPS FOR SUCCESS ON THE KETO DIET

Finding success in any new endeavor is all about forming new habits and settling into a new routine. Keto is no exception. With some prior planning and the following tips, you should be well on your way to transitioning to a keto lifestyle with ease.

Make a promise to yourself and keep it.

Commit to starting and staying the course even when life throws you curveballs. It's okay to fall down, as long as you always get back up. I know that might sound oversimplified, but it really is that simple. You have to commit to the process of lasting mental and physical change, even when it feels like the world is throwing you a lifetime of hardship.

Give yourself grace.

Agree to hold yourself to a standard of grace and not a standard of perfection. Slip-ups will happen. They are just part of life. They don't define you. Sometimes success is about meeting yourself where you are with acceptance, self-love, and forgiveness. If you take only one thing from this book, let it be the message of giving yourself more grace, more kindness, and more credit.

Find a support system.

I cannot overstate the importance of connection and community. Just as it's true that there is safety in numbers, there is also support in numbers. If you can't find the support you need from the people in your immediate circle of influence, there are some amazing resources online. You'll find strong and supportive keto communities on Instagram, Reddit, Facebook, and so on. While I know there are a lot of not-so-wonderful things about social media, you just might find the connection and support that you are looking for. You can also look for keto meet-ups in your area to connect in real life with people who share similar goals and interests.

"Perfectionism is self-abuse of the highest order."

—Anne Wilson Schaef

Get your family and friends involved.

Tell your family, friends, and coworkers what you are doing and ask for their support. People won't know that you are trying to make profound changes in your life unless you tell them. Avoid those office donut dilemmas by letting your coworkers in on your healthy lifestyle change. The more people you tell, the bigger the support system you will have.

Plan ahead.

Spend a little time each weekend setting your intentions and planning for the week ahead. Don't let it become a chore; think of it as a little personal time that you carve out for yourself to help you achieve your goals. (For help with meal planning, see pages 75 to 87.)

Set realistic expectations.

Be realistic about what you hope to achieve. Change doesn't happen overnight. If weight loss is your goal, it is important to remember that you didn't put the weight on over the course of one week, and you certainly aren't going to take it off in one week. The same is true of the path to healing.

Go beyond the food.

There is so much to health and wellness besides the food that you eat. The food is just one piece of a much larger puzzle. I think what causes many people to falter is putting all their time and attention into the food while ignoring other areas of their lives that are severely out of balance. Focus on all Five Foundations of Wellness (see pages 39 to 51). I promise that if you do, every area of your life will seem much more manageable.

Remove temptations.

Make sure to set yourself up for success! It starts in your kitchen. Clear your fridge and pantry of high-carb, sugary, gluten-filled foods. If you are like me and hate wasting food, donate it to a local shelter or to a family in need. But trust me when I tell you that it is imperative to start fresh. If there is bad food in your home, eventually you will give in and eat it. Why put yourself in tempting situations?

Keep it simple.

Don't overthink things. It is easy to end up in analysis paralysis. You are not perfect, and no one is expecting you to be. Just commit to making small changes over time. Don't feel like you have to have all the answers right away. Learn as you go and do what you can, when you can, with what you have.

2.

THE FIVE FOUNDATIONS OF WELLNESS

"The concept of total wellness recognizes that our every thought, word, and behavior affects our greater health and well-being. And we, in turn, are affected not only emotionally but also physically and spiritually.

—Greg Anderson

While nutrition plays a big role in health and wellness, it is only one piece of the puzzle. It is easy to get so fixated on food that you forget about the other areas of life that need attention. I believe that if you pay attention to all five of these foundations, you will begin to experience true fulfillment, wellness, and happiness. It's time to go beyond the food!

SLEEP

I cannot stress enough the importance of sleep. Sleep is what restores you and helps keep all areas of life in harmony and balance, not to mention that it is critical to your overall health and well-being.

I would guess that if you were honest with yourself, you would have to admit that you place more focus on keeping your phone, laptop, and other gadgets plugged in to recharge than you do on recharging your own body. I've definitely been guilty of treating sleep like a luxury rather than a necessity.

Why is sleep so important?

A lot takes place in your body while you slumber away. During sleep, your body works to repair damaged cells and tissue, boost your immune system, reduce systemic inflammation, heal your gut, and so much more. Sleep affects nearly every tissue in the human body.

Those restorative properties carry over into your waking hours as well. Being well rested can help improve memory, stave off anxiety and depression, lower stress levels, maintain a healthy weight, increase mental clarity and focus, and quicken reflexes, just to name a few of the benefits.

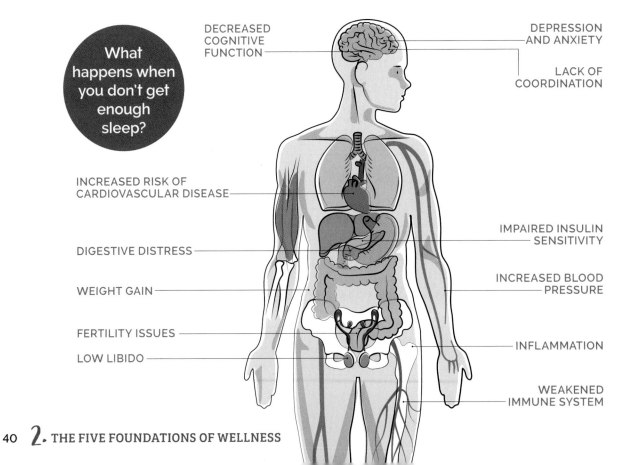

What happens when you don't get enough sleep?

DECREASED COGNITIVE FUNCTION

DEPRESSION AND ANXIETY

LACK OF COORDINATION

INCREASED RISK OF CARDIOVASCULAR DISEASE

DIGESTIVE DISTRESS

WEIGHT GAIN

FERTILITY ISSUES

LOW LIBIDO

IMPAIRED INSULIN SENSITIVITY

INCREASED BLOOD PRESSURE

INFLAMMATION

WEAKENED IMMUNE SYSTEM

Additionally, if you are sleep deprived, you may have trouble controlling your emotions, dealing with change, responding to stress, and managing cravings—all of which are necessary for finding success in any kind of lifestyle or dietary change.

Improving the quality of your sleep

You can implement a lot of small changes that won't feel disruptive to your everyday life and will vastly improve your quality of sleep over time. In fact, you may be sabotaging your shot at a restorative night's sleep without even realizing it. Here are my top ten tips for better sleep:

- Avoid caffeine and other stimulants within five hours of going to bed. Not only can they hinder your ability to fall asleep, but they can also disrupt your sleep throughout the night.

- Reestablish your natural circadian rhythm by having access to natural sunlight throughout the day. In the evening, dim the lights and reduce your exposure to artificial light.

- If evening screen time is unavoidable, purchase a pair of blue light–blocking glasses. Wear them while using your phone or laptop or watching TV. I wore them almost the entire time I was writing this book.

- Invest in a quality mattress. There is no point in saving money on a mattress if you aren't going to be able to get a good night's sleep on it. I like to tell people that you can never spend too much on a good pair of shoes or a bed, because you spend a third of your life in each of them.

- Turn your room into an optimal sleeping environment. Make it as dark as possible. This may require hanging blackout curtains or repositioning alarm clocks. Keep it cool and utilize sheets and blankets to find the perfect sleeping temperature. Lastly, keep it as quiet as possible. If your situation is anything like mine, then this may require earplugs. I sleep in a room with a snoring husband and three snoring pups. The last thing I do before turning in is pop in a pair of earplugs. You can also use a sound machine to block out noises that keep you from sleeping.

- Set aside twenty minutes or so before bedtime to induce relaxation. Go somewhere free of clutter and noise and take some time to focus on breathing techniques, meditation, or even yoga. Reading is another great way to calm your mind and ease yourself into a state of relaxation.

- Set a consistent sleeping schedule. If it is within your power, establish a set bedtime and commit to keeping it every night. Maintaining this pattern will help you fall asleep easier and wake up feeling restored and ready to tackle the day ahead.

- If you are having trouble sleeping, stop trying. What? But isn't that counterproductive? When you are suffering from sleepless nights or true insomnia, the idea of falling asleep can turn into an obsession, and your mind begins to race in a million different directions. Before you know it, it is time to get up, and you've barely slept a wink. Instead of tossing and turning, try getting up and spending fifteen to thirty minutes doing something else to induce sleep. Revisit some of the relaxation tactics I mentioned above, take a hot bath, or listen to soothing music.

- Try taking a natural melatonin supplement to help ease yourself into a state of slumber.

- Avoid alcohol at night. Alcohol can increase snoring, alter melatonin production, and negatively affect hormones. While a glass or two of wine can be really relaxing and help you fall asleep, it can also disrupt your sleep patterns throughout the night.

Keto-friendly foods to help promote a restful night's sleep

There may be nothing worse than trying to fall asleep when your body and brain just won't cooperate. Your thoughts racing, you toss and turn, go over to-do lists, and slowly edge further and further away from a restorative night of sleep. It might be that you can't power your brain down, and every thought that pops into your sleepy mind feels like it needs to be further examined at that very moment. So down the rabbit hole of insomnia you go, looking at the clock every two minutes. You try counting sheep, counting backwards, and all the other tricks, but nothing seems to work.

Before you resort to taking an over-the-counter sleeping pill, you might find relief right in your own kitchen. The following foods help relieve stress, regulate hormones, and induce relaxation. Perhaps natural relief is just a meal or two away.

Almonds: You've undoubtedly heard that almonds are a great source of energy. How could it be that the same food that provides you with natural energy could also be used as a natural sleep aid? In addition to the coenzyme Q10 that provides you with energy, almonds contain tryptophan, which helps relax you and promotes restful sleep.

Chamomile tea: German chamomile is proven to relieve stress and ease anxiety. When taken in large doses, it is also known to help with sleep issues.

Dark chocolate: Dark chocolate reduces cortisol in the brain. Cortisol, a stress hormone, can hinder your ability to let go of racing thoughts at night. Eat small amounts of dark chocolate throughout the day.

Elk: Elk contains twice the amount of tryptophan as turkey, making you much more likely to feel sleepy after consuming it.

Green tea: While green tea does have trace levels of caffeine, drinking green tea during the day can help calm your nerves. It has also been linked to improving symptoms of sleep apnea.

Halibut: Halibut is rich in vitamin B6, a natural sleep aid. B6 produces serotonin and is helpful in relieving leg cramps and restless leg syndrome, which commonly disrupt normal sleep patterns.

Kale: Kale is packed with calcium, which helps the brain use tryptophan to make melatonin and help you sleep.

Lettuce: A salad with dinner each night can go a long way toward correcting sleep issues. Lettuce contains lactucarium, which has natural sedative properties.

Saffron: Saffron aids in relaxation and helps balance mood disorders. Relieving anxiety enables you to fall asleep faster.

Shrimp and lobster: Crustaceans are another great source of tryptophan.

Tart cherries: Cherries increase the level of melatonin in the body and are loaded with antioxidants and phytonutrients. Try eating fresh tart cherries, snacking on no-sugar-added dried cherries, or drinking 100% cherry juice with no sugar added. (*Note:* Cherries have about 1 gram of carbohydrate each, but a few won't hurt, especially if they help you sleep.)

Tomatoes: Tomatoes are loaded with lycopene, which can help improve your quality of sleep.

Walnuts: Walnuts are a great source of serotonin and melatonin, both of which help regulate sleep.

MOVEMENT

Notice that I did not title this section "Fitness" or "Exercise." While those certainly count as movement, my goal here isn't to tell you that you need to jump into a rigorous workout routine or join a gym, but rather to talk about the importance of movement as a whole. Exercise is optional, but movement is essential to nearly every aspect of health and wellness. Movement affects everything from metabolism and immunity to circulation and digestion. And, unlike fitness, it doesn't require much effort.

Our modern society has almost turned sitting into an art form. People are more sedentary than ever. Technology and modern conveniences have made it so that we barely have to lift a finger. Everything is one click away. The agricultural revolution marked a rapid decline in hunter-gatherer lifestyles, making it no longer necessary to move in order to acquire the food needed for survival. Instead of gathering wild plants and hunting animals, people began relying on farmed crops and domesticated animals. Then the Industrial Revolution brought with it even more inactivity as machines began to replace physical labor and people began buying food instead of growing it. Fast-forward to today, and within thirty minutes, we can have food delivered to our doors; we have to move only a few steps to retrieve it before taking those same few steps to sit down and eat it. And, let me tell you, sitting is called the "silent killer" for a reason.

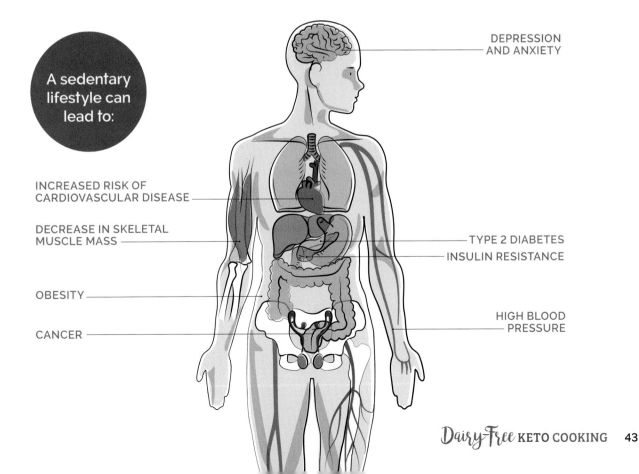

A sedentary lifestyle can lead to:

DEPRESSION AND ANXIETY

INCREASED RISK OF CARDIOVASCULAR DISEASE

DECREASE IN SKELETAL MUSCLE MASS

TYPE 2 DIABETES

INSULIN RESISTANCE

OBESITY

CANCER

HIGH BLOOD PRESSURE

Another reason I keep saying "movement" as opposed to "fitness" or "exercise" is because even if you work out for an hour a day, what you do in the other twenty-three hours matters, too. I'm sorry to tell you, but if you spend an hour in the gym and then drive to an office, sit in a chair all day, drive home, sit for dinner, unwind while sitting in front of the TV, and then go to bed just to do it all over again the next day, you are living a sedentary lifestyle. Now do you see how movement and fitness are not synonymous?

So let's get moving, shall we?

I know that I am always just one workout away from a good mood. I don't work out out of obligation or because I hate my body; I work out because I want to and because I love my body. I do it because it feels good, but more importantly because it is very good for my emotional well-being. But for me, movement doesn't stop after my daily workout. I make a conscious effort to keep moving throughout the day. Here are some things you can do to keep moving:

- Stand and move around at least once every hour that you are awake. An Apple Watch is great for this because it reminds you to stand, but you could just as easily set reminders on your phone.

- Utilize a standing desk or treadmill desk. I have a Surf Shelf on my treadmill. It cost around $30 and allows me to work while walking on the treadmill. I realize that not everyone works from home like I do, but the topic of a standing desk or a more active workplace is definitely worth bringing up with your employer.

- Take the stairs instead of using an elevator or escalator.

- Park farther away from entrances and get in some extra steps.

- Use a rebounder. I have a small trampoline in my garage, and I jump on it for several minutes each day. Not only is it fun, but it is great for circulatory and lymphatic systems.

- Walk while talking on the phone. There is no reason to stay seated when you are on a call; you could be getting in some extra steps instead.

- Walk instead of driving to do the things that are within walking distance of your house, such as shopping and dining out.

Once you start incorporating small bursts of intentional movement into your daily routine, movement will become second nature before you know it, and you won't have to give it a moment's thought. Your body will thank you. I think you will find that you sleep better, have fewer cravings, and feel more at ease, too. Give yourself the gift of movement. You won't regret it.

COMMUNITY AND CONNECTION

In a digital world where people are supposedly more connected than ever, I see a huge disconnect when it comes to personal relationships. Face-to-face meetings have been replaced by emails, and long heart-to-heart phone calls have been replaced by text messages. Even my own mother, who barely understands technology, only wished me happy birthday in an Instagram comment. With more ways to reach people than ever before, as a society we have never been more disconnected.

Your squad, tribe, team, or whatever you choose to call it is an integral part of achieving emotional stability and well-being. Knowing that you are cared for and supported enhances your self-esteem and leads to better coping skills when you hit those unexpected bumps in the road of life. Having people in your corner whom you trust and know you can turn to in times of joy and times of sorrow reduces stress and anxiety and promotes a general sense of contentment and happiness.

As you go through life, you are continually faced with heartbreak, unadulterated joy, and every emotion in between. But it's the people you experience these emotions with who truly affect the outcome.

Cultivating a community

If you don't feel like you have the right support system in place, then perhaps it is time to cultivate one. Whether you are new in town and don't really know anyone or you are seeking to leave toxic relationships, it is never too late to find your tribe. I realize that putting yourself out there can make you feel really exposed and vulnerable, but isn't it worth the effort if the end result is being surrounded by people who truly care for you and lift you up? Making new friends as an adult can seem like an overwhelming task. Here are a few ideas for putting yourself out there and meeting new people:

- **Volunteer:** Donate your time to a cause you are passionate about, and you are sure to find other like-minded individuals.

- **Get active in your local community:** Introduce yourself to your neighbors, participate in a local recreational sports league, attend community theater events, or even join local meet-up groups based on your hobbies and interests.

- **Take a class:** Check the daily deal sites and see what kinds of fun classes are being offered in your area, like a wine and painting night, pottery class, aerial yoga—anything!

- **Join a gym or fitness studio:** Not only is movement an important part of wellness, as discussed earlier in this chapter, but you just might make some health-minded friends in the process.

Choosing the right tribe

When it comes to the people in my life, I have always gone for quality over quantity. I never had the high school mentality of collecting friends, not even in high school. I have always sought to surround myself with people of high caliber. You should, too, and here's why: having the wrong people in your life is, dare I say, even worse than having no support system at all. Clean up your circle of influence and get rid of the toxins just as you would clean your home.

No one gets an automatic pass into your life. Just because you've been friends with someone for twenty years doesn't mean that you have to stay friends. If someone treats you poorly, makes you feel unsupported, or makes you feel bad about yourself, it is time to say goodbye. You are worth more than that. There comes a point when it becomes necessary to end the toxic relationships in your life if you want to begin to truly thrive. And sometimes you have to teach people how to treat you by setting clear and concise boundaries for what you will and will not accept for yourself. I'm not just talking about friends here, either. Biology does not automatically grant someone a place in your life.

In my book *Craveable Keto*, I talk a lot about your circle of influence—the people you associate with most frequently—and what the characteristics and traits of those people say about you. I love this quote by Jim Rohn, and I reflect on it often, both personally and professionally: "You are the average of the five people you spend the most time with." Who are the five people you spend the most time with? This doesn't have to mean face-to-face interaction. Who are you chatting online with the most? Who are you talking on the phone with? Who is in your ear and on your heart? Do you have your five people in mind? Are these people lifting you up and elevating you? Are they supportive, loving, and nurturing? Do they inspire and motivate you? Do they have qualities and characters that you admire and hope to emulate? If you aren't answering yes to these questions, you may need to reassess your circle of influence. Negativity breeds negativity. The same is true with positivity. So why not surround yourself with positive, supportive people? You deserve to be in the company of people who love and support you no matter what life throws your way.

Giving more than you take

I'd like to end this section with the gentle reminder that it is important to give more than you take from your relationships. If every person embodied this mindset, we would all feel so loved, cared for, and supported. No one likes being stuck in a one-way relationship.

- **Express gratitude:** Have an attitude of gratitude and show your appreciation.

- **Communicate openly:** Never assume you know what is going on or let long periods of time pass without speaking your heart. More often than not, the destruction of personal relationships is the result of unspoken assumptions, miscommunication, or no communication at all. Be vulnerable and speak up about the things that bother you.

- **Keep in touch:** Always let people know you care through your words and actions; never let there be any doubt.

- **Be a good listener:** Don't be the kind of listener who is merely waiting for your turn to talk. Engage in active listening.

- **Don't compete:** Relationships are not competitions, or at least they shouldn't be. Share in the successes of the people who matter most to you.

STRESS MANAGEMENT AND SELF-CARE

Self-care and stress management go hand in hand. What better way to relieve stress than by going the extra mile to take care of yourself? But before I dive into what self-care looks like and how to practice it, let's talk a little bit about stress and the negative effects it can have on the human body.

How stress affects your body

As I covered in the section "Breaking through the dreaded weight-loss plateau" (pages 31 to 33), prolonged stress can increase the body's production of cortisol. Cortisol is known as the stress hormone. At normal levels, it helps the body respond to stress, but in excess it can lead to weight gain, especially in the abdominal area. Elevated cortisol levels can also lower immune function, increase blood pressure, and impair learning and memory ability, among other things.

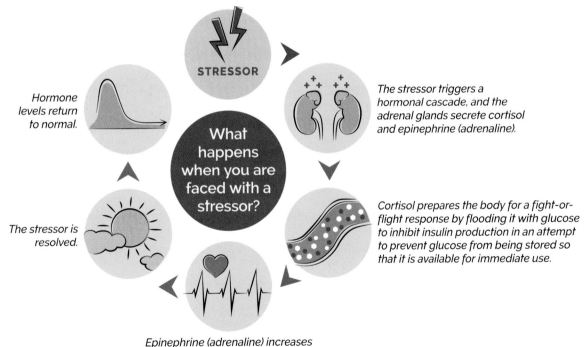

STRESSOR

What happens when you are faced with a stressor?

The stressor triggers a hormonal cascade, and the adrenal glands secrete cortisol and epinephrine (adrenaline).

Cortisol prepares the body for a fight-or-flight response by flooding it with glucose to inhibit insulin production in an attempt to prevent glucose from being stored so that it is available for immediate use.

Epinephrine (adrenaline) increases heart rate and blood pressure.

The stressor is resolved.

Hormone levels return to normal.

But this is a good thing, right? Well, in the case of a single stressful event, yes. This is what I meant when I said that at normal levels, cortisol helps the body respond to stress. But when you are subjected to chronic stress, you get stuck in this loop, and your body is constantly producing cortisol and adrenaline. When the stress response is stuck in the on position, it can wreak havoc on every system in your body. This can lead to metabolic syndrome, adrenal fatigue, and a whole host of other health issues.

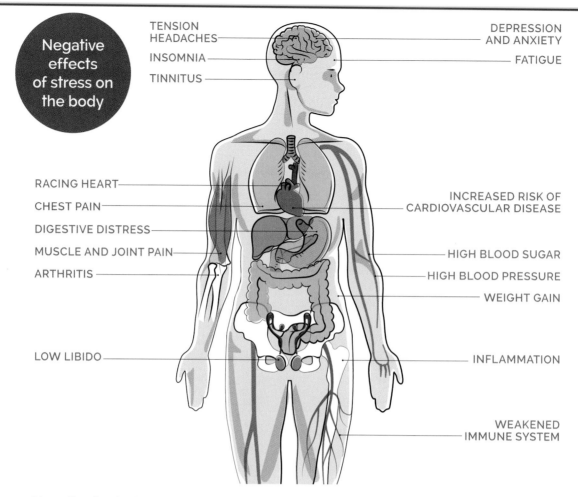

Negative effects of stress on the body

TENSION HEADACHES

INSOMNIA

TINNITUS

DEPRESSION AND ANXIETY

FATIGUE

RACING HEART

CHEST PAIN

DIGESTIVE DISTRESS

MUSCLE AND JOINT PAIN

ARTHRITIS

INCREASED RISK OF CARDIOVASCULAR DISEASE

HIGH BLOOD SUGAR

HIGH BLOOD PRESSURE

WEIGHT GAIN

LOW LIBIDO

INFLAMMATION

WEAKENED IMMUNE SYSTEM

You will notice that there are a lot of overlapping negative effects between chronic stress and sleep deprivation. Imagine the damage being done to your body if you live a high-stress lifestyle *and* are shorting yourself on precious sleep. Scary to think about, right? Well, the good news is that you have the power to change, and many of these negative effects can be reversed once you correct the imbalances. This is where self-care comes into play.

Self-care isn't selfish

I have come to believe that caring for myself is not self-indulgent. Caring for myself is an act of survival.

—Audre Lorde

The term *self-care* has almost become a social media buzzword. People are overspending, overindulging, and coming across as boastful, all in the name of "self-care." Well, that is not the type of self-care I am talking about here. I'm talking about taking care of yourself on a deeper level and doing things that truly nourish and restore you in mind, body, and spirit. I'm talking about getting yourself out of that stress response loop and into a cycle of well-being.

Self-care is more than just a set of actions or a list of ways to pamper yourself. It is about mindset and the habits you put into place to help combat stress, anxiety, depression, and anything in life that makes you unhappy. It doesn't have to mean spending hundreds of dollars at a spa; it can be as simple are saying no. I can't tell you how many times over the course of my life that I said yes when I really wanted to say no. Unfortunately, many of those yeses came at the cost of saying no to myself. Setting boundaries and reserving space for yourself can be the simplest act of self-care. I would even go so far as to call it self-preservation.

Self-care isn't selfish. Before you can do for others, you have to be able to do for yourself. You can't pour from an empty cup. Just like the keto diet itself, there is no one-size-fits-all approach to self-care, either. What restores balance and is relaxing for you might be anxiety-inducing to someone else.

Free ways to practice self-care

- Take a bubble bath.
- Meditate.
- Do yoga. (Check out Yoga With Adriene on YouTube.)
- Spend an entire day alone, free of work, to-do lists, and agendas.
- Give yourself a manicure and pedicure.
- Practice breathing exercises.
- Movement, movement, movement.
- Get lost in a good book.
- Banish the word *should* from your vocabulary. Live from a place of choice rather than obligation.
- Take a nap.
- Make more time for hobbies and passion projects.
- Build a little "me time" into every day, even if it is just fifteen minutes in the morning or before bedtime.
- Catch up with a loved one you have been missing.
- Go for a nice long walk.
- Plan a staycation.
- Get out in nature.
- Spend more time in natural light.
- Listen to soothing music that calms you.
- Take a break from social media.
- Create a list of the things you're grateful for.
- Learn to liberally use the word *no*.
- Dance it out to your favorite playlist.
- Take your time going through your shower and skincare routines and pamper yourself.
- Nourish your body with nutrient-dense foods.
- Practice mindfulness and being present.

None of the items on this list costs money, but they all will go a long way toward reducing stress and helping you find balance within all Five Foundations of Wellness. This is the only body you've got, and it's time to start taking better care of it. Think of yourself in terms of your car or other assets that require general care. You wouldn't run your car into the ground and skip all the necessary maintenance, would you? No, you want to protect your investment. Why should it be any different with your body? Keep those doctors' appointments. Get to the dentist. See a chiropractor if you need to. Invest in yourself. Your body is your most important asset. If you don't care for it, who will?

NUTRITION

While most of this book is about the nutrition part of the Five Foundations of Wellness, here I want to cover what I consider to be the six areas of nutrition that must be in balance in order to achieve optimal health and wellness, as outlined by the Nutritional Therapy Association.

> Don't eat anything your great-great grandmother wouldn't recognize as food. There are a great many foodlike items in the supermarket your ancestors wouldn't recognize as food (Go-Gurt? Breakfast-cereal bars? Nondairy creamer?); stay away from these.

—**Michael Pollan**

1. **Nutrient-dense, whole-food diet:** I use the term *nutrient-dense* throughout this book. But what does it mean to eat a nutrient-dense diet? Nutrients are chemical substances found in food that provide us with the nourishment essential to sustain life and the energy required to survive and thrive. A nutrient-dense, whole-food diet is comprised of minimally processed, unrefined foods in their natural state. It should be free of hydrogenated oils, trans fats, refined sugar and carbs, and chemical additives. A nutrient-dense, whole-food diet also includes local, seasonal, and organic vegetables as well as grass-finished meats, pastured poultry and eggs, and wild-caught seafood whenever possible.

2. **Digestion and elimination:** While eating a nutrient-dense, whole-food diet is essential, your diet is only as good as what your body is able to absorb. In order to absorb the nutrients from the food you eat, you need to be able to mechanically and chemically break down that food. Proper digestion of your food is what provides the essential nutrients to fuel your body and build every single cell that makes up all your tissues and organs. That means ensuring that your gut is healthy and populated with the right balance of good bacteria. (See pages 14 to 16 for more on how this affected me personally.)

3. **Blood sugar regulation:** As I covered on pages 26 and 27, regulating blood sugar levels and avoiding spikes and crashes is crucial to balanced energy levels. Not only does regulating blood sugar provide consistent and balanced energy levels, but it also reduces stress on the body and enables metabolic flexibility (the ability to switch between burning carbs and burning fat). Consistently eating a low-carb, high-fat diet ensures that blood glucose and insulin levels remain stable and that fat is burned for energy. In addition to eating a nutrient-dense, whole-food ketogenic diet, three of the other Five Foundations of Wellness play a big role in blood sugar regulation—getting quality sleep, focusing on movement, and reducing stress.

4. **Fatty acid balance:** Incorporating healthy unsaturated and saturated fats from plant and animal sources is another critical part of a nutrient-dense, whole-food diet. Healthy fats are crucial for blood sugar regulation, stable insulin levels, hormonal balance, optimal brain function, satiety, and regulation of the body's inflammatory response.

5. **Mineral balance:** Minerals make up approximately 5 percent of the human body, and they are critical for the proper function of every system in the body. Minerals transfer nutrients across cell membranes to build healthy bones, contract and relax muscles, and regulate nerve signaling. Common minerals include calcium, magnesium, potassium, and sodium. Your body is unable to make minerals on its own, so you must get them from the foods and beverages you consume. For more on the importance of minerals, check out the sections "Banishing the keto flu" on pages 33 and 34 and "Cracking the code on cravings" on pages 34 and 35.

6. **Hydration:** Water is the most important of all the nutrients and makes up approximately 60 percent of the human body. Drinking enough water is critical to overall hydration and health. Water helps regulate body temperature, cushion and lubricate joints, deliver nutrients and oxygen to cells, and transport waste away from cells and out of the body. Dehydration is the most common reason for mineral deficiency. To get all the amazing and critical life benefits of water, you have to actually absorb the water you drink, which requires a sufficient amount of minerals (electrolytes). Bottom line: drink up!

> All good food comes from the earth. And whether you get that food from a farmers' market, your local grocer, or your own backyard, this I know for sure: The pure joy of eating well is worth savoring.
>
> —**Oprah Winfrey**

3.

SETTING YOURSELF UP FOR SUCCESS ON KETO

DAIRY-FREE KETO-FRIENDLY FOODS

So now that we have discussed what keto is and the many ways to do it, let's talk about all the amazing foods you get to eat. Many people claim that keto is limiting, but if the recipes in this book prove nothing else, let it be that keto is far from restrictive. It's all about changing the way you look at food. Food should never be a punishment or a reward. It is meant to provide your body with the nourishment required to sustain life. That doesn't mean it can't also be enjoyable. It is okay to love food. The goal is to get to a place where the food you love to eat is also the food that loves you back. While you won't see all the foods on these lists used in the recipes in the book, I wanted to give you a full picture of the true variety of foods you can eat even when you are trying to cut back on carbs.

Fats and oils

For its versatility, avocado oil is always my first choice of oil in my recipes. Its neutral flavor and extremely high smoke point mean that it can be used for a range of cooking techniques and applications, from deep-frying to making salad dressings. I also love to save my bacon drippings and use them for recipes like Bacon Fat Hollandaise (page 372) and Cauliflower Alfredo Sauce (page 382). Bacon fat adds a nice smoky flavor to dishes. For baking, I primarily use coconut oil because it can replace butter at a one-to-one ratio. I use olive oil for medium-temperature cooking and in a lot of dressings and vinaigrettes.

Healthy keto fats and oils and their smoke points

FATS AND OILS	SMOKE POINT
Bacon fat	325°F
Butter	350°F
Coconut oil	350°F
Lard	370°F
Duck fat	375°F
Macadamia nut oil	390°F
Beef tallow	400°F
Plain sesame oil	410°F
Olive oil	420°F
Palm oil	450°F
Ghee	480°F
Avocado oil	520°F

What is a smoke point, and why does it matter? *If you have ever left a pan of oil preheating on the stove unattended only to see smoke billowing through your kitchen and the sound of the smoke alarm waging war on your ears, then you have likely taken an oil above its smoke point. Not only can an oil that is heated beyond its smoke point develop an acrid flavor, but the fat starts to break down, releasing harmful free radicals. The higher the smoke point of an oil, the more cooking methods you can use that oil for.*

FATS AND OILS TO AVOID ALTOGETHER

- *canola oil*
- *corn oil*
- *grapeseed oil*
- *peanut oil*
- *rice bran oil*
- *safflower oil*
- *soybean oil*
- *sunflower oil*
- *vegetable oil*

Proteins

Red meat
- beef
- bison
- goat
- lamb
- pork

Wild game
- alligator
- bear
- boar
- elk
- rabbit
- venison

Poultry
- chicken
- duck
- game hen
- ostrich
- pheasant
- quail
- turkey

Eggs
- chicken
- duck
- goose
- ostrich
- pheasant
- quail
- turkey

> *tip*: *When it comes to cured meats like bacon, sausage, pepperoni, salami, and lunch meats, it is best to look for brands that are free of added sugars, coloring, artificial flavors, and nitrates. A few clean brands that I really like are Aidells, Applegate, Isernio's, and Pederson's Natural Farms.*

Seafood

When it comes to seafood, I recommend buying wild-caught, sustainably sourced whenever possible. Wild-caught fish offers higher levels of beneficial omega-3 essential fatty acids, vitamins A and D, B-complex vitamins, iron, potassium, selenium, and zinc than farm-raised fish. Farm-raised fish can also contain high levels of contaminants that are strongly associated with several health problems.

Fish
- anchovies
- catfish
- cod
- flounder
- haddock
- halibut
- mackerel
- mahi mahi
- salmon
- sardines
- sea bass
- snapper
- sole
- swordfish
- tilapia
- trout
- tuna

Shellfish
- clams
- crab
- crayfish
- escargot
- langostinos
- mussels
- octopus
- oysters
- prawns
- scallops
- shrimp
- squid

> Hidden carbs in seafood: *While most fish have zero carbs, there are carbs in some shellfish. Many people do not realize this, and it can lead to a lot of extra carb consumption. The table below provides details on hidden carbs in certain types of seafood. Also, be sure to steer clear of imitation crab meat, or "Krab with a K," as it is typically nicknamed; it contains a hefty 13 grams of carbs per 3 ounces.*

SEAFOOD TYPE	SERVING SIZE	TOTAL CARBS
Oysters	1 medium	1g
Scallops	2 medium	1g
Escargot	6 ounces	3g
Octopus	6 ounces	4g
Clams	12 medium	5g
Mussels	10 medium	5g
Squid	6 ounces	5g

Fruits and vegetables

Can we all just stop demonizing fruits and vegetables already? I can't tell you how many times I have seen people become recreationally outraged on Instagram when I post my meals. Which, by the way, are usually loaded with fresh vegetables. The comments range from "not low-carb" and "vegetables aren't keto" to "I would gain so much weight if I ate that" and "are you really going to eat all that?" Three of these comments play right into diet dogma, and the fourth one is downright shaming. Heaven forbid I ever post a small serving of fresh berries; I think the internet might just implode and cease to exist.

Look, I get it. I really do. A lot of people want to throw down meat and cheese all day without a vegetable in sight. That is their prerogative. I am not the food police. What is on their plates is none of my business. But I can tell you one thing with absolute certainty: my lifelong struggles with my weight have never been the result of eating too many fresh fruits and vegetables. You will never hear anyone say, "I'm overweight because I just love carrots and broccoli so much." Doesn't that sound ridiculous? While we all may take different approaches to keto and to overall health and wellness, I think we can agree that eating real, whole, nutrient-dense foods is the best way to go. Don't you want to eat the foods that nourish you in mind, body, and spirit?

When it comes to the nonstarchy, lower-carb vegetables, I say go nuts! Er, go broccoli?

The following chart includes the most common lower-carb fruits and vegetables. I have listed their serving sizes, total carb counts, and net carb counts. This will give you a quick at-a-glance reference when you need help determining the carb count of a specific fruit or vegetable.

Per 100-g/3.5-Ounce Serving (unless otherwise noted)	TOTAL CARBS	FIBER	NET CARBS
Artichoke hearts	5.4g	1.5g	3.9g
Arugula	3.7g	1.6g	2.1g
Asparagus	3.9g	2.1g	1.8g
Avocado	8.6g	6.8g	1.8g
Bell peppers	4.6g	1.7g	2.9g
Blackberries	10g	5g	5g
Blueberries	14g	2.4g	11.6g
Broccoli	6.6g	2.6g	4g
Brussels sprouts	9g	4g	5g
Cabbage, green	6g	3g	3g
Cabbage, red	7.4g	2.1g	5.3g
Carrots	9.6g	2.8g	6.8g
Cauliflower	5g	2g	3g
Celery	3g	1.6g	1.4g
Chives	4.4g	2.5g	1.9g
Cranberries	12g	4.6g	7.4g
Cucumbers	3.6g	0.5g	3.1g
Eggplant	5.9g	3g	2.9g
Garlic (per clove)	1g	0g	1g
Ginger (per tablespoon grated)	1.2g	0g	1.2g

Per 100-g/3.5-Ounce Serving (unless otherwise noted)	TOTAL CARBS	FIBER	NET CARBS
Green beans	7g	2.7g	4.3g
Green onions	7g	2.6g	4.4g
Kale	8.8g	3.6g	5.2g
Lemons (per lemon)	5g	1.6g	3.4g
Lettuce	2.9g	1.3g	1.6g
Limes (per lime)	7g	2g	5g
Microgreens	4g	3g	1g
Mushrooms	3.3g	1g	2.3g
Olives	6g	3.2g	2.8g
Onions, white or yellow	9.3g	1.7g	7.6g
Oranges (per 1 small orange)	11g	2.3g	8.7g
Radishes	3.4g	1.6g	1.8g
Raspberries	12g	7g	5g
Red onions	8g	1.5g	6.5g
Shallots (per tablespoon chopped)	1.7g	0.3g	1.4g
Spaghetti squash	7g	1.5g	5.5g
Spinach	3.6g	2.2g	1.4g
Strawberries	8g	2g	6g
Tomatoes	3.9g	1.2g	2.7g
Zucchini	3.1g	1g	2.1g

In the Case of Fruits and Vegetables, Net Carbs or Total Carbs?

Personally, I have always landed smack dab in the middle of the total versus net debate. I count net carbs for fresh fruits and vegetables and total carbs for everything else. The reason is that fresh fruits and vegetables are loaded with fiber. Unlike other carbs, dietary fiber can't be broken down and absorbed by your digestive system. Instead, it passes relatively intact through the digestion process as it makes its way out of your body.

Herbs and spices

Herbs and spices are star of the show when it comes to cooking. There is nothing quite like a perfectly spiced, delicately balanced meal. Herbs and spices not only add flavor and aroma to dishes, but in some cases, they add texture, too. They are the ingredients that transform a dish from blah to aha!

• Store spices and dried herbs in airtight jars, away from heat and sunlight, to preserve freshness, extend shelf life, and ensure maximum flavor.

• Don't forget to account for the carbs in herbs and spices. People often ask me where the carbs in spices come from. Well, if fresh garlic has carbs, then naturally the dried, powdered form does as well.

I have quite a large collection of herbs and spices. They are some of my favorite ingredients to buy. I love walking through spice shops and inhaling the scent of each spice while silently dreaming up the dishes I would create with it. I have even been known to create an entire dish around the flavor profile of one specific spice.

The following are lists of the fresh herbs I grow in my kitchen window and the most commonly used dried herbs and spices in my pantry.

Fresh from the herb garden

Dried from the pantry

- basil
- bay leaves
- black pepper (ground and whole peppercorns)
- caraway seeds
- cayenne pepper
- celery salt
- chili powder
- Chinese five-spice
- cinnamon (ground and sticks)
- cloves (ground)
- cumin (ground)
- curry powder
- dill
- dried minced garlic
- dried minced onion
- fennel seeds
- garlic powder
- ground ginger
- Himalayan pink salt
- Italian seasoning
- lemon pepper seasoning
- mustard powder
- mustard seeds (yellow)
- nutmeg (ground)
- onion powder
- oregano leaves
- paprika
- parsley
- red pepper flakes
- rosemary leaves
- rubbed sage
- sea salt
- tarragon leaves
- thyme leaves
- toasted sesame seeds
- turmeric powder

Seasoning blends from this book

Blackening Seasoning (398)

Everyday Seasoning Blend (400)

Everything Bagel Seasoning (399)

Fajita Seasoning (397)

Pumpkin Pie Spice (396)

Nuts and seeds

Nuts and seeds can be tricky on keto (or in any style of eating) because it is easy to overindulge or snack away mindlessly. While they are a great source of healthy fats, they are also high in calories, and the carbs add up quickly. Nut and seed butters fall into this category, too. I recommend portioning out individual servings to help create good snacking habits.

NUTS Per ¼ Cup	TOTAL CARBS	FIBER	NET CARBS
Pecans	1g	0.7g	0.3g
Pili nuts	1.2g	0g	1.2g
Walnuts	3.4g	1.7g	1.8g
Brazil nuts	3.9g	2.5g	1.4g
Pine nuts	4.4g	1.2g	3.2g
Macadamia nuts	4.6g	2.9g	1.7g
Hazelnuts	5.6g	3.3g	2.4g
Peanuts*	5.9g	3.1g	2.8g
Almonds	7.7g	4.5g	3.2g
Pistachios	8.4g	3.3g	5.1g
Cashews	9.6g	1.1g	8.6g

SEEDS Per ¼ Cup	TOTAL CARBS	FIBER	NET CARBS
Hemp (hulled)	3.5g	2.3g	1.2g
Pepitas (pumpkin)	3.5g	1.9g	1.5g
Sunflower (hulled)	7g	3g	4g
Sesame (black and/or white)	8.4g	4.2g	4.2g
Flax	12.1g	11.5g	0.7g
Chia	15.2g	13.3g	1.9g

*peanuts are technically legumes

Condiments, dressings, and sauces

Many store-bought condiments, dressings, and sauces are low in carbs, but let's not forget that ingredients matter, too. Unfortunately, it can be really difficult to find products made with only clean, whole-food ingredients. But have no fear, I've got you covered! I've packed this book full of delicious, easy-to-make, homemade versions of the condiments, dressings, and sauces you love the most. Don't see what you're after? Be sure to check out my site, peaceloveandlowcarb.com, for an even wider selection of these types of recipes.

 372
Bacon Fat Hollandaise

 392
Balsamic Horseradish Chimichurri

 375
Caesar Dressing

 384
Classic Marinara Sauce

 367
Coconut Milk Whipped Cream

 393
Crack Sauce

 374
Creamy Avocado Dressing

 380
Dairy-Free Alfredo Sauce Two Ways

 388
Everything Bagel Aioli

 377
Lemon Basil Vinaigrette

 389
Lime Sriracha Aioli

 386
Mayo Ten Ways

 394
Peanut Sauce

 395
Pistachio Pesto

 376
Ranch Dressing

 390
Roasted Red Pepper Aioli

 391
Sweet and Spicy Barbecue Sauce

 378
Tomato Meat Sauce

Pantry items

Vinegars and flavorings

- apple cider vinegar
- balsamic vinegar
- coconut aminos
- cooking sherry
- distilled white vinegar
- fish sauce
- gluten-free soy sauce
- hot sauce
- maple extract
- mustard, Dijon and yellow
- pure almond extract
- pure lemon extract
- pure orange extract
- pure vanilla extract
- red wine vinegar
- Sriracha sauce
- toasted sesame oil
- unseasoned rice wine vinegar

Boxed, canned, and jarred goods

- artichoke hearts
- beef stock
- black olives
- capers
- chicken stock
- crushed tomatoes
- diced green chilies
- diced tomatoes
- diced tomatoes and green chilies
- dill pickles
- giardiniera
- green olives
- pepperoncini
- pork rinds
- pumpkin puree
- roasted red peppers
- stewed tomatoes
- sun-dried tomatoes
- sustainably caught canned salmon
- sustainably caught canned tuna
- tomato paste

Baking ingredients

- almond flour
- baking powder
- baking soda
- coconut flour
- nutritional yeast
- psyllium husk powder
- sugar-free dark chocolate chips
- sugar-free maple syrup
- unsweetened cocoa powder

Sweeteners

- brown sugar erythritol
- granular erythritol
- monk fruit
- powdered erythritol
- powdered stevia

Coffee boosters

- butter-flavored coconut oil
- collagen peptides
- dairy-free keto vanilla protein powder
- grass-fed gelatin
- MCT oil powder (flavored or unflavored)

Beverages

Low-carb beverages are one of the things I get asked about the most. Personally, I keep things pretty simple with water, sparkling water, coffee, kombucha, and the occasional (or sometimes more than occasional) keto-friendly alcoholic beverage—usually wine or vodka. If you crave more than just the basics or are looking for something sweeter in an attempt to slay the sugar dragon, I recommend checking out my book *Keto Happy Hour.* All the cocktails in that book can be mixed without alcohol to make delicious mocktails, too.

Low-carb beverages

- Almond Coconut Milk (page 346)
- Bone Broth (page 370)
- coffee (see "Ordering Keto at Starbucks" on pages 70 to 72)
- kombucha (higher in carbs, but great for the gut)
- sparkling water (with or without flavor enhancers)
- tea
- unsweetened almond milk
- unsweetened coconut milk
- water

Low-carb alcoholic beverages

Whether or not to include alcohol as part of your ketogenic lifestyle is completely up to you. I've read countless articles on the subject, and strong cases are made on both sides. Ultimately, it boils down to personal preference. If alcohol works for you, great. If it doesn't work for you, also great. If you notice one theme throughout this book, I hope it is that I truly believe there is no one-size-fits-all approach to life, and no one-size-fits-all approach to keto.

Wine: Wine is a great option whether you're entertaining at home or dining out. As long as you stick to dry or semisweet red, white, and sparkling wines, you can rest assured that in most cases a glass of wine will come in at less than 5 grams of carbs, which makes it a safe and easy go-to. It's also a great choice because you always know exactly what you are getting; when ordering a mixed drink, you run the risk of accidentally getting poured a high-carb alcohol or mixer.

Plus, wine is delicious. These days I mostly stick to champagne and dry sparkling wines. They are the lowest in carbs, plus I love the bubbles!

RED WINE	CARBS IN 5 FLUID OUNCES
Pinot Noir	3.5g
Merlot	3.7g
Cabernet	3.8g
Syrah	3.8g
Zinfandel	3.8g
WHITE WINE	
Sparkling white	1.5g
Brut champagne	2.5g
Sauvignon Blanc	2.8g
Pinot Grigio	3g
Chardonnay	3.1g
White Zinfandel	5g
Riesling	5.7g

Beer and spiked seltzer: I've compiled a list of beers that contain less than 6 grams of carbs per bottle. They are all easy to find at your local grocery store. However, please note that none of these beers is gluten-free. If you are living a strict gluten-free lifestyle, I would steer clear of beer. While I love a good craft beer, it doesn't love me back, and very rarely do I find it worth it to drink one.

BEER	CARBS IN 12 FLUID OUNCES
Bud Select 55	1.9g
Miller 64	2.4g
Rolling Rock Green Light	2.4g
Michelob Ultra	2.6g
Bud Select	3.1g
Busch Light	3.2g
Natural Light	3.2g
Miller Lite	3.2g
Michelob Ultra Amber	3.7g
Coors Light	5g
Corona Light	5g
Amstel Light	5g
Bud Light	6.6g
Heineken Light	6.8g
SPIKED SELTZER WATER	
Truly Spiked and Sparkling	2g
White Claw	4g
Spiked Seltzer	5g

tip: Check out beer brands like Omission that are crafted to remove gluten. If you have a higher carb allowance or are at a maintenance weight, hard cider can be a good option as well.

Liquor: Contrary to popular belief, not all liquors are low-carb and gluten-free. In fact, many are very high in carbs and contain added sugars. It is important to look at each brand individually for product and nutritional information. However, here are some basic guidelines for common types of liquor. The best rule to follow when crafting a low-carb cocktail is to stick to plain, unsweetened, unflavored clear liquors, like vodka, gin, and white rum. Tequila and whiskey are also safe bets.

LIQUOR	CARBS IN 1½ FLUID OUNCES
Dark rum	0g
Gin	0g
Light rum	0g
Tequila	0g
Vodka	0g
Whiskey/Bourbon	0–0.3g
Brandy	0–3g
Spiced rum	0.5g

For more information about alcohol on a keto diet, check out my book Keto Happy Hour.

INGREDIENTS USED IN THIS BOOK

I am a firm believer that you do not need a bunch of expensive, hard-to-find specialty ingredients to successfully live a ketogenic lifestyle. Keto should be about real, whole, nutrient-dense foods. I have made it my personal mission to keep all the recipes on my site and in my cookbooks accessible and approachable and to use only ingredients that can be found at a typical local grocery store. However, you may find better prices online at sites like Amazon and Thrive Market. Let's face it, everyone likes to save money.

That said, some of these common keto ingredients may be less than familiar to you, especially if you are still fairly new to ketogenic cooking. This list provides some tips on what to look for when purchasing these ingredients.

Almond flour: The recipes in this book call for blanched almond flour. *Blanched* simply means that the skins are removed from the almonds before they are ground into flour. Blanched almond flour is also typically ground finer, making it a better option for low-carb baking. My two favorite brands are Bob's Red Mill and Anthony's.

Apple cider vinegar: For maximum nutritional value, choose a raw, unfiltered version. My favorite brand is Bragg.

Avocado oil: I recommend avocado oil as the first choice for all the recipes in this book. This is because it is very light and mild-flavored, and it has a high smoke point. It is as stable for cooking at moderate temperatures as it is for high-temperature cooking, broiling, and frying, yet it is delicate enough to make the perfect base for a vinaigrette. My favorite brand is Chosen Foods.

Broths and stocks: If you don't have a batch of homemade bone broth (page 370) on hand, or you simply don't want to make it, there are several excellent brands of prepackaged stock. In fact, more often than not, that is what I use. When picking a store-bought stock, just be sure to read the labels. Many store-bought versions contain evaporated cane juice. What you

want is an ingredient list that includes only chicken or beef, vegetables, herbs, spices, and water. My favorite brand is Bonafide Provisions.

Butter-flavored coconut oil: This is a newer ingredient to me. With the exception of the Garlic and Herb Skillet Rib-Eyes (page 216) and Boosted Keto Coffee (page 340), I didn't list it as a required ingredient in any of the recipes in case you aren't able to find it, but I do mention it throughout the book, so I wanted to introduce it here. The product I use is made by Nutiva and contains no artificial ingredients, colors, or flavorings. When I saw "butter-flavored" on the label, I took pause because the word *flavor* in an ingredient list isn't usually a good thing, but in this case, the butter flavoring comes entirely from plant sources. If you are really missing butter, then this is an excellent addition to your dairy-free keto pantry. But I think the million-dollar question here is whether or not it tastes like coconut oil. It really doesn't. I personally don't enjoy the flavor of coconut, so you can guarantee that if I am recommending it, you won't be overpowered by the taste of coconut. The best prices I have seen for it are at Walmart and on Amazon and Thrive Market.

Cauliflower rice: In my book *Craveable Keto*, I cover some of the techniques for ricing your own cauliflower, like using a box grater or food processor. But for this book, I went the easier route and used store-bought riced cauliflower. It is widely available in nearly every grocery store these days and comes both fresh and frozen. For the recipes in the book, you can use either fresh or frozen and achieve the same results.

Coconut aminos: Coconut aminos is an excellent gluten-free and soy-free substitute for soy sauce. The recipes in this book call for gluten-free soy sauce (tamari) or coconut aminos. My favorite brands are Bali Tree Farm and Thrive Market. Note that if you are using coconut aminos in place of gluten-free soy sauce in these recipes, it may be necessary to season the dish with additional salt, because coconut aminos contains far less sodium than soy sauce.

Coconut flour: Nutiva is my favorite brand of coconut flour; I find it to be the most reliable for baking. Coconut flour is extremely absorbent, so when substituting coconut flour for another type, it is necessary to add more liquid and more egg. A good rule of thumb is to substitute 1 cup of almond flour with ¼ cup of coconut flour and one additional egg. If replacing more than 1 cup of almond flour, it is necessary to add one additional egg for each ¼ cup of coconut flour being used. It may be necessary to double the amount of liquid called for in the recipe as well. If the mixture seems too dry, simply add more liquid, a little at a time, until it reaches your desired consistency. If the mixture is too wet, add more coconut flour, mixing in 1 teaspoon at a time.

Coconut milk: I recommend buying unsweetened full-fat canned coconut milk. Trader Joe's sells a good-quality, affordable version. You can also get shelf-stable cartons of coconut milk, but be sure to buy only brands that are free of sugars and sweeteners and contain only coconut, water, and a natural stabilizer, such a guar gum.

Dairy-free keto vanilla protein powder: This ingredient is used in only a handful of recipes in the book, and I want to make it known that it is absolutely not a necessity. I have listed it here so that I could make brand suggestions to point you in the right direction. My favorite brand of dairy-free protein powder is Equip Foods. Their protein powders are dairy-free, gluten-free, soy-free, Paleo-friendly, and non-GMO and contain no artificial sweeteners, hormones, antibiotics, fillers, or preservatives.

Erythritol (granular, powdered, and brown sugar): My go-to brand for all my sweetening needs is Swerve. Swerve is a blended erythritol-based sweetener that measures cup for cup with sugar, has zero calories, and contains no artificial ingredients, flavors, or preservatives.

Golden flaxseed meal: Golden flaxseed meal has a mild, nutty flavor and is an excellent source of fiber and omega-3 fatty acids. It is a great low-carb and gluten-free option for breading mixes as well as baking. My favorite brand is Bob's Red Mill.

Grass-fed collagen peptides and gelatin: While both are extremely healthy for you and both are technically collagen, collagen peptides and gelatin are very different. Collagen peptides will not gel like gelatin does. Peptides merely dissolve into liquid, hot or cold. For the Boosted Keto Coffee (page 340), you will need collagen peptides, and for the Kombucha Gummy Snacks (page 136), you will need gelatin. I put collagen peptides in my coffee every day for the amazing benefits to gut health, joints, hair, skin, and nails. My favorite brand is Vital Proteins.

Meats: Whenever possible, I buy humanely raised meats from small family farms (local when I can)—grass-fed beef, organic pastured chicken, and pasture-raised heritage pork. It is important to me to know the history of my meat and to support companies that put the ethical treatment of animals at the forefront of their mission, vision, and values. I also have a monthly subscription to ButcherBox, a company that delivers clean meat right to my door, and absolutely love it.

Nutritional yeast: Since I transitioned to a dairy-free ketogenic lifestyle, nutritional yeast, or "nooch," as it is affectionately referred to, has been a lifesaver for me when the craving for cheese hits. It has a nutty, cheesy flavor resembling that of freshly grated Parmesan cheese. Nutritional yeast is gluten-free and contains a full spectrum of B vitamins. You will see it used throughout this book to add a cheesy flavor to recipes. I even love to sprinkle it over the tops of salads. While it may be a newer ingredient to you, you will soon wonder how you got on this far without it. My favorite brand is Bragg.

Pastured eggs: Buying pastured eggs (not to be confused with pasteurized eggs) is another case where I believe in "voting with my dollars." Not only are pastured eggs higher in omega-3 fatty acids, vitamins A and E, and beta-carotene, but the hens are raised with the freedom and space to roam outdoors in the sunshine and fresh air and feed on wild grasses and bugs as they are meant to do. If you do not have access to local farm-fresh eggs where you live, then I highly recommend buying Happy Eggs.

Psyllium husk powder: Not only is psyllium husk powder really good for digestive health, but it is also a dream for low-carb baking. In fact, without it, the bread recipes in this book wouldn't be possible. Note that some brands turn baked goods purple. I recommend Now Foods brand; not only is it one of the more affordable and accessible brands out there, but it doesn't turn foods purple. I find the best prices on Amazon and Thrive Market.

Sea salt: I used fine sea salt in all the recipes throughout this book, except where another type of salt is noted. My favorite brand (and the only one I use and recommend) is Redmond Real Salt. Real Salt is a great choice because it is unrefined and provides vital minerals that help support a healthy body. Best of all, it is mined from an ancient sea bed right here in the U.S.

Shirataki noodles: I have to be honest: initially, I was not a fan of shirataki noodles. I couldn't get past their fishy smell and slimy texture. (I'm really selling them here, I know!) But once I realized that I just hadn't been buying the right brands or preparing them correctly, everything changed. Now I am a huge fan! When cooking with shirataki noodles, it is imperative to drain the liquid that comes in the bag, soak the noodles in fresh water for at least 20 minutes, and then give them another good rinse and drain them again. If they still feel a little slimy, I recommend dry-frying them over medium heat for about 5 minutes. Taking these steps will drastically change the way they perform in a recipe. My favorite brand (and the only one I use and recommend) is House Foods.

Sugar-free dark chocolate chips: Many of the sweet treat recipes in this book call for sugar-free dark chocolate chips. My brand of choice is Lily's. Lily's chocolate chips are sweetened with erythritol and stevia and don't contain any artificial ingredients. They are vegan, non-GMO, and fair trade. I find the best pricing from Thrive Market.

Sugar-free syrups: Most store-bought sugar-free maple syrup substitutes contain aspartame, sucralose, sorbitol, and/or maltitol, which are artificial sweeteners/sugar alcohols that are known to cause digestive distress—not to mention that they also contain caramel color, artificial flavors, and preservatives, just to name a few of the other red flags. I like Lakanto maple syrup alternative, which is sweetened with monk fruit and has no funky, hard-to-pronounce ingredients. Lakanto also makes caramel- and vanilla-flavored coffee syrups.

SIMPLE FOOD SWAPS

Now you've got a better idea of the kinds of foods you can eat on a ketogenic diet, but you might still be wondering about how to replace some of your high-carb favorites. It takes time to change old habits, but I'm confident that with a little creativity, you'll be able to find low-carb substitutes for most, if not all, of those items. Here is a list of some simple swaps that you can make for everyday high-carb foods. I hope these substitutions help put some of your favorite foods back on the table.

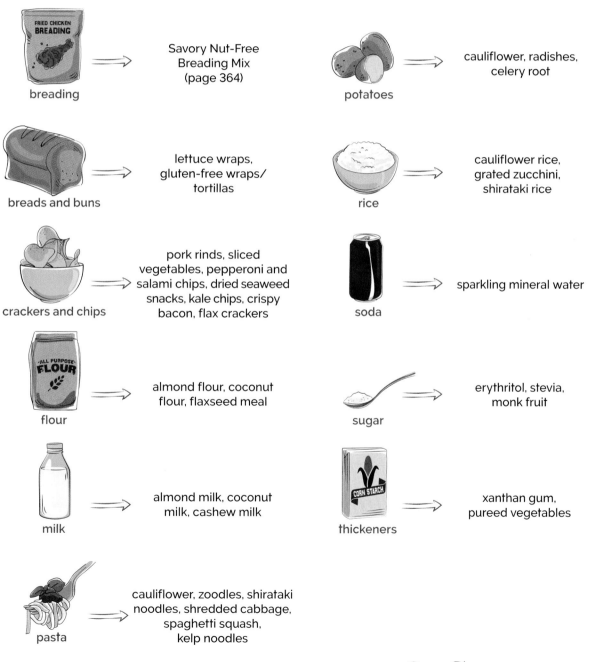

breading ⟶ Savory Nut-Free Breading Mix (page 364)

potatoes ⟶ cauliflower, radishes, celery root

breads and buns ⟶ lettuce wraps, gluten-free wraps/ tortillas

rice ⟶ cauliflower rice, grated zucchini, shirataki rice

crackers and chips ⟶ pork rinds, sliced vegetables, pepperoni and salami chips, dried seaweed snacks, kale chips, crispy bacon, flax crackers

soda ⟶ sparkling mineral water

flour ⟶ almond flour, coconut flour, flaxseed meal

sugar ⟶ erythritol, stevia, monk fruit

milk ⟶ almond milk, coconut milk, cashew milk

thickeners ⟶ xanthan gum, pureed vegetables

pasta ⟶ cauliflower, zoodles, shirataki noodles, shredded cabbage, spaghetti squash, kelp noodles

DAIRY-FREE KETO SNACKS

I am not much of a snacker. I am usually content between meals with one of the three beverages that can usually be found in front of me at all times: water, kombucha, and coffee. However, I always make sure to keep quality snacks on hand, especially when traveling, so that if the clock ticks past mealtime, I have a healthy option. This keeps me from reaching for the wrong things out of hanger and desperation. I also know that snacking is a tricky subject for many people, especially when first transitioning to a ketogenic lifestyle. After a while, you may find that you just aren't hungry for snacks. In the meantime, though, the following list provides some good choices.

Grab-and-go snacks

- canned tuna or salmon (sustainably caught)
- celery
- dark chocolate
- dried seaweed snacks
- flax crackers
- jerky
- kale chips
- keto-friendly snack bars
- meat sticks
- mixed berries
- nuts and seeds
- olives
- pickles
- pork rinds
- sardines
- unsweetened coconut chips

Snacks with minimal prep required

- bacon, pepperoni, or salami chips
- baked cucumber or zucchini chips
- Brussels sprouts chips
- hard-boiled eggs
- minute muffins
- mug cakes
- protein shakes
- sliced bell peppers or cucumbers

Snack options from this book

399
avocado sprinkled with Everything Bagel Seasoning

130
Bacon-Wrapped Avocado Fries

370
Bone Broth

340
Boosted Keto Coffee

132
Charcuterie Board

312
Chocolate Peanut Butter Coconut Fat Bombs

152
Crispy Oven-Fried Pickles

140
Cumin-Spiced Pecans

184
Egg Salad Prosciutto Cups

314
Fat-Boosted Chocolate Nut Butter

308
Fruit and Nut Chocolates

148
Garlic Dill Sauerkraut

136
Kombucha Gummy Snacks

350
PB&J Smoothie

330
Peanut Butter Chocolate No-Bake Granola Squares

154
Pickled Asparagus

144
Quick and Easy Chunky Guacamole

200
Ranch Chicken Salad Cups

156
Spicy Fried Ham Deviled Eggs

158
Sugar-Free Dried Cranberries

160
Sweet and Savory Trail Mix

336
Vanilla Chia Pudding

376
vegetables and Ranch Dressing

ORDERING KETO AT STARBUCKS

I was born and raised in Washington State, just outside Seattle. You could say that Seattle is the coffee capital of the U.S. The city of Seattle has the greatest concentration of coffeehouses in the country. The original Starbucks opened in 1971 in the Pike Place Market and has been iconic to this area ever since. It is part of our landscape. It's just something we do. I am surprised it is not used as a verb yet—like Facebooking, Googling, or tweeting. Friend: "Hey, what are you up to tomorrow?" Me: "Oh, you know, just Starbucking."

Now, it's rare to travel anywhere and not see a Starbucks. People get up early to grab it before work. They wait in long lines, preorder through the app, and even fork over cash they really don't have for a cup of that delicious bean juice. I find that the baristas there tend to get my drink order wrong far more often than they get it right. But when they do get it exactly right, it is oh so delicious.

So the big question on many low-carbers' minds is "Do I have to give up my daily Starbucks to maintain my low-carb, ketogenic lifestyle?" The answer is NO! You just have to get creative with your ordering. Don't be too shy to ask for exactly what you want. You are handing over your hard-earned money and paying a premium to go to Starbucks versus other coffee chains. Therefore, you should get exactly what you want, even if it is an off-menu or custom-made drink. Not once have I been met with anything but friendliness when requesting a special order. The baristas may not always get it right, but they certainly try, and they are always willing to remake it. I am here to help you get creative with your low-carb ordering. Starbucks is back on your low-carb menu!

So what can you order? Here are several options to get you started. Note that this list is not exclusively dairy-free; I wanted to include dairy options as well since this is a question I get asked so frequently.

What to know before you go

- Starbucks puts their signature Classic Syrup (liquid cane sugar) in a lot of their drinks. If you aren't sure whether the drink you are ordering normally contains it, err on the side of caution and ask for it without. Also note that not all stores make the drinks the same way. They should, but they don't. So just because one location makes your drink right doesn't mean that another location will. Always ask for exactly what you want, and don't be afraid to ask for clarification.

- Starbucks carries almond and coconut milk, but they are sweetened and contain about 5 grams of carbs per cup. This is substantially lower than dairy milk, but be aware before you order.

- While the drinks I've listed are better options for you, they aren't necessarily the best. Starbucks does use some questionable ingredients that I recommend avoiding. However, as I talked about at great length earlier in the book, I am a firm believer in doing the best you can, when you can, with what you have. No food police here. That being said, there are some things you can do to clean up your drink routine even further:

  • Add your own erythritol- or monk fruit–sweetened coffee syrups.

  • Add your own natural sweetener instead of the artificial sugar-free sweeteners that Starbucks offers. Many of their sugar-free syrups are made with sucralose, aspartame, saccharin, and maltitol. Try using erythritol, monk fruit, or stevia instead.

  • Use your own unsweetened coconut or almond milk. However, this works only for cold drinks, as the baristas aren't allowed to let any outside sources come into contact with their equipment.

The obvious choices

- **Cappuccino:** Cappuccino is just espresso and milk foam. If you like it wetter, it also has a little steamed milk in it. You can drink it plain or add sugar-free syrup to it, and you can substitute any type of nondairy milk. The lower the fat content of the milk, the higher the carbs. The higher the fat content, the less foamy the cappuccino will be. Coconut milk cappuccinos are delicious.

- **Cold brew:** This is made in house daily and in small batches. Get it early before it sells out.

- **Drip coffee:** You can drink it black or add coconut or almond milk (or heavy cream or half-and-half) and sugar-free syrup to it. This is how I drink my coffee at home on most days—when I am not drinking Boosted Keto Coffee (page 340), that is.

- **Espresso:** A shot of espresso has less than 1 gram of carbs. It is definitely an acquired taste, but it is always a viable option.

- **Hot tea:** Starbucks has a lot of great hot tea flavors. Drink the tea as is or add a little keto-friendly sweetener.

- **Iced coffee:** Again, you can add any sugar-free syrups you want. You can also add coconut or almond milk (or heavy cream or half-and-half).

Latte substitutions

- Order an americano (iced or hot) with a splash of coconut or almond milk (or heavy cream). If you want it flavored, add any of their sugar-free syrups.

- Order a latte and sub coconut or almond milk (or half-and-half [breve] or heavy cream). If you want it flavored, add any of their sugar-free syrups. This drink is very creamy. If you don't want it so rich, order the americano option above instead.

- Order a flat white, but substitute coconut or almond milk (or half-and-half [breve], or half heavy cream and half water) for the whole milk.

- Order a chai tea latte and ask for two brewed tea bags instead of the tea concentrate. Then add sugar-free vanilla syrup and a splash of coconut or almond milk (or heavy cream).

Mocha substitutions

- Order a Skinny Mocha made with coconut or almond milk (or half-and-half [breve], or half heavy cream and half water) instead of nonfat milk.

- Order an americano with Skinny Mocha Sauce and a splash of coconut or almond milk (or heavy cream).

- Order a coconut or almond milk mocha made with Skinny Mocha Sauce.

- Order a sugar-free peppermint mocha made with coconut or almond milk (or half-and-half [breve], or half heavy cream and half water) and Skinny Mocha Sauce.

Frappuccino substitutions

- This order took the baristas a couple of tries to get right. They looked at me like I was nuts, but once they got it, it became my favorite summer drink. Ask for a Coffee Light Frappuccino made with coconut or almond milk (or half water and half heavy cream) instead of nonfat milk. It has a subtle sweetness all on its own, but you can add any of their sugar-free syrups for a little more flavor.

- Ask for a Sugar-Free Cinnamon Dolce Light Frappuccino made with coconut or almond milk (or half water and half heavy cream) instead of nonfat milk. Trust me when I tell you that your low-carb blended coffee drink game just got elevated.

Non-coffee substitutions

- Order a hot chocolate made with coconut or almond milk (or half-and-half [breve]) and Skinny Mocha Sauce.

- For a keto Pink Drink, order an unsweetened Passion Tango Tea with no Classic Syrup (again with that pesky Classic Syrup!) and add sugar-free vanilla syrup and a splash of coconut or almond milk (or heavy cream). You can even add a little freeze-dried strawberries.

KITCHEN TOOLS AND APPLIANCES

Stocking and organizing your kitchen with the right tools and appliances can dramatically change your experience in the kitchen. Having the things you need on hand, and in the right place, makes cooking a much more enjoyable experience. In the culinary world, the term for this is *mise en place*, which translates literally to "put in place." It simply means to gather and arrange all the ingredients and tools you need for cooking. For me, this means setting out cutting boards with the proper knives, prepping all the ingredients and placing them in order of use, setting the pots and pans I will need on the stove, arranging all the cooking oils, spices, and herbs that I will need next to the stove, and so on. I want cooking to flow so seamlessly that it almost feels like I am floating through my kitchen.

The following are some of the kitchen items that I couldn't live without. These tools and appliances set me up for success every time I enter the kitchen.

Kitchen tools, gadgets, and miscellaneous

- colander
- cutting boards
- fine-mesh sieve
- graters and Microplane
- kitchen shears
- measuring cups
- measuring spoons
- meat chopper tool
- muffin liners (paper or silicone)
- pinch bowls or ramekins
- quality set of kitchen knives
- rubber spatulas
- silicone baking mats or parchment paper
- silicone splatter guard
- spiral slicer
- stainless-steel bench scraper
- stainless-steel nested mixing bowls
- tongs
- unbleached parchment paper
- whisks
- wooden spoons

Cookware and bakeware

- cast-iron skillets
- enameled cast-iron pan and Dutch oven
- large casserole dishes
- loaf pan (metal or silicone)
- muffin pan (metal or silicone)
- rimmed baking sheets and cookie sheets
- set of stainless-steel pots and pans
- wire cooling racks

Small kitchen appliances

- digital food scale
- food processor
- high-powered blender
- immersion blender
- slow cooker
- waffle iron

4.

MEAL
PLANNING

TIME- AND MONEY-SAVING TIPS

If there are two things that everyone loves saving, they are time and money. I am all about making keto a sustainable lifestyle and providing the resources to help others do the same.

Time-savers

- Set aside non-negotiable time each week for meal prep, even if it just means prepping all the things you eat regularly—making hard-boiled eggs, chopping lettuce, dicing vegetables, batch-cooking proteins, and so on. Meal prep does not have to mean spending hours in the kitchen cooking multiple meals at a time.

- Whenever possible, double the recipe and freeze the rest. Cook once, eat twice!

- Use store-bought rotisserie chicken in recipes that call for shredded chicken or cooked and chopped chicken.

- Batch-cook large quantities of meat on an outdoor grill. Then, when mealtime rolls around, you only have to worry about whipping up a salad or side dish.

- Make sheet pan meals like the Mini Meatloaves with Brussels Sprouts (page 244) and the Chicken Fajita Sheet Pan Meal (page 218). These meals require very little hands-on time and utilize only one pan, which drastically reduces cleanup time.

- Make quick and easy freezer meals. Combine a sauce like the Sweet and Spicy Barbecue Sauce (page 391) in a freezer bag with cut-up chicken and vegetables, and when you are ready to eat, just throw everything in a pan and sauté.

- Rice cauliflower and spiral-slice zucchini in large batches and freeze them. That way, you will always have them on hand for quick and easy weeknight meals.

- Pull out your slow cooker. By name alone, it doesn't sound like a time-saver, but you can throw ingredients into the slow cooker before you leave for work, and dinner will be ready when you get home.

- Create a mini salad bar in your fridge. Line glass storage containers with paper towels and fill them with your favorite salad ingredients for quick meals throughout the week. Some of my favorite ingredients are lettuces, bell peppers, cucumbers, mushrooms, olives, hard-boiled eggs, assorted meats, and Sugar-Free Dried Cranberries (page 158).

- Overlap ingredients across multiple recipes throughout the week so that you can prep them all at once. For example, plan to make multiple recipes that contain onions and bell peppers and prep all the vegetables for the week at the same time.

- Keep a stash of frozen organic vegetables on hand. They are perfect for quick and easy meals, and you don't have to worry about using them as quickly as fresh vegetables.

- Roast large batches of vegetables on a rimmed baking sheet, portion them into individual servings, and freeze them for reheating later.

Money-savers

- Set a meal plan for the week and stick to it. This will cut back on food waste and on expenses. Later in this chapter, I have provided five weekly plans for you to choose from.

- Make a shopping list and stick to it. Going to the store without a list can lead you to add a bunch of unnecessary items to your cart, and those extras add up fast at the register.

- Shop the perimeter of the store. This is where you will typically find the most nutrient-dense foods. It will also keep you from making impulse purchases in the center aisles.

- Scour the weekly ad circulars and shop according to store sales.

- Take advantage of sales on nonperishable items that you use regularly and stock up.

- Use coupons whenever possible. Many larger companies offer printable coupons on their websites.

- Ask for price matching. Most stores will happily match competitor pricing to keep your business.

- Skip the brand names and go for the generic equivalents.

- Buy meat in bulk and/or from the discounted meats section. Then portion it out and freeze it for later.

- Source your meat from local butchers or farmers. It will help you stretch your budget, and you typically get far better cuts of meat. This is also good practice for the environment. The shorter the distance your food has to travel, the less impact it has on the Earth.

- Substitute cheaper cuts of meat where possible—like chicken thighs for chicken breasts or sirloin for filet mignon or New York strip steaks.

- Buy whole chickens and cut them up yourself. You can save a lot of money by being willing to cut your own meat.

- Skip the bagged salad mixes and cut your own lettuces.

- Shop online sites like Amazon and Thrive Market for spices, condiments, nut flours, baking supplies, and other pantry staples. They are typically far less expensive and come with free shipping.

- Check dollar stores and discount grocery stores. Our local discount grocery store has a fairly large natural and organic section. I'm usually able to find some of my favorite brands for dirt cheap.

- Buy local pastured eggs whenever possible. They are healthier for you than factory-farmed eggs and can be considerably less expensive. Purchasing eggs from nearby farmers is also a great way to support your local economy.

- Join a local CSA or co-op to save on produce costs and get better-quality vegetables and fruits.

- Grow your own vegetables and herbs. Gardening comes with minimal upfront expense but pays off big-time.

- Skip the bottled water. Instead, buy a water filter; it will pay for itself over time, and using a filter is much better for the environment.

- Repurpose leftovers whenever possible. I am a big fan of taking the prior night's dinner and topping it with eggs for breakfast the next day. Another example is taking leftover casserole and mixing it with whisked eggs to bake a frittata.

WEEKLY MEAL PLANS

In this section, you'll find five different seven-day meal plans, which are designed to save you time and money. Each plan was created to meet a specific nutritional need—egg-free, nightshade-free, nut-free, and sweetener-free, along with a plan of meals that can be cooked in thirty minutes or less. These plans are designed to feed four people and utilize leftovers to reduce time spent in the kitchen. The idea is to cook once and eat twice. If you are cooking for only one or two people, simply scale the recipes down by cutting the entire ingredient list in half (unless the recipe already serves one or two, which is the case with a few of the recipes included in the plans).

Meal planning and meal prep were a game-changer for me in terms of finding success on my personal weight-loss journey. Knowing what I was going to eat each day took all the guesswork out of mealtime. It also helped me reach for the right foods instead of caving out of hunger and indecision and just grabbing something "easier." Hello, fast food drive-through, I'm talking to you!

Not only does taking the time to plan my meals help keep me on track, but it also saves me a lot of time and money. Spending a few concentrated hours in the kitchen over the weekend frees up a lot of my time throughout my busy work week. Opening up the fridge and seeing a bounty of precooked healthy choices staring back at me is so liberating. Planning my meals in advance also allows me to take advantage of sales at my local grocery stores. I began building my plans around the foods that were on sale each week. If a sale item didn't really fit into the plan I had put together for the week but was something I ate regularly, then I would buy it anyway knowing that I could freeze it for later. I am a sucker for a good sale and anything that helps stretch my grocery budget further.

A lot of people think that eating healthier means spending a lot more money on groceries, but I firmly believe that with a little effort and planning, it can actually *save* you money. In this chapter, I outline some of my favorite time- and money-saving tips to help you meal plan like a pro.

Egg-Free Meal Plan

	BREAKFAST	LUNCH	DINNER	SIDE, SOUP, SALAD	DESSERT OR SNACK
DAY 1	Fried Radish and Cauliflower Hash Browns (6) page 112 / Blueberry Maple Breakfast Sausage (8) page 96	Blackened Chicken Salad (2) page 182	Prosciutto Chicken and Broccoli Sheet Pan Meal (5) page 246	Kale and Cabbage Chopped Salad (10) page 194	Kombucha Gummy Snacks (30) page 136
DAY 2	Italian Spaghetti Squash Breakfast Skillet *(omit eggs)* (6) page 104	Chicken and "Rice" Soup (10) page 168	Dijon Paprika Pork Tenderloin (6) page 248	Cauliflower Rice Pilaf (12) page 280	Vanilla Chia Pudding (4) page 336
DAY 3	Fried Radish and Cauliflower Hash Browns (LEFTOVER) / Blueberry Maple Breakfast Sausage (LEFTOVER)	Mediterranean Slaw (8) page 196	Lemon and Herb Chicken Kebabs (4) page 256	Kale and Cabbage Chopped Salad (LEFTOVER)	Kombucha Gummy Snacks (LEFTOVER)
DAY 4	Italian Spaghetti Squash Breakfast Skillet (LEFTOVER)	Chicken and "Rice" Soup (LEFTOVER)	Gingered Pepper Steak Skillet (6) page 208	Cauliflower Rice Pilaf (LEFTOVER)	Jumbo Chocolate Peanut Butter Cups (12) page 318
DAY 5	Brussels Sprouts and Bacon Hash *(omit eggs)* (8) page 98	Mediterranean Slaw (LEFTOVER)	Chicken Fajita Sheet Pan Meal (4) page 218	"Goes with Everything" Garlicky Cauliflower Rice (6) page 288	Sweet and Savory Trail Mix (12) page 160
DAY 6	Boosted Keto Coffee (1) page 340	Easy Cuban Picadillo (8) page 222	Beef Ragout (6) page 206	Oven-Roasted Cabbage Steaks (6) page 300	Jumbo Chocolate Peanut Butter Cups (LEFTOVER)
DAY 7	Brussels Sprouts and Bacon Hash (LEFTOVER)	Beef Ramen *(omit eggs)* (4) page 164	Easy Cuban Picadillo (LEFTOVER)	"Goes with Everything" Garlicky Cauliflower Rice (LEFTOVER)	Sweet and Savory Trail Mix (LEFTOVER)

(0) - Servings

Nightshade-Free Meal Plan

	BREAKFAST	LUNCH	DINNER	SIDE, SOUP, SALAD	DESSERT OR SNACK
DAY 1	Green Eggs and Ham (2) page 114	Clam Chowder with Bacon (12) page 178	Beef and Broccoli Stir-Fry *(omit red pepper flakes)* (4) page 228	"Goes with Everything" Garlicky Cauliflower Rice (6) page 288	Lemon Blueberry Accidents (8) page 320
DAY 2	Vanilla Maple Pancakes (2) page 100	Lemon and Herb Chicken Kebabs (4) page 256	Prosciutto Chicken and Broccoli Sheet Pan Meal (5) page 246	Clam Chowder with Bacon (LEFTOVER) page	Mocha Chocolate Chip Muffins (8) page 328
DAY 3	Caramelized Onion and Pancetta Frittata (6) page 108	Egg Salad Prosciutto Cups (6) page 184	Chicken Adobo (6) page 234	"Goes with Everything" Garlicky Cauliflower Rice (LEFTOVER) page	Lemon Blueberry Accidents (LEFTOVER) page
DAY 4	Baked Zucchini Egg Nests *(omit red pepper flakes)* (4) page 94	Ranch Chicken Salad Cups *(omit tomatoes)* (4) page 200	Braised Bratwurst and Cabbage (6) page 232	Roasted Garlic and Chive Cauliflower Puree (8) page 284	Peanut Butter Chocolate Chip No-Bake Granola Squares (25) page 330
DAY 5	Caramelized Onion and Pancetta Frittata (LEFTOVER) page	Cranberry Almond Broccoli Salad (10) page 190	Steak David *(omit hot sauce from hollandaise)* (4) page 210	Kale and Cabbage Chopped Salad (10) page 194	Mocha Chocolate Chip Muffins (LEFTOVER) page
DAY 6	Everything Chimichurri Eggs (1) page 110	Bacon-Wrapped Avocado Fries (5) page 130	Garlic and Herb Skillet Rib-Eyes (2) page 216	Roasted Garlic and Chive Cauliflower Puree (LEFTOVER) page	Peanut Butter Chocolate Chip No-Bake Granola Squares (LEFTOVER) page
DAY 7	Boosted Keto Coffee (1) page 340	Cranberry Almond Broccoli Salad (LEFTOVER) page	Loco Moco (4) page 242	"Cheesy" Herbed Roasted Cauliflower (6) page 276	Vanilla Chia Pudding (4) page 336

(0) - Servings

Nut-Free Meal Plan

	BREAKFAST	LUNCH	DINNER	SIDE, SOUP, SALAD	DESSERT OR SNACK
DAY 1	Baked Zucchini Egg Nests (4) page 94	Pork Belly Wedge Salad (4) page 198	Loco Moco (4) page 242	Kale and Cabbage Chopped Salad (10) page 194	Vanilla Bean Custard (4) page 326
DAY 2	Taco Scotch Eggs (4) page 102	Kale and Cabbage Chopped Salad LEFTOVER page 100	Slow Cooker Pork Carnitas (10) page 266	Salt and Vinegar Roasted Radishes and Green Beans (6) page 304	Flourless Chocolate Lava Cakes (2) page 322
DAY 3	Pork Carnitas Eggs Benedict (4) page 122	Spicy Citrus Meatballs (5) page 272	Sweet and Spicy Barbecue Ribs (6) page 212	Cucumber Dill Broccoli Slaw (6) page 192	Sweet and Savory Trail Mix (12) page 160
DAY 4	Spicy Sausage Eggs in Purgatory (6) page 126	Ranch Chicken Salad Cups (4) page 200	Spaghetti Squash with Tomato Meat Sauce (6) page 270	Maple Bacon Brussels Sprouts (6) page 298	Spicy Fried Ham Deviled Eggs (6) page 156
DAY 5	Sausage and Kale Egg Muffins (6) page 106	Spaghetti Squash with Tomato Meat Sauce LEFTOVER page 270	Chorizo and Chicken Cauliflower Rice Paella (10) page 238	Oven-Roasted Vegetables (12) page 292	Sweet and Savory Trail Mix LEFTOVER
DAY 6	Spicy Sausage Eggs in Purgatory LEFTOVER	Egg Salad Prosciutto Cups (6) page 184	Garlic and Herb Skillet Rib-Eyes (2) page 216	Drunken Mushrooms with Caramelized Onions (6) page 294	Vanilla Chia Pudding (4) page 336
DAY 7	Sausage and Kale Egg Muffins LEFTOVER	Chorizo and Chicken Cauliflower Rice Paella LEFTOVER	Southwestern Pork Skillet (4) page 268	Oven-Roasted Vegetables LEFTOVER	Pickled Asparagus (10) page 154

(0) - Servings

Sweetener-Free Meal Plan

	BREAKFAST	LUNCH	DINNER	SIDE, SOUP, SALAD	DESSERT OR SNACK
DAY 1	Brussels Sprouts and Bacon Hash (8) page 98	Jalapeño Popper Chicken Salad (4) page 214	Chili Lime Chicken with Avocado Salsa (4) page 236	"Goes with Everything" Garlicky Cauliflower Rice (6) page 288	Crispy Oven-Fried Pickles (6) page 152
DAY 2	Taco Scotch Eggs (4) page 102	Blackened Chicken Salad (2) page 182	Crispy Five-Spice Chicken Thighs (4) page 240	Charred Lemon Pepper Broccolini (4) page 290	Bacon-Wrapped Avocado Fries (5) page 130
DAY 3	Brussels Sprouts and Bacon Hash LEFTOVER	Beef Ramen (4) page 164	Beef Ragout (6) page 206	Roasted Garlic and Chive Cauliflower Puree (8) page 284	Spicy Fried Ham Deviled Eggs (6) page 156
DAY 4	Baked Zucchini Egg Nests (4) page 94	Southwestern Pork Skillet (6) page 268	Lemon and Herb Chicken Kebabs (4) page 256	Lemon Pesto Cauliflower Rice with Artichokes (8) page 296	Crispy Baked Barbecue Dijon Wings (6) page 138
DAY 5	Fried Radish and Cauliflower Hash Browns with eggs (6) page 112	Egg Salad Prosciutto Cups (4) page 184	Beef Ragout LEFTOVER	Roasted Garlic and Chive Cauliflower Puree LEFTOVER	Charcuterie Board (10) page 132
DAY 6	Chorizo-Spiced Breakfast Sausage with eggs (5) page 124	Southwestern Pork Skillet LEFTOVER	Supreme Pizza Soup (14) page 176	Caesar Salad with Cumin-Spiced Pecans (4) page 180	Dinner Rolls (6) page 146
DAY 7	Fried Radish and Cauliflower Hash Browns with eggs LEFTOVER	Supreme Pizza Soup LEFTOVER	Puttanesca Pork Chops (4) page 262	Maple Bacon Brussels Sprouts (6) page 298	Charcuterie Board LEFTOVER

(0) - Servings

30-Minute Meals Meal Plan

	BREAKFAST	LUNCH	DINNER	SIDE, SOUP, SALAD	DESSERT OR SNACK
DAY 1	Green Eggs and Ham (2) page 114	Crab Salad–Stuffed Avocados (4) page 188	Sesame Chicken Egg Roll in a Bowl (8) page 204	"Goes with Everything" Garlicky Cauliflower Rice (6) page 288	Cumin-Spiced Pecans (16) page 140
DAY 2	Light and Fluffy Cinnamon Waffles (6) page 118	Chicago Dog Salad (6) page 186	Mini Meatloaves with Brussels Sprouts (6) page 244	Caesar Salad with Cumin-Spiced Pecans (4) page 180	Fruit and Nut Chocolates (10) page 308
DAY 3	Caramelized Onion and Pancetta Frittata (6) page 108	Pork Belly Wedge Salad (4) page 198	Sesame Chicken Egg Roll in a Bowl LEFTOVER page 204	"Goes with Everything" Garlicky Cauliflower Rice LEFTOVER page 288	Flourless Chocolate Lava Cakes (2) page 322
DAY 4	Light and Fluffy Cinnamon Waffles LEFTOVER page 118	Chicago Dog Salad LEFTOVER page 186	Blackened Shrimp Fettuccine Alfredo (4) page 230	Roasted Asparagus with Pancetta (6) page 302	Fruit and Nut Chocolates LEFTOVER page 308
DAY 5	Caramelized Onion and Pancetta Frittata LEFTOVER page 108	Lemony Greek Chicken Soup (8) page 172	Quick Braised Sausage and Peppers (6) page 264	Roasted Garlic and Chive Cauliflower Puree (8) page 284	Cumin-Spiced Pecans LEFTOVER page 140
DAY 6	Pesto Baked Eggs (2) page 120	Ranch Chicken Salad Cups (4) page 200	Garlic and Herb Skillet Rib-Eyes (2) page 216	Maple Bacon Brussels Sprouts (6) page 298	Vanilla Chia Pudding (4) page 336
DAY 7	Everything Chimichurri Eggs (1) page 110	Lemony Greek Chicken Soup LEFTOVER page 172	Puttanesca Pork Chops (4) page 262	Roasted Garlic and Chive Cauliflower Puree LEFTOVER page 284	Pickled Asparagus (10) page 154

(0) - Servings

Dairy-Free KETO COOKING   83

ALLERGEN INDEX

RECIPES	PAGE	◔	◉	◈	⚘	🌿	◷
Baked Zucchini Egg Nests	94			✓	✓		✓
Blueberry Maple Breakfast Sausage	96	✓		✓			✓
Brussels Sprouts and Bacon Hash	98	✓		✓	✓		
Vanilla Maple Pancakes	100		✓			✓	✓
Taco Scotch Eggs	102			✓	✓		
Italian Spaghetti Squash Breakfast Skillet	104			✓	✓		
Sausage and Kale Egg Muffins	106		✓		✓		
Caramelized Onion and Pancetta Frittata	108		✓		✓		
Everything Chimichurri Eggs	110			✓	✓	✓	✓
Fried Radish and Cauliflower Hash Browns	112	✓		✓	✓		✓
Green Eggs and Ham	114		✓		✓		
Leftover Breakfast Bowl	116			✓			✓
Light and Fluffy Cinnamon Waffles	118		✓	✓		✓	✓
Pesto Baked Eggs	120				✓	✓	✓
Pork Carnitas Eggs Benedict	122			✓	✓		✓
Chorizo-Spiced Breakfast Sausage	124	✓		✓	✓		✓
Spicy Sausage Eggs in Purgatory	126				✓		✓
Bacon-Wrapped Avocado Fries	130	✓	✓	✓	✓		✓
Charcuterie Board	132	✓			✓		✓
Strawberry Cucumber Mint Salsa	134	✓		✓	✓	✓	
Kombucha Gummy Snacks	136	✓		✓			✓
Crispy Baked Barbecue Dijon Wings	138	✓		✓			
Cumin-Spiced Pecans	140	✓				✓	✓
Restaurant-Style Salsa	142	✓		✓	✓	✓	✓
Quick and Easy Chunky Guacamole	144	✓		✓	✓	✓	✓
Dinner Rolls	146		✓		✓	✓	
Garlic Dill Sauerkraut	148	✓	✓	✓	✓	✓	✓
New Orleans–Style Olive Salad	150	✓		✓	✓	✓	✓
Crispy Oven-Fried Pickles	152		✓	✓	✓		✓
Pickled Asparagus	154	✓		✓		✓	✓
Spicy Fried Ham Deviled Eggs	156			✓	✓		✓
Sugar-Free Dried Cranberries	158	✓	✓	✓		✓	
Sweet and Savory Trail Mix	160	✓					✓
Beef Ramen	164			✓	✓		✓
Cabbage Roll Soup	166	✓		✓	✓		
Chicken and "Rice" Soup	168	✓		✓	✓		
Easy Peasy Wonton-Less Soup	170			✓	✓		
Lemony Greek Chicken Soup	172			✓	✓		✓
Spicy Bloody Mary Tomato Soup	174	✓		✓			
Supreme Pizza Soup	176	✓		✓	✓		

RECIPES	PAGE	🥚	🍅	🥥	🍄	🌿	⏱
Clam Chowder with Bacon	178	✓		✓	✓		
Caesar Salad with Cumin-Spiced Pecans	180						✓
Blackened Chicken Salad	182	✓		✓	✓		✓
Egg Salad Prosciutto Cups	184		✓	✓	✓		✓
Chicago Dog Salad	186			✓			✓
Crab Salad–Stuffed Avocados	188			✓	✓		✓
Cranberry Almond Broccoli Salad	190		✓				✓
Cucumber Dill Broccoli Slaw	192		✓	✓	✓	✓	✓
Kale and Cabbage Chopped Salad	194	✓	✓	✓	✓		✓
Mediterranean Slaw	196	✓		✓	✓		✓
Pork Belly Wedge Salad	198			✓	✓		✓
Ranch Chicken Salad Cups	200			✓	✓		✓
Sesame Chicken Egg Roll in a Bowl	204	✓		✓	✓		✓
Beef Ragout	206	✓		✓	✓		
Gingered Pepper Steak Skillet	208	✓		✓	✓		✓
Steak David	210			✓	✓		✓
Sweet and Spicy Barbecue Ribs	212	✓		✓			
Jalapeño Popper Chicken Salad	214			✓	✓		✓
Garlic and Herb Skillet Rib-Eyes	216	✓	✓	✓	✓		✓
Chicken Fajita Sheet Pan Meal	218	✓		✓	✓		✓
Beef Pot Roast	220	✓		✓	✓		
Easy Cuban Picadillo	222	✓		✓	✓		✓
Balsamic Shallot Pork Chops	224	✓	✓	✓	✓		✓
Barbecue Pulled Pork Sandwiches	226						
Beef and Broccoli Stir-Fry	228	✓		✓	✓		✓
Blackened Shrimp Fettuccine Alfredo	230	✓		✓	✓		✓
Braised Bratwurst and Cabbage	232	✓		✓	✓		
Chicken Adobo	234	✓	✓	✓	✓		
Chili Lime Chicken with Avocado Salsa	236	✓		✓	✓		✓
Chorizo and Chicken Cauliflower Rice Paella	238	✓		✓	✓		
Crispy Five-Spice Chicken Thighs	240	✓		✓	✓		✓
Loco Moco	242			✓			
Mini Meatloaves with Brussels Sprouts	244	✓					
Prosciutto Chicken and Broccoli Sheet Pan Meal	246	✓	✓	✓	✓		✓
Dijon Paprika Pork Tenderloin	248	✓		✓	✓		✓
Garlic Ginger Pork Noodle Bowl	250	✓		✓	✓		✓
Crispy Pork Fried Cauliflower Rice	252			✓	✓		✓
Grilled Steak with Chimichurri	254	✓		✓	✓		✓
Lemon and Herb Chicken Kebabs	256	✓	✓	✓	✓		✓
Meatloaf Burgers	258						✓

RECIPES	PAGE	🥚	🍅	🥥	🔪	🌿	🕐
Cold Brew Protein Shake	348	✓	✓	✓	✓	✓	✓
Lemon-Lime Soda	349	✓	✓	✓		✓	✓
PB&J Smoothie	350	✓	✓	✓		✓	✓
Shamrock Shake	351	✓	✓	✓		✓	✓
Strawberry Basil Bourbon Smash	352	✓	✓	✓		✓	✓
Strawberry Mojito	353	✓	✓	✓		✓	✓
Tart Cranberry Cooler	354	✓	✓	✓		✓	✓
Black Beauty	355	✓	✓	✓		✓	✓
Cucumber Lime Lavender Spritzer	356	✓	✓	✓		✓	✓
Everything Buns	360		✓		✓	✓	
Garlic and Herb Croutons	362		✓		✓	✓	
Savory Nut-Free Breading Mix	364	✓	✓				✓
Garlic and Herb–Infused Olive Oil	365	✓		✓	✓	✓	
Whole Roasted Garlic	366	✓	✓	✓	✓		
Coconut Milk Whipped Cream	367	✓	✓	✓		✓	✓
Pickled Red Onions	368	✓		✓		✓	✓
Bone Broth	370	✓	✓		✓		
Bacon Fat Hollandaise	372		✓		✓		✓
Creamy Avocado Dressing	374	✓		✓	✓	✓	✓
Caesar Dressing	375			✓			✓
Ranch Dressing	376		✓	✓	✓	✓	✓
Lemon Basil Vinaigrette	377	✓		✓	✓	✓	✓
Tomato Meat Sauce	378	✓		✓	✓		
Dairy-Free Alfredo Sauce Two Ways	380	✓		✓			✓
Classic Marinara Sauce	384	✓		✓	✓	✓	✓
Ketchup	385	✓		✓		✓	✓
Mayo Ten Ways	386		✓	✓	✓	✓	✓
Everything Bagel Aioli	388		✓	✓	✓	✓	✓
Lime Sriracha Aioli	389			✓		✓	✓
Roasted Red Pepper Aioli	390			✓	✓	✓	✓
Sweet and Spicy Barbecue Sauce	391	✓		✓			✓
Balsamic Horseradish Chimichurri	392	✓		✓	✓	✓	✓
Crack Sauce	393	✓		✓		✓	✓
Peanut Sauce	394	✓	✓	✓	✓	✓	✓
Pistachio Pesto	395	✓	✓		✓	✓	✓
Pumpkin Pie Spice	396	✓	✓	✓	✓	✓	✓
Fajita Seasoning	397	✓		✓			✓
Blackening Seasoning	398	✓		✓	✓	✓	✓
Everything Bagel Seasoning	399	✓	✓	✓	✓	✓	✓
Everyday Seasoning Blend	400	✓	✓	✓	✓	✓	✓

5.

RECIPES

HOW TO USE THE RECIPES

1   TITLE OF THE RECIPE

2   NET CARBS PER SERVING

3   **DIETARY AND ALLERGEN KEY:** These icons provide a quick and easy way to identify which recipes are egg-free, nightshade-free, nut-free, Paleo, and/or vegetarian or can be made in 30 minutes or less.

4   **SERVINGS, PREP TIME, AND COOK TIME:** This section tells you how many servings the recipe provides, as well as how long it will take you to prepare and cook the recipe.

5   **INGREDIENT LIST:** Everything you will need, and in the exact proportions, to prepare the recipe.

6   **DIRECTIONS:** This section takes you through the step-by-step preparation of the recipe.

7   **TIPS:** This is where you will find helpful hints, tips, and tricks, as well as substitution recommendations.

8   **NUTRITIONAL ANALYSIS:** At the bottom of each recipe, you will find the calories, fat, protein, total carbs, dietary fiber, net carbs, and erythritol (if applicable) per serving.

Notes:

- *Recipes that have the 30 Minutes or Less icon can be cooked in 30 minutes and involve minimal prep time. Note that the time needed to prepare a required subrecipe, such as a sauce or spice blend, is not factored into the prep and cook times.*

- *Ingredients listed as optional are not factored into the nutritional analysis for each recipe.*

- *Because erythritol is a natural sugar alcohol and is not known to cause blood sugar spikes, it is not factored into the total or net carbs, but rather is broken down into its own category in the nutritional analysis.*

- *Some recipes give two ingredient options, like "gluten-free soy sauce or coconut aminos." My preferred ingredient is always listed first, and that is the ingredient upon which the nutritional analysis is based.*

CHARRED LEMON PEPPER BROCCOLINI

MAKES: **4 servings** · PREP TIME: **5 minutes** · COOK TIME: **10 minutes**

Broccoli was the one vegetable that I loved as a child. My parents never had to force me to eat it because it was always the first thing gone from my plate. However, it wasn't until I was much older that I realized broccoli isn't in fact supposed to be cooked until it is mushy. Broccoli is still my favorite vegetable, but now I serve it cooked perfectly crisp-tender. Broccolini is a cross between broccoli and Chinese broccoli. It has a mildly sweet, earthy taste. This charred broccolini has a deliciously smoky flavor that pairs perfectly with the fresh lemon.

INGREDIENTS

- 1 pound broccolini
- 2 tablespoons avocado oil, divided
- 2 tablespoons grated lemon zest
- Juice of 1 lemon
- 1 teaspoon sea salt
- 1 teaspoon ground black pepper
- ½ teaspoon garlic powder
- 1 lemon, halved

DIRECTIONS

1. Put the broccolini in a large shallow bowl.

2. Put 1 tablespoon of the avocado oil, the lemon zest, lemon juice, salt, pepper, and garlic powder in a small bowl. Mix to combine, then pour the mixture over the broccolini and toss to coat evenly.

3. Heat the remaining tablespoon of oil in a large cast-iron or other skillet over medium-high heat. Once hot, add the broccolini and cook until it is charred and crisp-tender, tossing every 20 seconds to keep it from burning.

4. Plate the broccolini and pour any remaining pan juices over the top.

5. Put the lemon halves cut side down in the hot pan and char just slightly. Serve alongside the broccolini.

> **tip**: *Because you are charring this broccolini over high heat, it will smoke quite a bit. Be sure to turn your vent fan on before cooking. Alternatively, you can roast the broccolini on a broiler pan in a 475°F oven until it has a nice char and is crisp-tender.*

PER SERVING: ⎯⎯⎯⎯⎯⎯⎯
CALORIES: **107**   TOTAL CARBS: **8.3g**
FAT: **7g**   FIBER: **5.7g**
PROTEIN: **4.2g**   NET CARBS: **2.5g**

Breakfast

BAKED ZUCCHINI EGG NESTS

NET CARBS 4.9g

MAKES: 4 servings
PREP TIME: 15 minutes, plus time to rest zucchini noodles · **COOK TIME:** 15 minutes

These zucchini nests are one of my favorite ways to sneak an extra serving of vegetables into my day. Zucchini noodles, or zoodles, as they are often called in the low-carb community, make an excellent substitute for pasta or, in this case, hash browns. Another great option for these nests is spaghetti squash. To use spaghetti squash, simply cook it as you would per the directions for the Italian Spaghetti Squash Breakfast Skillet (page 104) and then follow the directions below, beginning with Step 2, using the cooked spaghetti squash where zoodles are referenced.

INGREDIENTS

- 3 medium zucchini, spiral sliced
- 2½ teaspoons sea salt
- 6 slices bacon, cooked crisp and crumbled
- 2 tablespoons bacon drippings (reserved from cooking bacon)
- 2 cloves garlic, minced
- 1 tablespoon chopped fresh basil
- ¼ teaspoon red pepper flakes, plus more for garnish
- 4 large eggs
- 1 teaspoon black and/or white sesame seeds
- 1 large avocado, peeled, pitted, and sliced, for serving

DIRECTIONS

1. Lay the zucchini noodles in a single layer on a bed of paper towels. Sprinkle them with the salt and let rest for 10 to 15 minutes. The salt will help draw out the excess moisture so that the nests aren't soupy. When the zoodles have released liquid, put a layer of fresh paper towels on top and dab away the excess moisture, then set the zoodles aside.

2. Preheat the oven to 350°F. Line a rimmed baking sheet with parchment paper or a silicone baking mat.

3. Toss the zoodles, bacon, bacon drippings, garlic, basil, and red pepper flakes together in a large mixing bowl, coating the zoodles evenly in the bacon drippings.

4. Divide the mixture into 4 equal portions and form into nests on the prepared baking sheet, making a well in the center of each nest.

5. Crack an egg into each well. Bake for 15 minutes, or until the whites are set but the yolks are still runny.

6. Garnish with the sesame seeds and red pepper flakes and serve with avocado slices.

> *tip*: To make this dish nightshade-free, omit the red pepper flakes.

PER SERVING:

CALORIES: **265** TOTAL CARBS: **9.9g**
FAT: **19.7g** FIBER: **5g**
PROTEIN: **14.6g** NET CARBS: **4.9g**

BLUEBERRY MAPLE BREAKFAST SAUSAGE

NET CARBS 2.7g

MAKES: 16 patties (2 per serving) · PREP TIME: 15 minutes · COOK TIME: 24 minutes

Sausage patties were one of those foods that used to have a permanent spot on my grocery list, right there alongside the bacon. For years I bought them without ever considering making my own. What a missed opportunity that was. I had no idea what I was missing out on. The taste of store-bought breakfast sausage doesn't even remotely compare to the taste of a perfectly spiced, homemade sausage patty. Once you start making this recipe and the Chorizo-Spiced Breakfast Sausage (page 124), I think you will know exactly what I mean, and the store-bought version may be banished from your grocery list forever, too.

INGREDIENTS

- 2 pounds ground pork
- ½ cup fresh blueberries
- ¼ cup sugar-free maple syrup
- 3 cloves garlic, minced
- 2 teaspoons dried rubbed sage
- 2 teaspoons sea salt
- 1 teaspoon ground black pepper
- 1 teaspoon dried thyme leaves
- ¼ teaspoon ground nutmeg
- ¼ teaspoon smoked paprika
- 2 tablespoons avocado oil or olive oil, for the pan

DIRECTIONS

1. Mix all the ingredients, except the oil, in a large mixing bowl until they are well incorporated.

2. Form the mixture into patties, about 2 inches in diameter. You should have 16 patties.

3. Heat the oil in a large skillet over medium heat. Fry the patties in batches until they are browned on both sides and cooked through, about 4 minutes per side.

tip: These sausage patties are perfect for meal prep. You can make a batch and freeze them cooked or raw for quick and easy breakfasts throughout the week.

PER SERVING:
CALORIES: **289**   FIBER: **0.9g**
FAT: **21.7g**   NET CARBS: **2.7g**
PROTEIN: **20.6g**   ERYTHRITOL: **1.5g**
TOTAL CARBS: **3.6g**

BRUSSELS SPROUTS AND BACON HASH

MAKES: 8 servings · **PREP TIME:** 20 minutes · **COOK TIME:** 30 minutes

I was well into adulthood before I learned to appreciate Brussels sprouts. It took me years to realize that I had just never tasted them prepared the right way. When I was a child, my mom would boil frozen Brussels sprouts until they were brown and mushy, then salt them and force us to eat them. The smell and taste of this experience were burned into my brain, so much so that even though my husband and kids love Brussels sprouts, I couldn't even stand to have them in the house. That all changed just a few short years ago. If, in my late thirties, I can come to appreciate a food that once made my stomach flip, then I honestly feel like just about anyone can be converted. This was one of the recipes that helped change my mind. I started making it for my family, but I still wouldn't eat it. Then I realized just what I was missing. This hash is amazing served on its own, but I like to top it with perfectly fried eggs.

INGREDIENTS

- 10 slices bacon, chopped
- 1½ pounds Brussels sprouts, trimmed and shaved
- 1 small red bell pepper, seeded and chopped
- 3 cloves garlic, minced
- 2 tablespoons balsamic vinegar
- 1 tablespoon apple cider vinegar
- 1 teaspoon ground cumin
- 1 teaspoon sea salt
- ½ teaspoon ground black pepper

DIRECTIONS

1. Heat a large skillet over medium heat. Cook the bacon in the preheated pan until it is crispy. Use a slotted spoon to remove the bacon from the pan and set aside. Drain half of the bacon drippings, leaving the rest in the pan.

2. Add the Brussels sprouts, bell pepper, garlic, balsamic vinegar, apple cider vinegar, cumin, salt, and pepper to the skillet. Mix to combine the ingredients and coat them in the bacon drippings.

3. Sauté until the vegetables are tender and slightly caramelized, about 15 minutes.

4. Mix in the cooked bacon before serving.

PER SERVING: ——————————
CALORIES: **151**   TOTAL CARBS: **9.3g**
FAT: **9.8g**   FIBER: **3.5g**
PROTEIN: **8.2g**   NET CARBS: **5.9g**

NET CARBS
5.9g

VANILLA MAPLE PANCAKES

NET CARBS 2.5g

MAKES: eight 6-inch pancakes (2 per serving)
PREP TIME: 10 minutes · **COOK TIME:** 20 minutes

I love a good pancake recipe. I'm talking breakfast, lunch, and dinner kind of love. I top them with reduced-sugar peanut butter and sugar-free maple syrup; it's like dessert and breakfast wrapped into one.

INGREDIENTS

- ½ cup coconut flour
- 3 tablespoons granular erythritol
- 1 teaspoon ground cinnamon
- 1 teaspoon baking powder
- ½ teaspoon sea salt
- 5 large eggs
- 1 cup unsweetened almond or coconut milk
- ¼ cup coconut oil, melted but not hot
- 1½ teaspoons maple extract
- 1 teaspoon pure vanilla extract
- Avocado oil or coconut oil, for the pan

DIRECTIONS

1. In a large mixing bowl, whisk together the coconut flour, erythritol, cinnamon, baking powder, and salt until well combined.

2. Crack the eggs into a separate bowl and whisk together with the almond milk, coconut oil, and extracts.

3. Slowly pour the egg mixture into the dry ingredients, a little at a time, mixing as you go. Stir until the ingredients are well incorporated and there are no visible lumps.

4. Heat the avocado oil in a large skillet over medium-low heat. When the pan is hot, pour ¼ cup of the batter at a time into the pan. Depending on the size of your skillet, you should be able to cook 2 or 3 pancakes at a time. Cook until the bottom is golden brown and the top begins to bubble, about 3 minutes. Carefully flip and cook until the other side is golden brown.

tip: I love to top these pancakes with butter-flavored coconut oil.

PER SERVING:
CALORIES: **282**
FAT: **22.4g**
PROTEIN: **10.8g**
TOTAL CARBS: **5.7g**
FIBER: **3.2g**
NET CARBS: **2.5g**
ERYTHRITOL: **9g**

TACO SCOTCH EGGS

NET CARBS 2.6g

MAKES: 4 Scotch eggs (1 per serving) · **PREP TIME:** 20 minutes · **COOK TIME:** 30 minutes

Traditional Scotch eggs just got a Taco Tuesday makeover, making them the perfect meal for breakfast, lunch, or dinner. They are crispy on the outside, soft on the inside, and bursting with flavor. I like to eat them taco salad style, serving them up on a bed of greens with olives, tomatoes, avocado, jalapeños, and a side of Lime Sriracha Aioli (page 389).

INGREDIENTS

- 2 large eggs
- 1 batch Savory Nut-Free Breading Mix (page 364)
- 1 pound ground pork
- 3 tablespoons Fajita Seasoning (page 397)
- 4 soft-boiled eggs, peeled
- Oil, for frying

DIRECTIONS

1. Preheat the oven to 375°F. Put a cooling rack on a rimmed baking sheet.

2. Set up 2 shallow bowls in a row. Whisk the eggs in the first bowl and put the breading in the second bowl.

3. In a large mixing bowl, mix the ground pork and fajita seasoning until well incorporated.

4. Divide the meat into 4 equal portions and roll into balls, then flatten into patties. Put an egg in the center of each patty and gently mold the meat around the egg, pinching it together until the egg is fully encased and there are no openings in the meat.

5. Roll each Scotch egg in the egg wash, then in the breading mix, generously coating it with breading all around.

6. Heat 2 to 3 inches of oil in a large 4-inch-deep (or deeper) skillet or Dutch oven over medium-high heat. When the oil is hot (375°F) and begins to bubble slightly, gently drop the breaded Scotch eggs into the oil and fry until golden brown and crispy, 2 to 3 minutes on each side.

7. Transfer the Scotch eggs to the cooling rack on the baking sheet.

8. Bake the Scotch eggs until the sausage is cooked through and the breading is golden brown and crispy, about 20 minutes.

PER SERVING: —————————
CALORIES: **567** TOTAL CARBS: **7.6g**
FAT: **39.4g** FIBER: **5g**
PROTEIN: **39.6g** NET CARBS: **2.6g**

ITALIAN SPAGHETTI SQUASH BREAKFAST SKILLET

NET CARBS 10.3g

MAKES: 6 servings · **PREP TIME:** 15 minutes · **COOK TIME:** 1 hour

I love recipes born out of a desperate need to go grocery shopping. When I made this dish for the first time, we had been traveling a lot and our fridge was slim pickings. I started my day in the kitchen knowing only one thing for sure: that I was going to use the lone spaghetti squash in our vegetable bowl. From there, it quickly took on an Italian theme—which was fitting because we had just returned home from visiting Italy, Greece, Croatia, and Turkey. For this recipe, I like the meat and vegetables to be the stars of the show, so I put only four eggs in the skillet, but feel free to add as many eggs as you wish. Another delicious option is to cook a big pan of scrambled eggs and then serve them alongside the skillet.

INGREDIENTS

- 1 small spaghetti squash (about 2 pounds), halved lengthwise and seeded
- 3 tablespoons avocado oil or olive oil, divided
- Sea salt and ground black pepper
- 1 medium onion, diced (about 1 cup)
- 2 cloves garlic, minced
- 4 ounces sliced Italian salami, cut into strips
- ½ cup diced tomatoes
- ½ teaspoon dried Italian seasoning
- ½ cup halved Kalamata olives
- 4 large eggs
- Handful of fresh flat-leaf parsley, roughly chopped, for garnish

DIRECTIONS

1. Preheat the oven to 400°F.

2. Put the spaghetti squash halves cut side up on a rimmed baking sheet. Drizzle 1 tablespoon of the oil over the squash. Sprinkle generously with salt and pepper. Bake for 45 minutes, or until tender and the squash shreds easily pull away from the skin with a fork.

3. While the spaghetti squash is baking, heat the remaining 2 tablespoons of oil in a large ovenproof skillet over medium heat. When the pan is hot, add the onion and garlic and cook until they are soft and tender, about 8 minutes.

4. Add the salami, tomatoes, and Italian seasoning. Cook for an additional 10 minutes, then mix in the olives.

5. When the spaghetti squash is finished roasting, use a fork to scrape the flesh from both halves into the skillet. Combine the squash with the onion and salami mixture.

6. Use a large spoon to create 4 deep wells in the mixture. Crack an egg into each well.

7. Transfer the skillet to the oven and bake until the egg whites are set and the yolks have reached the desired level of doneness. (About 10 minutes of baking time will provide runny yolks; bake longer if you prefer set yolks.)

8. Garnish with parsley before serving.

PER SERVING:
CALORIES: **260**   TOTAL CARBS: **13.6g**
FAT: **19.2g**   FIBER: **3.3g**
PROTEIN: **9.7g**   NET CARBS: **10.3g**

SAUSAGE AND KALE EGG MUFFINS

NET
CARBS
2g

MAKES: 12 egg muffins (2 per serving) · **PREP TIME:** 10 minutes · **COOK TIME:** 40 minutes

Egg muffins are my favorite way to meal prep breakfasts for the week. You can literally just grab one out of the fridge, heat, and eat. Because they are individual sized, you don't even have to worry about cutting a portion out of a casserole dish. They make breakfasts on hectic weekday mornings a breeze.

INGREDIENTS

- 1 tablespoon avocado oil or olive oil
- 1 shallot, chopped
- ½ teaspoon sea salt
- ½ teaspoon ground black pepper
- ¼ teaspoon ground nutmeg
- 1 pound bulk sweet Italian sausage
- 3 packed cups baby kale
- 8 large eggs
- ½ cup unsweetened almond milk

DIRECTIONS

1. Preheat the oven to 350°F. Put 12 standard-sized silicone muffin cups on a rimmed baking sheet. Alternatively, lightly grease a standard-sized 12-well muffin pan.

2. Heat the oil in a large skillet over medium heat. When the oil is hot, add the shallot, salt, pepper, and nutmeg and sauté until the shallot is translucent.

3. Add the sausage to the pan and sauté until it is cooked through, breaking up the meat as it cooks, about 8 minutes.

4. Add the kale to the pan and cook until wilted, about 3 minutes.

5. Divide the meat and vegetable mixture among the 12 muffin cups or wells.

6. In a large mixing bowl, whisk together the eggs and almond milk. Pour the mixture evenly over the meat and vegetables in the muffin cups or wells, filling them about three-quarters of the way full.

7. Bake for 20 minutes, or until the eggs are set.

> *tips*: For a nut-free version, simply omit the almond milk. I like to add it because it makes the egg muffins fluffier.
>
> If you are not avoiding dairy, you can substitute heavy cream for the almond milk for even airier and fluffier egg muffins.

PER SERVING:

CALORIES: 392	TOTAL CARBS: 3.1g
FAT: 32.6g	FIBER: 1.1g
PROTEIN: 20.4g	NET CARBS: 2g

CARAMELIZED ONION AND PANCETTA FRITTATA

NET CARBS
2.7g

 MAKES: 6 servings · **PREP TIME:** 10 minutes · **COOK TIME:** 55 minutes

I simply adore caramelized onions. They add such amazing flavor to dishes. Not to mention that their sweetness pairs perfectly with salty meats like pancetta. Putting the onions and pancetta together in this frittata was a no-brainer. I love to serve this dish with a pinch of red pepper flakes and a side of fresh avocado.

INGREDIENTS

- 8 ounces thinly sliced pancetta
- 2 tablespoons avocado oil or olive oil, divided
- 1 large onion, thinly sliced
- ½ teaspoon sea salt
- ¼ teaspoon ground black pepper
- 3 cloves garlic, minced
- ½ teaspoon dried rubbed sage
- 10 large eggs
- ¼ cup unsweetened almond milk
- 2 tablespoons roughly chopped fresh flat-leaf parsley, for garnish

DIRECTIONS

1. Chop the pancetta, reserving 4 slices to put on top of the frittata.

2. Heat 1 tablespoon of the oil in a 10-inch ovenproof sauté pan over medium-low heat. When the oil is hot, add the onion slices, salt, and pepper and cook until the onions are nice and caramelized, about 25 minutes. Remove the onions from the pan and set aside.

3. To the same pan, add the remaining tablespoon of oil and the chopped pancetta. Cook over medium heat until the pancetta is just starting to brown. Add the garlic and sage to the pan and continue cooking until the pancetta is crispy and golden brown.

4. Preheat the oven to 350°F.

5. Return the caramelized onions to the pan, reserving some for the top of the frittata. Mix the onions in with the pancetta.

6. Crack the eggs into a mixing bowl, add the almond milk, and whisk with a fork. Pour the egg mixture over the pancetta and onions in the skillet. Mix just slightly.

7. Cook, without stirring, until the sides and bottom begin to set, 6 to 8 minutes.

8. Transfer the skillet to the oven and bake for 10 minutes. Remove from the oven and top the frittata with the remaining pancetta slices and caramelized onions. Return to the oven and bake for an additional 10 to 15 minutes, until the eggs are firm and cooked through.

9. Garnish with parsley before serving.

> *tips:* As the onions are caramelizing, they may start to stick to the pan. Simply add a little water and then use a rubber spatula to scrape up and mix in any browned bits from the bottom of the pan. This really helps develop depth of flavor.
>
> If you aren't avoiding dairy, top this frittata with some crumbled feta or goat cheese before serving.

PER SERVING:
CALORIES: **296**
FAT: **23.3g**
PROTEIN: **17.6g**
TOTAL CARBS: **3.3g**
FIBER: **0.5g**
NET CARBS: **2.7g**

EVERYTHING CHIMICHURRI EGGS

NET CARBS 4.9g

🥑 🔪 🌿 🕐 **MAKES:** 1 serving · **PREP TIME:** 5 minutes · **COOK TIME:** 10 minutes

If you have a copy of my book *Craveable Keto,* then you know all about how I love to cook my eggs low and slow and load them up with fresh herbs and spices. Well, I can tell you that not much has changed; I still love doing that. If fried eggs aren't your thing, this combination is also excellent with light and fluffy scrambled eggs.

INGREDIENTS

- 2 tablespoons Balsamic Horseradish Chimichurri (page 392), divided
- 3 large eggs
- 2 teaspoons Everything Bagel Seasoning (page 399)

DIRECTIONS

1. Heat 1 tablespoon of the chimichurri in a small skillet over medium-low heat. When the sauce is hot, crack the eggs into the pan.

2. When the whites are just barely starting to set and turn white, reduce the heat to low, spoon the remaining sauce over the eggs, and sprinkle the Everything Bagel Seasoning over the top.

3. Continue cooking over low heat until the whites are completely set but the yolks are still runny.

PER SERVING:

CALORIES: **338**   TOTAL CARBS: **6.4g**
FAT: **25.3g**   FIBER: **1.5g**
PROTEIN: **20.1g**   NET CARBS: **4.9g**

FRIED RADISH AND CAULIFLOWER HASH BROWNS

NET CARBS 2.6g

MAKES: 6 servings · PREP TIME: 20 minutes · COOK TIME: 15 minutes

Ever since I was a small child, potatoes have been my favorite food. Mashed, fried, hash browns, French fries, tater tots . . . you name it, and I love it. When I first started a low-carb lifestyle, potatoes were the food I missed the most. I instantly knew that I needed to find a satisfying solution for when the craving for crispy hash browns struck. After making a few different variations, this one became my favorite. I hope you like it as much as I do.

INGREDIENTS

- 1 pound radishes (without greens), shredded and pressed to remove excess moisture (see tip)
- 3 cups riced cauliflower
- 6 slices bacon, cooked crisp and crumbled
- 3 cloves garlic, minced
- 1 teaspoon sea salt
- ½ teaspoon smoked paprika
- ¼ teaspoon ground black pepper
- 3 tablespoons avocado oil or olive oil

DIRECTIONS

1. In a large mixing bowl, toss the radishes, cauliflower, bacon, garlic, salt, paprika, and pepper until well combined.

2. Heat the oil in a large skillet over medium-high heat. When the oil is hot, spread the hash in a thin, even layer across the whole skillet. If you do not have a large enough skillet, you may need to cook the hash browns in two batches in order to get them crispy. Alternatively, you can cook them on a griddle.

3. Fry until the hash browns are cooked through and crispy, about 15 minutes. Flip halfway through, or as needed to avoid burning.

> tip: *Radishes have a high water content and are very wet when shredded. To make sure they cook up nice and crispy, it is necessary to place them in cheesecloth or between paper towels and squeeze out the excess moisture before cooking.*

PER SERVING: ————————
CALORIES: **178**   TOTAL CARBS: **5.2g**
FAT: **14.6g**   FIBER: **2.7g**
PROTEIN: **6.1g**   NET CARBS: **2.6g**

GREEN EGGS AND HAM

NET CARBS 1.8g

MAKES: 2 servings · **PREP TIME:** 10 minutes · **COOK TIME:** 10 minutes

"Say! I like green eggs and ham! I do! I like them, Sam-I-Am! And I would eat them in a boat. And I would eat them with a goat . . . And I will eat them in the rain. And in the dark. And on a train. And in a car. And in a tree. They are so good, so good, you see!" —Dr. Seuss

INGREDIENTS

- 6 large eggs
- 4 tablespoons dairy-free pesto, store-bought or homemade (page 395), divided
- 2 tablespoons avocado oil or olive oil, divided
- 4 ounces thinly sliced ham
- ¼ cup microgreens, for garnish

DIRECTIONS

1. Crack the eggs into a small bowl and whisk with a fork. Add 3 tablespoons of the pesto and whisk until well combined.

2. Heat 1 tablespoon of the oil in a large skillet over medium heat. When the oil is hot, add the ham and sear until it is heated through and golden brown on both sides, about 2 minutes on each side. Remove from the pan and cover to keep warm.

3. Heat the remaining tablespoon of oil in the skillet and add the eggs. Use a rubber spatula to gently stir and fold the eggs. Let them begin to set, then fold them again. Repeat this process until the eggs are cooked to your desired level of doneness. Scrambling them slowly and not overworking them will produce amazingly fluffy eggs.

4. Divide the eggs between 2 plates and top with the remaining tablespoon of pesto, the fried ham, and the microgreens.

> *tip*: *This dish is delicious served with Restaurant-Style Salsa (page 142) and fresh avocado.*

PER SERVING: —————————
CALORIES: **428** TOTAL CARBS: **1.9g**
FAT: **33g** FIBER: **0.2g**
PROTEIN: **28.9g** NET CARBS: **1.8g**

LEFTOVER BREAKFAST BOWL

NET CARBS 6g

MAKES: 1 serving · **PREP TIME:** 10 minutes

This is more of a concept than an actual recipe. I frequently post big bowls of random food on my Instagram, and the response is always "Recipe?" I never considered that people might want a recipe simply comprised of leftovers and other colorful foods all thrown into a bowl together. So this recipe was born from that. It's a great way to combine leftovers you may have from making various recipes in this book. The other great thing about it is that you can use any meat and vegetables you want, store-bought or from this book. Get creative with the sauces, dips, and dressings in your fridge, too.

INGREDIENTS

- 1 cup mixed salad greens
- 2 Blueberry Maple Breakfast Sausage patties (page 96), warmed
- 1 large egg, cooked to your liking
- 6 slices Pickled Red Onions (page 368)
- ½ small avocado, peeled and pitted
- 1 teaspoon Everything Bagel Seasoning (page 399)
- ¼ cup Garlic Dill Sauerkraut (page 148)
- 2 tablespoons roasted red peppers
- 2 tablespoons pitted green olives
- 2 tablespoons halved Kalamata olives

DIRECTIONS

Plate the salad greens in a large salad bowl and pile the rest of the ingredients on top.

PER SERVING:
CALORIES: **623**
FAT: **52.2g**
PROTEIN: **23.2g**
TOTAL CARBS: **17.5g**
FIBER: **11.5g**
NET CARBS: **6g**

LIGHT AND FLUFFY CINNAMON WAFFLES

NET CARBS 1.7g

MAKES: 6 waffles (1 per serving) · **PREP TIME:** 15 minutes · **COOK TIME:** 30 minutes

These light and fluffy waffles make for the ultimate weekend breakfast. I top them with reduced-sugar peanut butter and sugar-free preserves; it's like dessert and breakfast wrapped into one. I love to pair them with Blueberry Maple Breakfast Sausage (page 96) and some perfectly poached eggs topped with Bacon Fat Hollandaise (page 372).

INGREDIENTS

- ½ cup coconut flour
- ¼ cup granular erythritol
- 1 teaspoon ground cinnamon
- 1 teaspoon baking powder
- ½ teaspoon sea salt
- 5 large eggs
- 1 cup unsweetened coconut or almond milk
- ¼ cup coconut oil, melted but not hot
- 1 teaspoon pure vanilla extract

DIRECTIONS

1. Preheat a waffle iron.

2. In a large mixing bowl, whisk the coconut flour, erythritol, cinnamon, baking powder, and salt until combined.

3. In a separate mixing bowl, whisk together the eggs, coconut milk, coconut oil, and vanilla extract.

4. Slowly pour the wet ingredients into the dry ingredients, mixing as you pour. Mix until the ingredients are well incorporated and the batter is smooth.

5. Lightly grease the hot waffle iron. Ladle the batter onto the center of the waffle iron; consult the manufacturer's directions for the recommended amount of batter to use.

6. Cook for 5 minutes, or until the waffle iron stops steaming. Repeat this process until all the batter is gone, regreasing the iron after each waffle, as needed. For a crispier waffle, drop it in the toaster before serving.

PER SERVING: ─────────
CALORIES: **110** FIBER: **2.1g**
FAT: **6.5g** NET CARBS: **1.7g**
PROTEIN: **7.2g** ERYTHRITOL: **8g**
TOTAL CARBS: **3.9g**

PESTO BAKED EGGS

NET CARBS 1.5g

MAKES: 2 servings · **PREP TIME:** 5 minutes · **COOK TIME:** 15 minutes

Baking the eggs is a simple way to jazz up your morning egg routine. It adds loads of flavor without requiring a lot of hands-on time. You can simply throw your favorite meats, vegetables, herbs, and spices in a little baking dish or ramekin, crack an egg or two over the top, and pop it in the oven. Easy peasy and delicious!

INGREDIENTS

- 4 tablespoons unsweetened almond or coconut milk, divided
- 4 large eggs
- 4 tablespoons dairy-free pesto, store-bought or homemade (page 395), divided
- ½ teaspoon dried minced onion
- ¼ teaspoon red pepper flakes
- Fresh basil, for garnish (optional)

DIRECTIONS

1. Preheat the oven to 425°F. Lightly oil two 8-ounce quiche dishes or ramekins and put them on a rimmed baking sheet.

2. Pour 2 tablespoons of almond milk into each dish, then crack 2 eggs into each dish.

3. Add 2 tablespoons of pesto to each dish. Sprinkle the dried minced onion and red pepper flakes over the top.

4. Bake for 15 minutes, or until the egg whites are set.

5. Garnish with fresh basil before serving, if desired.

> *tip: If you are not avoiding dairy, use heavy cream in place of the almond milk for even creamier baked eggs.*

PER SERVING:
CALORIES: **181**   TOTAL CARBS: **1.7g**
FAT: **13.1g**   FIBER: **0.3g**
PROTEIN: **13.1g**   NET CARBS: **1.5g**

PORK CARNITAS EGGS BENEDICT

NET CARBS 7.3g

MAKES: 4 servings · PREP TIME: 15 minutes · COOK TIME: 20 minutes

Eggs Benedict is my all-time favorite breakfast dish. There is something so dreamy about a perfectly poached egg that is quite literally topped with more eggs. The fresh taste of hollandaise pairs perfectly with just about any protein, which is why you commonly see a wide variety of eggs Benedict offerings on restaurant breakfast menus. Here I've swapped out the traditional Canadian bacon for carnitas and added avocado. While you may be asking where the muffin is, I have a few suggestions that just might make you ask, "Muffin, who?" Instead of the traditional English muffin, I like to use a layer of avocado slices, fresh tomato slices, or a bed of greens, or even just double the meat. This is a great tip for dining out as well. Most restaurants are more than happy to accommodate. But if you really want that breadlike feel, serve it on top of a toasted Everything Bun (page 360).

INGREDIENTS

- 1 large avocado, peeled, pitted, and sliced
- 1½ pounds Slow Cooker Crispy Pork Carnitas (page 266), warmed
- 8 large eggs
- ¼ teaspoon distilled white vinegar
- 1 cup Bacon Fat Hollandaise (page 372), freshly made
- Chopped fresh chives, for garnish
- Pinch of cayenne pepper, for garnish (optional)

DIRECTIONS

1. Divide the avocado slices evenly among 4 serving plates. Top each portion with 6 ounces of the carnitas.

2. Crack the eggs into individual small bowls or ramekins.

3. Bring a small pot of water to a rapid boil. Add the vinegar to the water. Give the water a swirl to create a whirlpool effect. Gently slip an egg into the center of the whirlpool. After 2 minutes, use a slotted spoon to remove the egg from the water. Repeat this process with all 8 eggs.

4. Put 2 poached eggs on top of the carnitas on each plate. Top each serving with ¼ cup of the hollandaise and garnish with chives. Sprinkle with a pinch of cayenne pepper before serving, if desired.

PER SERVING: ───────────

CALORIES: 811	TOTAL CARBS: 11.7g
FAT: 68.1g	FIBER: 4.4g
PROTEIN: 63.6g	NET CARBS: 7.3g

CHORIZO-SPICED BREAKFAST SAUSAGE

NET CARBS 2.6g

MAKES: 10 patties (2 per serving)
PREP TIME: 20 minutes, plus 2 hours to refrigerate · **COOK TIME:** 15 minutes

These spiced breakfast sausage patties are perfectly juicy on the inside and delightfully crispy on the outside. They have all the warm flavors of chorizo in a quick and easy sausage patty. These are great to have on hand for hectic weekday mornings when you need something you can just heat and eat before heading out the door. I like to make a double or triple batch, portion them out, and freeze them for later use. You can freeze them cooked or raw. To cook or reheat, simply defrost and then pan-fry the patties.

INGREDIENTS

- 3 tablespoons avocado oil or olive oil, divided
- 1 small onion, finely diced (about ½ cup)
- 3 cloves garlic, minced
- 2 teaspoons dried oregano leaves
- 1½ teaspoons ground cumin
- 1 teaspoon smoked paprika
- ¼ teaspoon cayenne pepper
- Pinch of ground cinnamon
- ⅓ cup apple cider vinegar
- ¼ cup cold water
- 1½ pounds ground pork
- 1½ teaspoons sea salt
- ½ teaspoon ground black pepper

DIRECTIONS

1. Heat 2 tablespoons of the oil in a sauté pan over medium heat. Add the onion and garlic and cook until the onion is translucent and the garlic is fragrant.

2. Add the oregano, cumin, paprika, cayenne, and cinnamon and cook for 1 additional minute.

3. Add the vinegar and cook until reduced by half, about 5 minutes.

4. Remove the onion mixture from the heat and transfer it to a blender or food processor. Add the water and blend until smooth.

5. In a large bowl, mix the ground pork, blended onion mixture, salt, and pepper until the ingredients are well incorporated. Cover and refrigerate for 2 hours or up to 24 hours to let the flavors come together.

6. Form the pork mixture into 12 equal-sized patties, about 3 inches in diameter.

7. Heat the remaining tablespoon of oil in a cast-iron skillet over medium heat. When the pan is hot, cook the patties in batches, being careful not to overcrowd the pan, until they are browned and cooked through, about 4 minutes on each side.

8. Transfer the cooked patties to a paper towel–lined plate to absorb the excess grease before serving.

PER SERVING:

CALORIES: **387**	TOTAL CARBS: **3.4g**
FAT: **30.4g**	FIBER: **0.7g**
PROTEIN: **24.9g**	NET CARBS: **2.6g**

SPICY SAUSAGE EGGS IN PURGATORY

NET CARBS
2.7g

MAKES: 6 servings · PREP TIME: 10 minutes · COOK TIME: 20 minutes

There are many different variations of eggs cooked in tomato sauce—eggs in purgatory, shakshuka, and so on—but I just call it delicious. This recipe is a quick and easy way to fancy up your morning eggs.

INGREDIENTS

- 1 tablespoon avocado oil or olive oil
- ½ small onion, chopped (about ¼ cup)
- 2 cloves garlic, minced
- 1 pound bulk spicy Italian sausage
- ¾ cup marinara sauce, store-bought or homemade (page 384)
- 2 tablespoons dairy-free pesto, store-bought or homemade (page 395)
- 6 large eggs
- 3 to 4 fresh basil leaves, torn, for garnish
- 1 tablespoon finely chopped fresh flat-leaf parsley, for garnish
- Pinch of red pepper flakes, for garnish (optional)

DIRECTIONS

1. Heat the oil in a large skillet over medium heat. When the oil is hot, add the onion and garlic and cook for 2 to 3 minutes, until the onion is soft.

2. Add the sausage to the skillet and cook, breaking it up with a spatula, until it is browned, about 5 minutes. Drain the excess grease.

3. Add the marinara and pesto to the skillet and mix in.

4. Use the back of a spoon to make 6 shallow wells in the tomato mixture; carefully crack an egg into each well.

5. Reduce the heat to medium-low and let the eggs simmer in the sauce until the whites are set but the yolks are still runny, about 8 minutes.

6. Top with the basil, parsley, and red pepper flakes, if desired, before serving.

Tips: To cut down on prep time, you can use a store-bought marinara sauce. Be sure to read the labels and look for a sauce that contains only vegetables, healthy fats, and seasonings. Rao's is a great brand of clean, keto-friendly marinara sauce. In addition to the recipe in this book, I have a couple of different low-carb marinara sauces on my website.

If you are not avoiding dairy, this dish is fantastic topped with Parmesan, Romano, or even feta cheese.

PER SERVING:
CALORIES: **366**   TOTAL CARBS: **3.3g**
FAT: **28.8g**   FIBER: **0.6g**
PROTEIN: **24.5g**   NET CARBS: **2.7g**

Snacks and Starters

BACON-WRAPPED AVOCADO FRIES

NET
CARBS
1.8g

MAKES: 5 servings (4 fries per serving)
PREP TIME: 15 minutes · **COOK TIME:** 25 minutes

It doesn't get much simpler than a recipe with just two main ingredients. And it doesn't get much more delicious than when those two ingredients are bacon and avocados. For this recipe, it is important to par-cook the bacon to prevent the avocados from spending too much time in the oven and becoming dry and bitter-tasting.

INGREDIENTS

- 20 slices bacon
- 2 large avocados
- Everything Bagel Aioli (page 388), for serving (optional)

DIRECTIONS

1. Preheat the oven to 425°F. Line a rimmed baking sheet with parchment paper or a silicone baking mat.

2. Line the slices of bacon across the parchment paper and bake for 10 minutes, or until slightly cooked but still bendable without breaking.

3. While the bacon is cooking, slice the avocados in half lengthwise and remove the peels and pits, then slice each half into 5 equal-sized wedges to make a total of 20 fries.

4. Line the baking sheet with a fresh piece of parchment paper or a clean silicone baking mat.

5. Wrap each avocado slice tightly with a slice of par-cooked bacon and lay the wrapped fries on their sides in a single layer across the baking sheet.

6. Bake for 15 minutes, or until the bacon is crispy, flipping the fries over halfway through.

7. Serve with Everything Bagel Aioli, if desired.

PER SERVING:

CALORIES: **582**	TOTAL CARBS: **8.6g**
FAT: **52.4g**	FIBER: **6.7g**
PROTEIN: **22.6g**	NET CARBS: **1.8g**

CHARCUTERIE BOARD

MAKES: 10 servings · **PREP TIME:** 20 minutes

A charcuterie board is the perfect way to enjoy a delicious appetizer with friends and family. Pour a glass of wine or two and dig in! There is sure to be a little something on there for everyone. The thing I love most about a good charcuterie board, besides how visually stunning it is, is that there are no rules. You can fill the board with literally anything you want. The traditional offerings are meats and cheeses, but I think those of us who live a dairy-free keto lifestyle are used to doing things in a less-than-traditional fashion.

INGREDIENTS

- 8 ounces sliced Italian dry salami
- 3 ounces sliced capicola
- 3 ounces sliced pancetta
- 3 ounces sliced prosciutto
- 10 marinated artichoke heart quarters
- 10 mini dill pickles
- 10 garlic-stuffed queen olives
- 10 pepperoncini
- 10 fresh blackberries
- 5 fresh strawberries, hulled and halved
- 2 tablespoons stone-ground mustard
- ⅓ cup giardiniera
- ⅓ cup mixed nuts
- ¼ cup sugar-free dried cranberries, store-bought or homemade (page 158)
- ¼ cup Pickled Red Onions (page 368)
- ¼ cup pitted Kalamata olives
- ¼ cup Garlic Dill Sauerkraut (page 148)

DIRECTIONS

Arrange all the ingredients on a large platter or cutting board. Be sure to put any watery ingredients or ingredients that might roll off the plate in little dishes of their own.

> *tip*: *If you aren't avoiding dairy, you can also load up this tray with a variety of your favorite cheeses.*

PER SERVING:

CALORIES: **209**	TOTAL CARBS: **4.3g**
FAT: **16.5g**	FIBER: **2g**
PROTEIN: **10.5g**	NET CARBS: **2.3g**

STRAWBERRY CUCUMBER MINT SALSA

NET CARBS 1.5g

MAKES: about 6 cups (¼ cup per serving) · **PREP TIME:** 15 minutes, plus 1 hour to chill

Strawberries and tomatoes together? Am I crazy? You might think so until you take your first bite of this fresh and light summer salsa. While it is a shining star all on its own, it is even better when it is paired with Grilled Steak with Chimichurri (page 254). I also love to serve it with an array of crunchy dippers, like bell peppers, celery, pork rinds, and low-carb crackers. If you have leftover salsa, it is amazing added to salads and the Leftover Breakfast Bowl (page 116).

INGREDIENTS

- 1 medium English cucumber, diced (about 2 cups)
- 1 medium tomato, seeded and diced (about 1 cup)
- 1 pound strawberries, hulled and diced (about 2 cups)
- ½ cup diced red onions
- 10 fresh mint leaves, chopped
- 5 fresh basil leaves, chopped
- 1 tablespoon fresh lime juice
- 1 tablespoon balsamic vinegar
- Pinch of sea salt
- Pinch of ground black pepper

DIRECTIONS

1. Put all the ingredients in a large mixing bowl and toss to combine. Refrigerate for 1 hour before serving to allow the flavors to come together.

2. Store leftovers in the refrigerator for up to a week.

tips: Seeding the tomato before chopping it helps you avoid having a soupy mess of a salsa. To quickly and easily remove the seeds from the tomato, put the tomato on its side so that the stem is facing to the right and slice the tomato in half. Use a small spoon to scoop out the seeds from all four sections of each tomato half.

If you aren't avoiding dairy, this salsa is amazing with some feta cheese added to the mix.

PER SERVING:

CALORIES: **9**	TOTAL CARBS: **1.9g**
FAT: **0.1g**	FIBER: **0.5g**
PROTEIN: **0.3g**	NET CARBS: **1.5g**

KOMBUCHA GUMMY SNACKS

NET CARBS 1.1g

MAKES: 300 gummies (15 per serving)
PREP TIME: 15 minutes, plus 1 hour to set · COOK TIME: 5 minutes

Is it a snack or a health supplement? I'll never tell. These kombucha gummies are packed full of healthy collagen and probiotics, so while you are snacking away on a delicious treat, you will be doing wonders for your gut health, too. You can make these with any brand and flavor of kombucha that you like. My favorite is GT's Trilogy, flavored with lemon, raspberry, and ginger.

INGREDIENTS

- 8 ounces kombucha of choice
- 1 cup frozen mixed berries, thawed
- 2 tablespoons powdered erythritol
- ⅓ cup grass-fed gelatin

SPECIAL EQUIPMENT:

Silicone gummy molds with 300 cavities

DIRECTIONS

1. Puree the kombucha, berries, and erythritol in a blender or food processor.

2. Transfer the mixture to a small saucepan over low heat. Whisk in the gelatin and continue whisking until it has dissolved. It will form a thick paste. Heat until the mixture is warm and pourable. You want it just warm enough that the gelatin will dissolve, but not so warm that the heat kills the probiotics in the kombucha.

3. Transfer the mixture to a liquid measuring cup or bowl with a pour spout, then quickly pour it into the silicone gummy molds.

4. Transfer to the refrigerator to cool and solidify, about 1 hour. Pop the gummies out of the molds and enjoy!

5. Store leftovers in a sealed jar in the refrigerator for up to 2 weeks.

PER SERVING: —————————
CALORIES: **13**   FIBER: **0.3g**
FAT: **0g**   NET CARBS: **1.1g**
PROTEIN: **2g**   ERYTHRITOL: **1.2g**
TOTAL CARBS: **1.3g**

CRISPY BAKED BARBECUE DIJON WINGS

NET CARBS 2.1g

MAKES: 6 servings · PREP TIME: 10 minutes, plus 20 minutes to rest · COOK TIME: 1 hour 15 minutes

I'm sure *crispy* and *baked* aren't words you are used to seeing together. But let me just tell you that this cooking method delivers perfectly crispy baked wings every time. For a couple of different variations, like garlic and Parmesan and teriyaki, be sure to check out my website, peaceloveandlowcarb.com.

INGREDIENTS

- 2 pounds chicken wings
- 1 teaspoon sea salt
- 2 tablespoons baking powder
- ¾ cup Sweet and Spicy Barbecue Sauce (page 391)
- ¼ cup Dijon mustard
- Celery sticks, for serving (optional)
- Dairy-free ranch dressing, store-bought or homemade (page 376), for serving (optional)

DIRECTIONS

1. Spread the wings in a single layer across paper towels and sprinkle with the salt. Cover with another layer of paper towels and let rest for 20 minutes.

2. Put one oven rack in the middle-lower position and another rack in the middle-upper position. Preheat the oven to 250°F. Set a cooling rack on a rimmed baking sheet.

3. Put the wings and baking powder in a resealable plastic bag. Shake to coat the wings evenly.

4. Spread the wings in a single layer across the cooling rack. Bake on the middle-lower rack for 30 minutes.

5. Increase the oven temperature to 425°F and bake on the middle-upper rack for an additional 45 minutes, or until the skin is nice and crispy.

6. Warm the barbecue sauce and mustard in a small saucepan over medium heat. Mix to combine. Toss the wings in the sauce before serving.

7. Serve with celery sticks and ranch dressing, if desired.

PER SERVING:
CALORIES: **304**   TOTAL CARBS: **2.5g**
FAT: **19.8g**   FIBER: **0.4g**
PROTEIN: **26.9g**   NET CARBS: **2.1g**

CUMIN-SPICED PECANS

NET CARBS 0.9g

 MAKES: 4 cups (¼ cup per serving) · PREP TIME: 5 minutes · COOK TIME: 20 minutes

Although these roasted nuts make the perfect keto-friendly snack, my favorite way to enjoy them is on top of a salad. They add a great crunch and a boost of flavor.

INGREDIENTS

- 2 tablespoons powdered erythritol
- 1 teaspoon sea salt
- 2 teaspoons ground cumin
- 1 teaspoon smoked paprika
- Pinch of cayenne pepper
- 3 tablespoons avocado oil
- 10 ounces raw pecan halves

DIRECTIONS

1. Preheat the oven to 300°F. Line a rimmed baking sheet with parchment paper or a silicone baking mat.

2. Put the erythritol, salt, and spices in a large bowl and mix to combine.

3. Whisk in the avocado oil until the mixture is smooth and there are no clumps of seasoning.

4. Add the pecans to the bowl and toss until all the nuts are evenly coated.

5. Spread the pecans in a single layer across the prepared baking sheet. Bake for 20 minutes, or until the nuts are toasted.

> *tip: Mix things up and use any combination of your favorite lower-carb nuts. See page 59 for a breakdown of the total and net carbs in different kinds of nuts.*

PER SERVING:

CALORIES: **147**	FIBER: **1.8g**
FAT: **15.4g**	NET CARBS: **0.9g**
PROTEIN: **1.7g**	ERYTHRITOL: **1.5g**
TOTAL CARBS: **2.6g**	

RESTAURANT-STYLE SALSA

NET CARBS 1.9g

MAKES: 3 cups (¼ cup per serving) · PREP TIME: 10 minutes · COOK TIME: 15 minutes

Fresh salsa is so quick and easy to make that there really is no excuse for having that jar of store-bought salsa in your refrigerator right now. Once you start making your own, there is no turning back. You will never buy it again. The roasted tomatoes, garlic, and chili peppers in this recipe are brought to life by the bright acidity of the lime juice. To make this salsa truly shine, I recommend refrigerating it for a few hours before serving to let the flavors really come together.

INGREDIENTS

- 4 vine-ripened tomatoes, quartered
- 2 cloves garlic, halved
- 2 small serrano peppers, stemmed and halved lengthwise
- 1 small onion, cut into large chunks
- 3 tablespoons avocado oil or olive oil
- 2 teaspoons sea salt, divided
- ¼ cup loosely packed fresh cilantro leaves
- Juice of ½ lime, or more to taste
- ½ teaspoon ground cumin

FOR SERVING (OPTIONAL):

- Sliced bell peppers
- Sliced cucumbers
- Pork rinds
- Low-carb crackers

SPECIAL EQUIPMENT:

Food processor or high-powered blender

DIRECTIONS

1. Put an oven rack in the top position. Preheat the oven to broil-high.

2. Arrange the tomatoes, garlic, peppers, and onion across a rimmed baking sheet. Drizzle the oil over the top and sprinkle with 1 teaspoon of the salt. Toss to evenly coat and spread out in a single layer.

3. Broil on the top rack until the tomatoes and onion are soft and charred, about 10 minutes.

4. Transfer everything from the baking sheet, juices included, to a food processor or high-powered blender (see tips below). Add the cilantro, lime juice, cumin, and remaining teaspoon of salt. Pulse until mostly smooth but still slightly chunky. Taste and add more lime juice, if desired.

5. Store leftovers in the refrigerator for up to a week.

> *tips: Add the roasted serranos to the food processor one at a time to make sure you are happy with the heat level. Serrano peppers range in spiciness, and it would be a shame for your salsa to be so spicy that you don't want to eat it.*
>
> *For an even quicker version of this salsa, you can replace the charred tomatoes and peppers with a 28-ounce can of whole, fire-roasted tomatoes and a 14.5-ounce can of diced tomatoes and green chilies.*

PER SERVING:
CALORIES: **42**   TOTAL CARBS: **2.6g**
FAT: **3.6g**   FIBER: **0.7g**
PROTEIN: **0.5g**   NET CARBS: **1.9g**

QUICK AND EASY CHUNKY GUACAMOLE

NET CARBS
2.6g

MAKES: about 4 cups (½ cup per serving) · PREP TIME: 10 minutes, plus 1 hour to chill

I'd like to hug whoever thought of mashing up avocados, mixing them with amazing Mexican flavors, and making a dip out of it. They are true champions in my book. Of course, I think that would mean going all the way back to Aztec times. I would love to have been around for that very first bowl of guacamole ever made.

INGREDIENTS

- 3 large avocados, peeled and pitted
- Juice of ½ lime, or more to taste
- ¼ cup restaurant-style salsa, store-bought or homemade (page 142)
- ¼ cup chopped red onions, plus more for garnish if desired
- 3 cloves garlic, minced
- 2 teaspoons Maldon sea salt flakes
- ¼ teaspoon ground cumin
- 2 tablespoons chopped fresh cilantro, plus more for garnish if desired (optional)
- 2 tablespoons chopped bell peppers (any color), for garnish (optional)

DIRECTIONS

1. Put the avocado flesh in a bowl and mash it with a fork until it is mostly smooth but there are still visible chunks.

2. Add the lime juice, salsa, onions, garlic, salt, cumin, and cilantro, if using, to the bowl. Using a rubber spatula, fold in the ingredients until they are well incorporated.

3. Refrigerate for 1 hour before serving. Garnish with chopped cilantro, bell peppers, and red onions, if desired.

> tip: I love to serve this guacamole with crunchy dippers like bell pepper slices, cucumber slices, and pork rinds.

PER SERVING:
CALORIES: **127**   TOTAL CARBS: **7.9g**
FAT: **11.1g**   FIBER: **5.3g**
PROTEIN: **1.7g**   NET CARBS: **2.6g**

DINNER ROLLS

NET CARBS 3.4g

MAKES: 6 rolls (1 per serving) · **PREP TIME:** 10 minutes · **COOK TIME:** 55 minutes

These dinner rolls are a variation of the Everything Buns recipe on page 360, and they are the perfect accompaniment to any meal. I like to slice mine in half and serve them with butter-flavored coconut oil, or even use them for making sliders.

INGREDIENTS

- 1¼ cups blanched almond flour
- ¼ cup plus 2 teaspoons psyllium husk powder
- 2 tablespoons nutritional yeast
- 2 teaspoons baking powder
- ½ teaspoon sea salt
- ½ teaspoon garlic powder
- ½ teaspoon onion powder
- ½ teaspoon dried Italian seasoning
- 2 teaspoons apple cider vinegar
- 3 large egg whites
- 1 cup hot water
- 2 teaspoons black and/or white sesame seeds

DIRECTIONS

1. Put an oven rack in the lower third position. Preheat the oven to 350°F. Line a rimmed baking sheet with parchment paper or a silicone baking mat.

2. Whisk together the almond flour, psyllium husk powder, nutritional yeast, baking powder, salt, garlic powder, onion powder, and Italian seasoning in a large mixing bowl. Mix until the ingredients are well combined with no visible clumps.

3. Add the vinegar and egg whites to the bowl and, using a rubber spatula, mix while slowly pouring in the hot water. You want to mix just enough that the ingredients are well combined, but no longer or the dough will become overmixed.

4. Moisten your hands and divide the dough into 6 equal portions. Roll each portion into a ball. Put the dough balls on the prepared baking sheet and sprinkle the sesame seeds over the top.

5. Bake for 55 minutes, or until the rolls have doubled in size and are crisp on top, making a hollow sound when you thump them. Allow to cool before slicing.

> *tip*: Some brands of psyllium husk powder will cause these rolls to turn purple. I recommend using Now Foods brand.

PER SERVING:

CALORIES: **241**	TOTAL CARBS: **12.6g**
FAT: **20.8g**	FIBER: **9.2g**
PROTEIN: **9.1g**	NET CARBS: **3.4g**

GARLIC DILL SAUERKRAUT

NET CARBS 3.2g

MAKES: about 2 cups (¼ cup per serving)
PREP TIME: 20 minutes, plus time to ferment

Fermented sauerkraut is an excellent way to get a dose of gut-healing probiotics. Not only are probiotics good for gut health, but they also help improve immune function, detoxify the body, control inflammation, and support brain function and cognitive health. Sauerkraut truly is a nutritional powerhouse.

INGREDIENTS

- 1 small to medium head green cabbage (about 1½ pounds), finely shredded (reserve 1 leaf before shredding)
- 3 cloves garlic, peeled
- 2 teaspoons sea salt
- ½ ounce fresh dill, chopped

DIRECTIONS

1. Combine the shredded cabbage, garlic, salt, and dill in a large mixing bowl. Using your hands, massage the cabbage, squeezing it to help draw out the moisture.

2. Put another slightly smaller bowl on top of the cabbage and place something heavy inside the smaller bowl to weight it down. The pressure will help draw more moisture out of the cabbage. Let sit for 2 hours.

3. Pack the cabbage mixture and all the liquid into a clean 32-ounce wide-mouth mason jar. Put the reserved cabbage leaf on top of the cabbage mixture, tucking the sides of the leaf down around the side of the jar, and press down until all the cabbage mixture is submerged.

4. Put a smaller jar inside the mason jar to pack the cabbage down and keep it below the liquid line. You need all the cabbage to be submerged or it will not ferment. It will create more liquid as time goes on.

5. Cap the jar and leave it on the counter for 3 to 5 days, burping it twice a day. To burp the jar, simply open the lid to release built-up pressure, push the cabbage back down below the liquid line, and recap.

6. On day 3, taste the sauerkraut. If the taste and texture are to your liking, transfer the jar to the refrigerator. I like a very acidic sauerkraut, so I like to ferment mine on the counter for a minimum of 2 weeks or up to a month before transferring it to the refrigerator. (The longer it ferments, the more sour the taste and the softer the texture.) Putting it in the refrigerator will stop the fermentation process, so it is important to make sure that your cabbage has turned to kraut and that you are happy with the taste and texture.

PER SERVING:
CALORIES: **19**   TOTAL CARBS: **5.3g**
FAT: **0.1g**   FIBER: **2.2g**
PROTEIN: **1g**   NET CARBS: **3.2g**

NEW ORLEANS–STYLE OLIVE SALAD

NET CARBS 0.4g

MAKES: 5¼ cups (¼ cup per serving) · **PREP TIME:** 10 minutes, plus 1 hour to chill

If you have ever been to New Orleans, then you know that just about every menu you see has muffuletta on its pages. One of the things that makes muffuletta so uniquely special in the sandwich world is the olive salad. It's paired with delectable meats and cheeses and piled high on a giant round Sicilian sesame bun. There is nothing like it in the world. But if you ask me, the star of the show is the olive salad. I keep a jar of this in my refrigerator at all times. I love to put it on salads, sandwiches, eggs, and lettuce wraps, or even just eat it with a spoon!

INGREDIENTS

- 1½ cups giardiniera
- 1 cup pimiento-stuffed green olives
- 1 cup pitted Kalamata olives
- ½ cup pepperoncini, stems removed
- ¼ cup roasted red peppers
- ¼ cup red wine vinegar
- ¼ cup olive oil
- 4 cloves garlic, peeled
- 1 teaspoon dried basil
- 1 teaspoon dried oregano
- ½ teaspoon ground black pepper
- Pinch of red pepper flakes
- ⅓ cup capers

SPECIAL EQUIPMENT:

Food processor or high-powered blender

DIRECTIONS

1. Put the giardiniera, green and Kalamata olives, pepperoncini, roasted red peppers, vinegar, olive oil, garlic, basil, oregano, black pepper, and red pepper flakes in a food processor or high-powered blender. Pulse until all the ingredients are in small pieces about the size of the capers.

2. Stir in the capers.

3. Cover and refrigerate for at least 1 hour before serving. Store leftovers in the refrigerator for up to 3 weeks.

PER SERVING: ──────────
CALORIES: **25**   TOTAL CARBS: **0.5g**
FAT: **2.6g**   FIBER: **0.1g**
PROTEIN: **0.1g**   NET CARBS: **0.4g**

CRISPY OVEN-FRIED PICKLES

NET CARBS 1.8g

MAKES: 36 fried pickles (6 per serving) · PREP TIME: 15 minutes · COOK TIME: 15 minutes

It simply wouldn't be one of my books if it didn't have some sort of pickle recipe in it, now would it? Fried pickles were always one of my favorite bar appetizers. I would order them every time I saw them on a menu. They were one of the foods I missed the most when I switched to a low-carb lifestyle, and I knew right away that I wanted to re-create them in a low-carb version.

INGREDIENTS

- 36 large dill pickle chips
- ½ cup mayonnaise, store-bought or homemade (page 386)
- 1 batch Savory Nut-Free Breading Mix (page 364)
- Lime Sriracha Aioli (page 389), for serving (optional)

DIRECTIONS

1. Put the pickle chips between layers of paper towels to absorb the moisture. You want the pickles to be as dry as possible when you bread them.

2. Preheat the oven to 450°F. Put a cooling rack on a rimmed baking sheet.

3. Set up two shallow bowls in a row. Put the mayonnaise in the first bowl and the breading mix in the second bowl.

4. Dip each pickle chip in the mayonnaise and then coat generously in the breading.

5. Line the breaded pickles in a single layer across the cooling rack. Baking the chips on the cooling rack rather than directly on the baking sheet allows them to get crispy on both sides.

6. Bake for 15 minutes, or until crispy and browned. Let cool just slightly before serving to let the breading finish crisping. Serve with aioli, if desired.

---

tips: *If you are slicing whole pickles to make your own "chips," slice them slightly on a bias for larger pickle chips.*

If you aren't avoiding dairy, you can use ¼ cup heavy cream whisked with 1 large egg in place of the mayonnaise in this recipe.

PER SERVING:

CALORIES: **131**	TOTAL CARBS: **6.6g**
FAT: **13.9g**	FIBER: **4.8g**
PROTEIN: **0.7g**	NET CARBS: **1.8g**

PICKLED ASPARAGUS

NET CARBS
1.3g

MAKES: about 40 spears (4 per serving)
PREP TIME: 10 minutes, plus at least 2 hours to pickle · **COOK TIME:** 5 minutes

Not only are these pickled asparagus spears a delicious snack, but they also pack a major health punch. They are full of antioxidants and are a great source of vitamins A, B6, C, E, and K, as well as folate, iron, copper, calcium, protein, and fiber. Add that to the immune-boosting properties from the garlic, and I'd say we have ourselves a winner!

INGREDIENTS

- 1 pound pencil-thin asparagus, trimmed
- 3 sprigs fresh dill
- 1½ cups distilled white vinegar
- ¼ cup apple cider vinegar
- 1¼ cups water
- 2 tablespoons sea salt
- 1 tablespoon granular erythritol
- 1 tablespoon black peppercorns
- 1 tablespoon yellow mustard seeds
- 1 teaspoon red pepper flakes
- 5 cloves garlic, smashed with the side of a knife

DIRECTIONS

1. Pack the asparagus and dill into a 32-ounce mason jar.

2. In a saucepan over medium heat, bring the vinegars, water, salt, erythritol, peppercorns, mustard seeds, red pepper flakes, and garlic to a light boil, stirring to dissolve the erythritol and salt.

3. Pour the brine, including the garlic and spices, over the asparagus and dill in the jar.

4. Let the jar sit on the counter for 1 hour to cool to room temperature. Cap and shake gently to surround the asparagus with the spices.

5. Put the jar in the refrigerator for at least 2 hours. You can eat the asparagus after 2 hours, but they get better and better the longer they are in the fridge. Store in the refrigerator for up to 2 months.

tip: If you aren't a fan of spicy foods, simply omit the red pepper flakes. Doing so will also make this dish nightshade-free.

PER SERVING:

CALORIES: **41**   TOTAL CARBS: **2.3g**
FAT: **2.9g**   FIBER: **1g**
PROTEIN: **1.1g**   NET CARBS: **1.3g**

SPICY FRIED HAM DEVILED EGGS

NET CARBS
1.2g

MAKES: 12 deviled eggs (2 per serving) · **PREP TIME:** 10 minutes · **COOK TIME:** 15 minutes

I have been known to eat a plate of deviled eggs as a meal on more than one occasion. They are one of my favorite foods of all time. You can prepare them in countless ways, and for me that never gets boring. On the off chance I have leftovers, I like to chop them up into an egg salad and wrap it in lettuce leaves or slices of prosciutto.

INGREDIENTS

- 1 tablespoon avocado oil or olive oil
- 2 ounces ham, finely diced
- 6 hard-boiled eggs
- ¼ cup mayonnaise, store-bought or homemade (page 386)
- 2 tablespoons dill pickle relish
- 1 tablespoon Dijon mustard
- 1 tablespoon Sriracha sauce
- 1 teaspoon dried minced onion
- ¼ teaspoon garlic powder
- Microgreens, for garnish

DIRECTIONS

1. Heat the oil in a skillet over medium heat. When the pan is hot, add the ham and fry until browned on all sides. Remove the ham from the pan and set aside.

2. Slice the eggs in half lengthwise and scoop the yolks into a medium mixing bowl. Mash the yolks with a fork. Set the whites aside.

3. To the yolks, add the mayonnaise, relish, mustard, Sriracha, and dried minced onion. Mix until the ingredients are well combined.

4. Transfer the yolk mixture to a pastry bag or resealable plastic bag. If using a plastic bag, snip off one corner of the bag. Pipe the yolk mixture into the egg whites.

5. Top the deviled eggs with the fried ham and garnish with microgreens.

> *tips: This is how I make the perfect hard-boiled eggs: Put the eggs in a large saucepan and cover with cold water. Be sure to add enough water so that the eggs are fully submerged. Over high heat, bring the water to a rolling boil. When the water is boiling, remove the pan from the heat, cover, and let sit for 12 minutes. Submerge the eggs in a cold-water bath before peeling.*
>
> *Don't like spicy foods? Skip the Sriracha!*

PER SERVING:

CALORIES: **172**	TOTAL CARBS: **1.4g**
FAT: **14.8g**	FIBER: **0.2g**
PROTEIN: **8.1g**	NET CARBS: **1.2g**

SUGAR-FREE DRIED CRANBERRIES

NET CARBS 5g

MAKES: about 3 cups (¼ cup per serving) · PREP TIME: 15 minutes · COOK TIME: 3 to 4 hours

I love adding dried cranberries to dishes. They add the perfect hint of sweetness without being overbearing. What I don't love is how high in sugar and carbs the store-bought versions are. Did you know that just ¼ cup of the average store-bought brand of dried cranberries contains 33 grams of carbs and 29 grams of sugar? No thanks! I think I will keep making my own.

INGREDIENTS

- 2 (12-ounce) bags fresh cranberries
- 1 cup granular erythritol
- 3 tablespoons avocado oil
- ½ teaspoon pure orange extract (optional)

DIRECTIONS

1. Preheat the oven to 200°F. Line two rimmed baking sheets with parchment paper or silicone baking mats.

2. Rinse and dry the cranberries and remove any brown or soft ones. Slice the cranberries in half and put them in a large mixing bowl.

3. Add the erythritol, avocado oil, and orange extract, if using. Toss to evenly coat all the berries.

4. Line the berries in single layers across the baking sheets.

5. Bake for 3 to 4 hours, rotating the racks halfway through, until the cranberries are fully dried and no longer releasing juices.

6. Store in an airtight container in the refrigerator for up to 2 months.

PER SERVING:
CALORIES: 61   FIBER: 2g
FAT: 0g   NET CARBS: 5g
PROTEIN: 0.3g   ERYTHRITOL: 16g
TOTAL CARBS: 7g

SWEET AND SAVORY TRAIL MIX

NET CARBS
1.4g

MAKES: **3 cups (¼ cup per serving)** · PREP TIME: **10 minutes**

Having been born and raised in the Pacific Northwest, I am an avid hiker. I love being out in nature, without a care in the world. This trail mix is one of my favorite snacks to throw in my pack and take with me on the trails. I don't have to stop to eat it, I don't have to cook it, and it gives me an added boost of energy to keep pushing along the trail.

INGREDIENTS

- 3 ounces no-sugar-added beef jerky, chopped
- ½ cup roasted pecans
- ¼ cup roasted pepitas (pumpkin seeds)
- ¼ cup slivered almonds
- ¼ cup unsweetened coconut flakes
- ¼ cup sugar-free dried cranberries, store-bought or homemade (page 158)
- ¼ cup sugar-free dark chocolate chips
- 3 tablespoons hulled sunflower seeds

DIRECTIONS

Combine all the ingredients and store in an airtight container for up to 3 weeks.

tip: Mix it up with any of your favorite low-carb nuts and seeds.

PER SERVING:
CALORIES: **116**   TOTAL CARBS: **3.7g**
FAT: **9.2g**   FIBER: **2.3g**
PROTEIN: **6.6g**   NET CARBS: **1.4g**

Soups and Salads

BEEF RAMEN

NET CARBS
5.8g

🍲 🍴 🕐 **MAKES:** 4 servings · **PREP TIME:** 15 minutes · **COOK TIME:** 20 minutes

I certainly don't want to offend any traditionalists or ancient cultures with my very Americanized low-carb version of ramen, but ramen has been one of my favorite foods ever since I started eating solids. Granted, it used to come in the form of Top Ramen, with the dried noodles and little seasoning packets, but I loved it nonetheless. In fact, Top Ramen was the first thing I learned to cook on my own. These days, I am eating more traditional, freshly made versions of ramen, but I still love it in all its many shapes, sizes, flavors, and styles.

INGREDIENTS

- 1 pound boneless top sirloin steak, cut into ¼-inch-thick slices
- Sea salt and ground black pepper
- 4 (8-ounce) packages spaghetti-style shirataki noodles (see page 66)
- 5 cups beef stock or bone broth (page 370)
- 2 cloves garlic, minced
- 1 teaspoon grated fresh ginger
- 1 tablespoon toasted sesame oil
- 1 tablespoon unseasoned rice wine vinegar
- 1 tablespoon fish sauce
- Pinch of red pepper flakes
- 5 tablespoons gluten-free soy sauce or coconut aminos, divided
- 12 cremini mushrooms, thinly sliced
- 4 green onions, sliced on a bias, white and green parts separated

- 4 soft-boiled eggs
- 1 tablespoon black and/or white sesame seeds

DIRECTIONS

1. Season the steak generously with salt and pepper and set aside.

2. Rinse the shirataki noodles, soak them in fresh water for 10 minutes, and then drain them.

3. Heat a large skillet over medium heat. Add the noodles to the pan and dry-fry them for 3 to 4 minutes, tossing frequently.

4. While the noodles are frying, bring the beef stock to a simmer in a stockpot or Dutch oven over medium heat, then reduce the heat to medium-low.

5. To the noodles, add the garlic, ginger, sesame oil, vinegar, fish sauce, red pepper flakes, and 4 tablespoons of the soy sauce. Stir-fry for 5 minutes, or until the noodles turn brown from absorbing the sauce. Add the noodles and sauce to the pot with the stock.

6. Return the skillet to the stovetop over medium-high heat. Sear the steak in the hot pan for 1 to 2 minutes on each side. Remove the steak from the pan and cover to keep warm.

7. Reduce the heat under the skillet to medium and add the mushrooms, the white parts of the green onions, and the remaining tablespoon of soy sauce. Stir-fry until the mushrooms are tender and the onions are soft.

8. Divide the noodle mixture among 4 bowls. Top each bowl with the steak and the mushroom mixture. Pour the broth over each bowl, dividing it evenly among the bowls. Finish each bowl with an egg, some sesame seeds, and the green parts of the green onions.

PER SERVING:

CALORIES: **419**	TOTAL CARBS: **8.5g**
FAT: **24g**	FIBER: **2.7g**
PROTEIN: **42.1g**	NET CARBS: **5.8g**

tips: *Use this recipe as a base to create your own spin on ramen. Add whatever type of protein—seafood, chicken, beef, pork—and any low-carb vegetables you want. Some of my favorites are bean sprouts, bell peppers, bok choy, broccoli slaw, cabbage, and leeks.*

If you need this recipe to be nightshade-free, make sure to choose a brand of stock that is free of nightshades.

CABBAGE ROLL SOUP

NET CARBS 6.2g

MAKES: 4 quarts (1 cup per serving) · **PREP TIME:** 20 minutes · **COOK TIME:** 1 hour

I cannot hear the word *cabbage* without thinking of the Cabbage Patch Dolls that I had as a child. Eleanor and Sybil were beautiful with their puffy nylon faces and braidable yarn hair. They used to spend their time playing with my Glo Worm and my G.I. Joes—that is, when my G.I. Joes weren't busy playing with my Transformers and Barbies. Oh, to be a kid in the early 1980s. At any rate, you probably did not come here to hear about my childhood toys. This soup is a brothy, comforting version of deconstructed cabbage rolls.

INGREDIENTS

- 2 tablespoons avocado oil or olive oil
- 1 medium onion, diced (about 1 cup)
- 4 cloves garlic, minced
- 1½ pounds ground beef
- ½ pound ground pork
- 6 cups beef stock or bone broth (page 370)
- 3 teaspoons dried oregano leaves
- 2 teaspoons sea salt
- 2 teaspoons smoked paprika
- 2 teaspoons garlic powder
- 2 teaspoons onion powder
- 1 teaspoon ground black pepper
- ½ teaspoon dried thyme leaves
- 2 (14.5-ounce) cans diced tomatoes, drained
- 1 (6-ounce) can tomato paste
- 2 tablespoons chopped fresh flat-leaf parsley
- 1 large head green cabbage, halved and shredded
- 3 cups riced cauliflower

DIRECTIONS

1. Heat the oil in a stockpot or Dutch oven over medium heat. Add the onion and garlic. Sauté until the onion is translucent and the garlic is fragrant.

2. Add the ground beef and pork to the pot. Cook until browned, using a spatula to break up the meat, then drain any excess grease.

3. Add the rest of the ingredients to the pot. Bring to a boil, then reduce the heat to low and simmer for 40 minutes to allow the flavors to come together.

tip: *This recipe makes a large batch of soup, but it is excellent for separating into portions and freezing for later meals.*

PER SERVING:

CALORIES: **211**	TOTAL CARBS: **8.4g**
FAT: **13.4g**	FIBER: **2.2g**
PROTEIN: **13.7g**	NET CARBS: **6.2g**

CHICKEN AND "RICE" SOUP

NET CARBS 2.7g

MAKES: 10 cups (1 cup per serving) · **PREP TIME:** 20 minutes · **COOK TIME:** 50 minutes

This is my go-to feel-good soup. As soon as anyone in my house even remotely starts to feel under the weather, I am in the kitchen whipping up a batch. From time to time, I even make a double batch and freeze half so that we always have an emergency stash on hand. While it might not take the cold and flu symptoms away entirely, it sure is comforting and soothing.

INGREDIENTS

- 2 tablespoons avocado oil or olive oil
- 1 small onion, diced (about ½ cup)
- 4 cloves garlic, minced
- 1 bay leaf
- ½ teaspoon ground ginger
- ½ teaspoon turmeric powder
- ½ teaspoon dried basil
- ½ teaspoon dried oregano leaves
- ½ teaspoon dried rosemary leaves
- ¼ teaspoon dried thyme leaves
- ¼ teaspoon ground black pepper
- 1 teaspoon sea salt
- 1½ pounds boneless, skinless chicken breasts or thighs
- 6 cups chicken stock or bone broth (page 370)
- 4 cups riced cauliflower
- 1 medium red bell pepper, seeded and diced
- 4 ribs celery, sliced
- 6 slices bacon, cooked crisp and crumbled
- Fresh thyme sprigs, for garnish (optional)

DIRECTIONS

1. Heat the oil in a stockpot or Dutch oven over medium heat. Add the onion and garlic and sauté until the onion is translucent and the garlic is fragrant.

2. Add the spices, salt, and chicken to the pot and cook until the chicken is cooked through and browned, about 6 minutes.

3. Deglaze the pan with a splash of the chicken stock and use a rubber spatula to scrape up and mix in any browned bits from the bottom of the pan.

4. Add the cauliflower to the pot and cook for 10 minutes, stirring occasionally, until it is tender.

5. Add the bell pepper, celery, and remaining chicken stock to the pot and bring to a boil over high heat, then reduce the heat to low and simmer for 30 minutes to allow the flavors to come together.

6. Remove the bay leaf and mix in the bacon before serving. Garnish with thyme, if desired.

PER SERVING:

CALORIES: **176**   TOTAL CARBS: **4.6g**
FAT: **10.1g**   FIBER: **1.8g**
PROTEIN: **17.3g**   NET CARBS: **2.7g**

EASY PEASY WONTON-LESS SOUP

NET CARBS 5.3g

MAKES: 5 quarts (2 cups per serving) · **PREP TIME:** 30 minutes · **COOK TIME:** 40 minutes

This wonton-less soup will leave you wondering why you ever needed the wonton wrappers in the first place. Making low-carb Chinese food recipes can be a little tricky. Many traditional Asian-inspired dishes contain sugar, gluten, and other ingredients that I try to avoid. But with a little creativity and a willingness to cook your own food, you can have a delicious low-carb version that tastes just as good as takeout, if not better.

INGREDIENTS

FOR THE MEATBALLS:

- 1½ pounds ground pork
- 3 tablespoons gluten-free soy sauce or coconut aminos
- 2 tablespoons plus 1 teaspoon toasted sesame oil, divided
- 1 teaspoon gluten-free oyster sauce
- 1 teaspoon fish sauce
- 2 green onions, chopped
- 2 cloves garlic, minced
- 1 teaspoon grated fresh ginger
- ¼ teaspoon red pepper flakes
- 1 large egg

FOR THE BROTH:

- 2 quarts chicken stock or bone broth (page 370)
- 2 cups water
- 2 tablespoons fish sauce
- 2 tablespoons gluten-free oyster sauce
- 2 tablespoons gluten-free soy sauce or coconut aminos
- 2 teaspoons grated fresh ginger
- ½ teaspoon red pepper flakes

- 1 (14-ounce) bag coleslaw mix, or 1 small head green cabbage (about 1 pound), shredded

- 5 large cremini mushrooms, thinly sliced
- 4 green onions, thinly sliced on a bias, for garnish (optional)

DIRECTIONS

1. Make the meatballs: Put the ground pork, soy sauce, 1 teaspoon of the sesame oil, the oyster sauce, fish sauce, green onions, garlic, ginger, red pepper flakes, and egg in a large mixing bowl. Mix until the ingredients are well incorporated. Form the mixture into bite-sized meatballs. You should have about 40 meatballs.

2. In a stockpot or Dutch oven, heat the remaining 2 tablespoons of sesame oil over medium-high heat. Add the meatballs to the pot and cook until they are browned all over and cooked through. If they start to stick, splash a little chicken stock into the pot. Remove the meatballs from the pot and set aside.

3. Make the broth: In the same pot, bring the chicken stock, water, fish sauce, oyster sauce, soy sauce, ginger, and red pepper flakes to a boil. Once at a boil, reduce the heat to low and simmer for 10 minutes.

4. Add the meatballs, coleslaw mix, and mushrooms to the broth. Simmer for an additional 10 minutes, or until the cabbage and mushrooms are tender.

5. Garnish with the green onions before serving, if desired.

> *tip: This soup is amazing served with a soft-boiled egg.*

PER SERVING:
CALORIES: **260**   TOTAL CARBS: **6.4g**
FAT: **16g**   FIBER: **1.1g**
PROTEIN: **21g**   NET CARBS: **5.3g**

LEMONY GREEK CHICKEN SOUP

NET CARBS 4.9g

MAKES: 4 quarts (2 cups per serving) · PREP TIME: 10 minutes · COOK TIME: 20 minutes

My favorite thing about this soup is how delightfully creamy it is. It gives the illusion that it contains dairy, all from tempering whisked eggs into the broth. The flavors come together in under thirty minutes, but the soup tastes like it simmered away all day.

INGREDIENTS

- 2 tablespoons avocado oil or olive oil
- 1 medium orange bell pepper, seeded and diced (about 1 cup)
- 1 medium onion, diced (about 1 cup)
- 3 cloves garlic, minced
- ½ teaspoon red pepper flakes
- 1½ teaspoons sea salt, or more to taste
- ½ teaspoon ground black pepper, or more to taste
- 2 quarts chicken stock or bone broth (page 370)
- 2 cups riced cauliflower
- 4 large eggs
- ¼ cup fresh lemon juice
- 4 cups shredded rotisserie chicken
- 3 cups fresh baby spinach
- 3 tablespoons chopped fresh dill

DIRECTIONS

1. Heat the oil in a stockpot or Dutch oven over medium heat. Add the bell pepper and onion and sauté until they are tender, about 4 minutes. Add the garlic, red pepper flakes, salt, and black pepper. Cook, stirring constantly, until the garlic is fragrant, about 2 minutes.

2. Add the chicken stock and increase the heat to high. Bring to a boil, then add the riced cauliflower and cook for 5 minutes.

3. While the cauliflower is cooking, whisk the eggs and lemon juice together in a medium bowl until they are frothy.

4. Remove 1 cup of the boiling stock from the pot and very gradually pour it into the lemon-egg mixture, whisking constantly to temper the eggs. If you do this step too quickly, you'll end up with scrambled eggs. Once all the stock is added, whisk for 1 additional minute, then pour the mixture into the pot and stir to combine.

5. Reduce the heat to medium-low and mix in the chicken, spinach, and dill. Cook, stirring constantly, until the spinach is wilted.

6. Taste and add more salt and pepper, if desired.

> *tip*: One large rotisserie chicken should be the perfect size to yield 4 cups of shredded chicken. When selecting your chicken, be sure to check for added sugars. Many store-bought rotisserie chickens have evaporated cane juice added.

PER SERVING:
CALORIES: **177**   TOTAL CARBS: **6.6g**
FAT: **7.9g**   FIBER: **1.7g**
PROTEIN: **19.1g**   NET CARBS: **4.9g**

SPICY BLOODY MARY TOMATO SOUP

NET CARBS 6.6g

MAKES: 2 quarts (1 cup per serving) · PREP TIME: 10 minutes · COOK TIME: 50 minutes

Your favorite Sunday morning hangover cocktail is about to become your favorite tomato soup recipe. All the rich and delicious flavors of a scratch-made bloody Mary, but in the form of a warm and comforting soup. Here's a little pairing suggestion for you, too—if you happened to make the Blackened Shrimp Fettuccine Alfredo (page 230) and have any leftover blackened shrimp, it goes fantastically with this soup.

INGREDIENTS

- 2 tablespoons avocado oil or olive oil
- 2 ribs celery, chopped
- 1 small onion, chopped (about ½ cup)
- 3 cloves garlic, minced
- ½ teaspoon sea salt
- ¼ teaspoon ground black pepper
- 1 (15-ounce) can tomato sauce
- 1 (14.5-ounce) can stewed tomatoes
- 1 quart chicken stock or bone broth (page 370)
- 2 tablespoons Worcestershire sauce
- 2 teaspoons prepared horseradish, or more to taste
- ½ teaspoon celery salt

FOR GARNISH (OPTIONAL):

- Garlic and Herb Croutons (page 362)
- Bacon, chopped and cooked until crispy

DIRECTIONS

1. Heat the oil in a stockpot or Dutch oven over medium heat. When the oil is hot, add the celery, onion, garlic, salt, and pepper. Sauté until the vegetables are translucent and tender.

2. Add the tomato sauce, stewed tomatoes, chicken stock, Worcestershire sauce, horseradish, and celery salt to the pot. Bring to a boil over medium-high heat, then reduce the heat to medium-low and simmer for 30 minutes to allow the flavors to come together.

3. Transfer the soup to a blender and puree until smooth. Depending on the size of your blender, you may need to do this in batches, as hot liquid expands while blending. Alternatively, you can puree the soup directly in the pot using an immersion blender.

4. Return the blended soup to the pot and simmer for an additional 10 minutes.

5. Garnish with croutons and bacon, if desired.

> *tips: If the soup is too acidic for you, add a little low-carb sweetener, like erythritol or monk fruit.*
>
> *For a vegetarian option, substitute vegetable stock for the chicken stock.*
>
> *If you aren't a fan of spicy foods, use less horseradish or skip it altogether.*

PER SERVING:

CALORIES: **69**	TOTAL CARBS: **8.2g**
FAT: **3.8g**	FIBER: **1.7g**
PROTEIN: **1.8g**	NET CARBS: **6.6g**

SUPREME PIZZA SOUP

NET CARBS 2.6g

MAKES: 14 cups (1 cup per serving) · **PREP TIME:** 15 minutes · **COOK TIME:** 45 minutes

If you have followed my site, peaceloveandlowcarb.com, or any of my cookbooks over the years, then you already know that I am a big fan of pizza and of trying to come up with creative low-carb pizza variations. There is a reason that there are more than twenty different pizza recipes on my site alone. This soup is another delicious spin on a favorite comfort food. I love to garnish it with Garlic and Herb Croutons (page 362) to get that whole pizza crust vibe going. If you aren't avoiding dairy, top the soup with the croutons and then with some mozzarella and Parmesan cheeses. It takes the soup to the next level and almost gives it a French onion feel. Yum!

INGREDIENTS

- 1 tablespoon avocado oil or olive oil
- 1 small onion, diced (about ½ cup)
- 4 cloves garlic, minced
- 1 teaspoon dried parsley
- ½ teaspoon dried oregano leaves
- ½ teaspoon sea salt
- ¼ teaspoon ground black pepper
- 1 pound bulk Italian sausage
- 6 ounces pepperoni slices, halved
- 3 ounces cremini mushrooms, quartered
- 6 cups beef stock or bone broth (page 370)
- 1 (14.5-ounce) can diced tomatoes, with juices
- ½ cup marinara sauce, store-bought or homemade (page 384)
- 1 small orange bell pepper, seeded and diced

- 1 small green bell pepper, seeded and diced
- ¼ cup sliced black olives

DIRECTIONS

1. Heat the oil in a stockpot or Dutch oven over medium heat. Add the onion, garlic, parsley, oregano, salt, and black pepper and sauté until the onion is translucent and the garlic is fragrant.

2. Add the sausage, pepperoni, and mushrooms and cook until the sausage is cooked through and the mushrooms have released their liquid. Drain the excess grease.

3. Add the beef stock, tomatoes, marinara sauce, and bell peppers. Bring to a boil, then reduce the heat to a simmer.

4. Simmer, stirring occasionally, for 30 minutes. Taste and add more salt and pepper, if needed.

5. Stir in the black olives in before serving.

tips: To cut down on preparation time, you can use a store-bought marinara sauce. Be sure to read the labels and look for a sauce that contains only vegetables, healthy fats, and seasonings. Rao's is a great brand for clean, keto-friendly marinara sauce. In addition to the recipe in this book, I have a couple of different low-carb marinara sauce recipes on my website.

If you have leftover Drunken Mushrooms with Caramelized Onions (page 294), toss them into this soup for an extra burst of flavor.

PER SERVING:

CALORIES: **192**	TOTAL CARBS: **3.9g**
FAT: **13.4g**	FIBER: **2.3g**
PROTEIN: **12.9g**	NET CARBS: **2.6g**

CLAM CHOWDER WITH BACON

MAKES: 3 quarts (1 cup per serving) · **PREP TIME:** 15 minutes · **COOK TIME:** 40 minutes

I am a huge fan of clam chowder—especially when it is loaded up with smoky bacon. When I set out to write a dairy-free keto cookbook, my wheels immediately began turning about how I could create a perfectly creamy clam chowder without using any dairy. I have to say, I am pretty impressed with the end result. For those of you who are not avoiding dairy, add a cup and a half of heavy cream into the final simmer. It is heavenly.

INGREDIENTS

- 1 extra-large head cauliflower (about 2½ pounds), trimmed into large florets, divided
- 1 quart chicken stock or bone broth (page 370), divided
- 2 teaspoons sea salt, divided
- ½ teaspoon ground black pepper
- 2 tablespoons avocado oil or olive oil
- 1 medium onion, chopped (about 1 cup)
- 1 shallot, chopped
- 4 cloves garlic, minced
- 2 ribs celery, chopped
- 1 small leek, washed, trimmed, and thinly sliced
- 1 teaspoon dried thyme leaves
- 1 tablespoon fish sauce
- 3 (10-ounce) cans fancy whole baby clams, with juices
- 1 cup clam juice

SPECIAL EQUIPMENT:

High-powered blender or food processor

DIRECTIONS

1. Cut one-quarter of the cauliflower florets into bite-sized pieces and set aside. Put the remaining cauliflower florets, 3 cups of the chicken stock, 1½ teaspoons of the salt, and the pepper in a large saucepan. Cover and bring to a boil over medium-high heat. When the stock reaches a boil, reduce the heat to medium and steam the cauliflower until it is fork-tender, about 10 minutes.

2. While the cauliflower is steaming, heat the oil in a stockpot or Dutch oven over medium heat. Add the onion, shallot, garlic, celery, leek, thyme, and remaining ½ teaspoon of salt and sauté until the vegetables are tender and fragrant, about 7 minutes.

3. Put the steamed cauliflower, along with any remaining cooking liquid, half of the sautéed vegetables, and the fish sauce in a high-powered blender or food processor. Pulse until smooth and creamy.

4. Add the remaining 1 cup of chicken stock to the pot with the remaining vegetables. Use a rubber spatula to scrape up and mix in any browned bits on the bottom of the pan.

5. Add the reserved bite-sized cauliflower, the clams, and the clam juice to the pot. Bring to a boil over medium-high heat.

6. Pour the pureed cauliflower mixture in the blender back into the pot and return the soup to a boil. Reduce the heat to medium-low and simmer, stirring often, until the cauliflower florets are tender and the flavors have come together, about 30 minutes.

tip: If you do not have a high-powered blender or food processor, you can also use an immersion blender. Simply add half of the sautéed vegetables and the fish sauce to the pot with the steamed cauliflower and stock and use an immersion blender to puree it right in the pot.

PER SERVING:

CALORIES: **87**	TOTAL CARBS: **6.4g**
FAT: **2.6g**	FIBER: **1.9g**
PROTEIN: **9.4g**	NET CARBS: **4.6g**

CAESAR SALAD WITH CUMIN-SPICED PECANS

NET CARBS 2.9g

MAKES: 4 servings · PREP TIME: 10 minutes

I seriously love Caesar salad. In fact, I almost always have one when we dine out. Minus the croutons, they are typically keto-friendly no matter where you order them. Often I order a large Caesar salad as my entree and add blackened salmon or chicken. There is something so crave-worthy about crunchy romaine tossed with a really garlicky Caesar dressing. In my world, there is no such thing as too much garlic. Or too much Caesar salad, for that matter.

INGREDIENTS

- 1 large head romaine lettuce, chopped
- ¼ cup dairy-free Caesar dressing, store-bought or homemade (page 375)
- 4 slices bacon, cooked crisp and chopped
- ¼ cup halved Kalamata olives
- ½ cup Cumin-Spiced Pecans (page 140)

DIRECTIONS

Put the lettuce and dressing in a large serving bowl and toss to coat the lettuce with the dressing. Top with the bacon, olives, and pecans.

tip: In place of, or in addition to, the nuts, this salad is also amazing with Garlic and Herb Croutons (page 362).

PER SERVING:
CALORIES: **285**   FIBER: **4.7g**
FAT: **26.4g**   NET CARBS: **2.9g**
PROTEIN: **7.6g**   ERYTHRITOL: **1g**
TOTAL CARBS: **7.5g**

BLACKENED CHICKEN SALAD

NET CARBS 4.7g

MAKES: 2 servings · **PREP TIME:** 15 minutes · **COOK TIME:** 20 minutes

Colorful food just tastes better. After all, we eat with our eyes first. I believe a big bowl of real food like this is what the phrase "taste the rainbow" should mean. I eat a hearty salad nearly every day. I like to prep all the vegetables in advance and batch-cook my proteins so that I can quickly throw a big, beautiful salad together. I have an entire drawer in my fridge that I call my salad bar drawer. It has glass storage containers filled with all my favorite salad toppings, already cut into bite-sized pieces. I line the bottoms of the containers with paper towels to absorb the moisture and keep the vegetables fresh longer. Having these ingredients already prepped reduces the chance of me getting hangry when it goes past mealtime.

INGREDIENTS

- 1 pound boneless, skinless chicken breasts or thighs
- 1 tablespoon avocado oil or olive oil
- 2 tablespoons Blackening Seasoning (page 398)
- 4 cups mixed lettuce
- ½ medium avocado, peeled, pitted, and sliced
- ½ small tomato, cut into wedges
- ¼ cup diced yellow bell peppers
- ¼ cup diced orange bell peppers
- ¼ cup Pickled Red Onions (page 368)
- 1 mini cucumber, diced
- Fresh cilantro, for garnish (optional)
- ½ lime, cut into wedges, for serving (optional)

DIRECTIONS

1. Preheat the oven to 375°F.

2. Put the chicken on a plate and drizzle on both sides with the oil. Sprinkle the blackening seasoning on both sides.

3. Heat a grill pan or cast-iron skillet over medium-high heat. When the pan is hot, add the chicken and sear for 1 to 2 minutes on each side. Transfer the chicken to a rimmed baking sheet. Bake for 15 minutes, or until cooked all the way through. Let rest for 10 minutes and then slice.

4. Divide the lettuce between 2 salad bowls and put the chicken on top.

5. Divide the avocado, tomato, yellow and orange bell peppers, red onions, and cucumber evenly between the bowls and arrange beside the chicken.

6. Garnish with fresh cilantro and serve with lime wedges, if desired.

PER SERVING:
CALORIES: **537**   TOTAL CARBS: **11.8g**
FAT: **22.3g**   FIBER: **7.1g**
PROTEIN: **69.9g**   NET CARBS: **4.7g**

EGG SALAD PROSCIUTTO CUPS

NET CARBS 1g

MAKES: 12 egg salad cups (2 per serving) · **PREP TIME:** 15 minutes · **COOK TIME:** 12 minutes

Egg salad is one of my favorite lunches when I look in the refrigerator and see bare shelves staring back at me. Even when I am in desperate need of a trip to the grocery store, I always have eggs, condiments, and spices on hand. So egg salad is always an option, and it's an option I love to take. If you don't want to take the time to bake the prosciutto, you can just chop it up and mix it into the egg salad or use it as wraps for the salad.

INGREDIENTS

- 10 ounces thinly sliced prosciutto
- 6 hard-boiled eggs, roughly chopped
- ½ cup mayonnaise, store-bought or homemade (page 386)
- 2 tablespoons dill pickle relish
- 1 tablespoon Dijon mustard
- 1 teaspoon apple cider vinegar
- 1 tablespoon dried minced onion
- 1 tablespoon chopped fresh chives, plus more for garnish
- ½ teaspoon chopped fresh dill, plus more for garnish

DIRECTIONS

1. Preheat the oven to 400°F. Lightly oil a standard-sized 12-well muffin pan.

2. Make the prosciutto cups: Line each of the 12 wells of the muffin pan with a slice of prosciutto, or two if needed for coverage. Bake for 12 minutes, or until the prosciutto is crispy and slightly browned. Remove the prosciutto cups from the pan and let cool and crisp up.

3. Make the egg salad: In a medium bowl, mix the eggs, mayonnaise, relish, mustard, vinegar, dried minced onion, chives, and dill until the ingredients are well incorporated.

4. Divide the egg salad evenly among the 12 prosciutto cups. Garnish with fresh chives and dill before serving. Store leftovers in the refrigerator for up to 3 days.

> *tip: This is how I make the perfect hard-boiled eggs: Put the eggs in a large saucepan and cover with cold water. Be sure to add enough water so that the eggs are fully submerged. Over high heat, bring the water to a rolling boil. When the water is boiling, remove the pan from the heat, cover, and let sit for 12 minutes. Submerge the eggs in a cold-water bath before peeling.*

PER SERVING: ——————

CALORIES: **298**   TOTAL CARBS: **1.2g**

FAT: **23.6g**   FIBER: **0.2g**

PROTEIN: **18.6g**   NET CARBS: **1g**

CHICAGO DOG SALAD

NET CARBS 3.4g

MAKES: 6 servings · PREP TIME: 20 minutes · COOK TIME: 5 minutes

Hot dog salad? Am I crazy? Well, maybe a little, but certainly not for making this recipe. I'd say I knocked it out of the park with this one. (See what I did there?) It has all the delicious flavors of a classic Chicago dog, but in an addictively creative salad. I suppose if you are really missing the bun, you could pile a mess of this on top of an Everything Bun (page 360) and really hit a home run.

INGREDIENTS

FOR THE DRESSING:

- 3 tablespoons prepared yellow mustard
- 3 tablespoons mayonnaise, store-bought or homemade (page 386)
- 2 tablespoons apple cider vinegar
- 2 tablespoons avocado oil
- 1 teaspoon granular erythritol
- 1½ garlic dill pickles, chopped

FOR THE SALAD:

- 8 ounces coleslaw mix or shredded green cabbage
- 1 head romaine lettuce, shredded
- 1½ garlic dill pickles, chopped
- ½ small red onion, thinly sliced
- 1 small tomato, cut into wedges
- 6 pepperoncini (optional)
- 2 tablespoons avocado oil or olive oil, for the pan
- 6 large grass-fed hot dogs, sliced on a bias
- Celery salt, for finishing

DIRECTIONS

1. Make the dressing: In a large mixing bowl, whisk together the mustard, mayonnaise, vinegar, avocado oil, and erythritol. Mix in the chopped pickles.

2. Add the coleslaw mix and lettuce to the bowl with the dressing and toss to coat.

3. Arrange the additional pickles, onion slices, tomato wedges, and pepperoncini, if using, on top of the salad.

4. Heat the oil in a large skillet or grill pan over medium-high heat and sear the hot dogs until they are slightly charred and warmed through. Arrange them on top of the salad.

5. Sprinkle the salad with a pinch of celery salt before serving.

PER SERVING: ———————
CALORIES: **306**   FIBER: **3.7g**
FAT: **27.2g**   NET CARBS: **3.4g**
PROTEIN: **14.3g**   ERYTHRITOL: **1.5g**
TOTAL CARBS: **7.2g**

CRAB SALAD–STUFFED AVOCADOS

NET CARBS 3.6g

MAKES: **4 servings** · PREP TIME: **15 minutes**

This crab salad is one of my favorite quick and easy weekday lunches. It is fresh and light and super easy to whip up at a moment's notice. The crunch from the vegetables in the salad combined with the buttery texture of fresh avocado is a match made in keto heaven.

INGREDIENTS

- 8 ounces lump crab meat
- 1 small shallot, finely chopped
- 1 rib celery, chopped
- ½ cup chopped red bell peppers
- 1 teaspoon chopped fresh chives
- ½ teaspoon chopped fresh dill
- ¼ teaspoon smoked paprika
- ¼ teaspoon sea salt
- ¼ teaspoon ground black pepper
- ¼ cup mayonnaise, store-bought or homemade (page 386)
- 1 teaspoon Dijon mustard
- 2 large avocados, halved and pitted

DIRECTIONS

1. Make the crab salad: In a large bowl, mix together the crab meat, shallot, celery, bell peppers, chives, dill, paprika, salt, and pepper. Add the mayonnaise and mustard and, using a rubber spatula, gently mix until the ingredients are well incorporated.

2. Use a large spoon to scoop the crab salad on top of each avocado half, dividing the mixture evenly among the 4 halves.

> *tip*: This recipe is also great with chopped cooked shrimp or even chicken in place of the crab meat. Add more mayonnaise for a creamier salad.

PER SERVING: ───────

CALORIES: **291**   TOTAL CARBS: **11.2g**

FAT: **24.9g**   FIBER: **7.6g**

PROTEIN: **8.5g**   NET CARBS: **3.6g**

CRANBERRY ALMOND BROCCOLI SALAD

NET CARBS
2.6g

 MAKES: 10 servings · **PREP TIME:** 15 minutes

If you would have told me when I was younger that someday I would crave a dish that had raw broccoli as the main ingredient, I would have told you that you were crazy. But there is something about this salad that makes you want to return to it time and time again. It is the perfect summer side dish.

INGREDIENTS

- 1 pound broccoli florets, roughly chopped
- 6 slices bacon, cooked crisp and chopped
- ½ cup slivered almonds
- ¼ cup chopped red onions
- ¼ cup sugar-free dried cranberries, store-bought or homemade (page 158)
- ⅓ cup mayonnaise, store-bought or homemade (page 386), or more if desired
- 2 tablespoons apple cider vinegar (see tip)
- 1 tablespoon powdered erythritol (optional)
- ½ teaspoon sea salt
- ¼ teaspoon ground black pepper

DIRECTIONS

1. Put the broccoli, bacon, almonds, red onions, and dried cranberries in a large mixing bowl and toss to combine.

2. Put the mayonnaise, vinegar, erythritol (if using), salt, and pepper in a separate small bowl and mix until well incorporated.

3. Add the mayonnaise mixture to the bowl with the broccoli mixture and toss until all the pieces of broccoli are well dressed. Store leftovers in the refrigerator for up to a week.

tip: *If omitting the erythritol, cut the vinegar in half. But that slight hint of sweetness is what gives this salad its classic flavor.*

PER SERVING:

CALORIES: **148**   TOTAL CARBS: **4.5g**
FAT: **12.8g**   FIBER: **1.9g**
PROTEIN: **4.9g**   NET CARBS: **2.6g**

CUCUMBER DILL BROCCOLI SLAW

NET CARBS 2g

MAKES: 6 servings · **PREP TIME:** 10 minutes

Cucumber and dill is one of my favorite flavor combinations. If you own any of my other cookbooks, then you likely have noticed that there is a common theme here. It's just such a fresh and light pairing. I love making slaws with broccoli because it adds a wonderful texture and crunch, and, because of its heartiness, it holds up well against heavy sauces.

INGREDIENTS

- 10 ounces broccoli slaw
- 1 mini cucumber, thinly sliced
- ½ small red onion, diced (about ¼ cup)
- ½ cup mayonnaise, store-bought or homemade (page 386)
- 1 tablespoon apple cider vinegar
- 1 tablespoon chopped fresh dill
- ½ teaspoon garlic powder
- ½ teaspoon sea salt
- ¼ teaspoon ground black pepper

DIRECTIONS

Put all the ingredients in a large mixing bowl and mix until well incorporated. For the best flavor, refrigerate for at least 1 hour before serving.

tip: Broccoli slaw is a mix of shredded broccoli stems, carrots, and purple cabbage. You can find bagged broccoli slaw in the produce department of most grocery stores. You will typically find it with the bagged lettuces and coleslaw mix. If you are not able to find it, you can substitute coleslaw mix or make your own by shredding broccoli stalks, carrots, and purple cabbage.

PER SERVING:

CALORIES: **139**	TOTAL CARBS: **3.8g**
FAT: **13.3g**	FIBER: **1.8g**
PROTEIN: **1.4g**	NET CARBS: **2g**

KALE AND CABBAGE CHOPPED SALAD

NET CARBS
4g

MAKES: 10 servings · **PREP TIME:** 15 minutes

The heartiness of cabbage, kale, and Brussels sprouts makes this the perfect salad for weekly meal prep because it keeps in the refrigerator longer than a premade lettuce-based salad would. The natural bitterness of the kale pairs perfectly with the saltiness of the pancetta, the slight sweetness of the dried cranberries, and the burst of freshness from the vinaigrette, making this salad well balanced in both flavor and texture.

INGREDIENTS

- 8 ounces pancetta, chopped and cooked crisp
- 1 bunch Lacinato kale (about ½ pound), shredded
- 8 ounces Brussels sprouts, trimmed and shaved
- 8 ounces coleslaw mix or shredded green cabbage
- 8 ounces shredded purple cabbage
- ¼ cup sugar-free dried cranberries, store-bought or homemade (page 158)
- ¼ cup hulled sunflower seeds
- Lemon Basil Vinaigrette (page 377) or dressing of choice, for serving (optional)

DIRECTIONS

Put all the ingredients, except the vinaigrette, in a large mixing bowl and toss to combine. Serve with the vinaigrette or other dressing of your choice, if desired. Store leftover salad undressed in the refrigerator for up to a week.

tip: If you aren't avoiding dairy, this salad is amazing with feta cheese.

PER SERVING:
CALORIES: **108**   TOTAL CARBS: **6.5g**
FAT: **7.2g**   FIBER: **2.5g**
PROTEIN: **6g**   NET CARBS: **4g**

MEDITERRANEAN SLAW

NET CARBS 2.7g

MAKES: 8 servings · **PREP TIME:** 15 minutes

The amazing thing about this slaw is that it works with just about any dressing. In fact, it has so much flavor, you just might opt to not add dressing at all. But should you decide to, my favorite is actually a combination of two dressings—Caesar Dressing (page 375) mixed with balsamic vinaigrette. This slaw is amazing with Creamy Avocado Dressing (page 374) as well.

INGREDIENTS

- 1 (14-ounce) bag coleslaw mix
- 4 ounces sliced Italian salami, quartered
- ½ cup sliced and quartered English cucumbers
- ½ cup chopped canned artichoke hearts
- ½ cup halved grape tomatoes
- ¼ cup halved Kalamata olives
- 2 tablespoons capers
- 2 tablespoons chopped red onions
- Sea salt and ground black pepper

DIRECTIONS

Put all the ingredients, except the salt and pepper, in a large mixing bowl and toss to combine. Taste and season with salt and pepper. Store leftovers in the refrigerator for up to 3 days.

> *tip: If you are not a fan of cabbage or you want to lower the carb count even further, you can substitute shredded lettuce for the coleslaw mix.*

PER SERVING:

CALORIES: **96**   TOTAL CARBS: **4.6g**
FAT: **7.1g**   FIBER: **1.9g**
PROTEIN: **4.3g**   NET CARBS: **2.7g**

PORK BELLY WEDGE SALAD

NET CARBS 2.5g

 MAKES: 4 servings · **PREP TIME:** 15 minutes

I am a huge fan of wedge salads. There is something so satisfying about cutting into a big, crunchy wedge of iceberg lettuce. Plus, the topping possibilities are endless.

INGREDIENTS

- 1 large head iceberg lettuce, quartered
- 1 cup dairy-free ranch dressing, store-bought or homemade (page 376)
- 12 ounces precooked pork belly, cooked crisp and chopped
- 12 grape tomatoes, halved
- 3 tablespoons chopped red onions or Pickled Red Onions (page 368)
- A few sprigs of fresh dill
- 2 tablespoons Everything Bagel Seasoning (page 399)

DIRECTIONS

Put each iceberg wedge on a salad plate, drizzle with ¼ cup of the ranch dressing, and then divide the toppings equally among the wedges.

tip: For this recipe, I like to use precooked pork belly from Trader Joe's. I slice it up and pan-fry it in a dry skillet until it is nice and crispy. It tastes delicious and is a lot faster than preparing raw, uncured pork belly.

PER SERVING:
CALORIES: **152**   TOTAL CARBS: **5g**
FAT: **10g**   FIBER: **2.5g**
PROTEIN: **8.5g**   NET CARBS: **2.5g**

RANCH CHICKEN SALAD CUPS

NET CARBS 1.6g

🥑 🍴 🕐   **MAKES:** 8 salad cups (2 per serving) · **PREP TIME:** 15 minutes

Why make chicken salad with mayonnaise when you can make it with ranch dressing? If you were to look in my fridge on any given day, two of the things that you would be sure to find are chopped cooked chicken and cooked bacon. It's amazing how many different things you can make if you have just those two ingredients already cooked and prepped. This chicken salad is one of them.

INGREDIENTS

- 1 pound boneless, skinless chicken breasts or thighs, cooked and cut into bite-sized pieces
- 6 slices bacon, cooked crisp and chopped
- ⅓ cup dairy-free ranch dressing, store-bought or homemade (page 376)
- 1 medium avocado, peeled, pitted, and cubed
- 8 grape tomatoes, quartered
- 8 romaine lettuce leaves
- Chopped fresh dill, for garnish (optional)
- Chopped fresh chives, for garnish (optional)

DIRECTIONS

1. Put the chicken, bacon, ranch dressing, avocado, and tomatoes in a mixing bowl and gently toss until the ingredients are well combined.

2. Divide the chicken salad evenly among the romaine lettuce leaves.

3. Garnish with dill and chives, if desired.

PER SERVING: ——————
CALORIES: **333**   TOTAL CARBS: **5.3g**
FAT: **32.1g**   FIBER: **3.7g**
PROTEIN: **7.5g**   NET CARBS: **1.6g**

Main Dishes

SESAME CHICKEN EGG ROLL IN A BOWL

NET CARBS 3.3g

MAKES: 8 servings · **PREP TIME:** 15 minutes · **COOK TIME:** 20 minutes

Anyone who knows me knows that I am obsessed with the Pork Egg Roll in a Bowl recipe from my book *Craveable Keto*. I eat it multiple times per week. When I find a recipe I like, I stick with it. I am the type of person who can eat the same foods over and over without getting tired of them. This chicken and broccoli variation is a delicious spin on the original. It has definitely been in high rotation in our house.

INGREDIENTS

- 3 tablespoons toasted sesame oil
- 1 small red onion, chopped (about ½ cup)
- 4 cloves garlic, minced
- 5 green onions, sliced on a bias (white and green portions separated)
- 1½ pounds boneless, skinless chicken breasts or thighs, cut into bite-sized pieces
- 1 teaspoon ground ginger
- 1 teaspoon sea salt
- ½ teaspoon ground black pepper
- 1 tablespoon plus 1 teaspoon Sriracha sauce or garlic chili sauce
- 20 ounces broccoli slaw
- ¼ cup gluten-free soy sauce or coconut aminos
- 2 tablespoons unseasoned rice wine vinegar
- 2 tablespoons sesame seeds, for garnish
- Crack Sauce (page 393) or Sriracha sauce, for serving (optional)

DIRECTIONS

1. Heat the sesame oil in a large skillet over medium-high heat.

2. Add the onion, garlic, and white portion of the green onions to the pan. Sauté until the green onions are translucent and the garlic is fragrant.

3. Add the chicken, ginger, salt, pepper, and Sriracha to the pan. Sauté until the chicken is cooked through, about 5 minutes.

4. Add the broccoli slaw, soy sauce, and vinegar and sauté until the broccoli is crisp-tender, about 8 minutes.

5. Top with the green parts of the green onions and the sesame seeds before serving. Drizzle some Crack Sauce or Sriracha over the top, if desired.

> *tip*: *Broccoli slaw is a mix of shredded broccoli stems, carrots, and purple cabbage. You can find bagged broccoli slaw in the produce department of most grocery stores, typically with the bagged lettuces and coleslaw mix. If you are unable to find it, you can substitute coleslaw mix, or you can make your own by shredding broccoli stalks, carrots, and purple cabbage.*
>
>

PER SERVING:
CALORIES: **267**	TOTAL CARBS: **4.9g**
FAT: **19.5g**	FIBER: **1.6g**
PROTEIN: **4.9g**	NET CARBS: **3.3g**

BEEF RAGOUT

MAKES: 6 servings · **PREP TIME:** 20 minutes · **COOK TIME:** 40 minutes

The savory meat sauce in this recipe reminds me of a cross between sloppy Joe mix and beef stew. It is good old-fashioned comfort food at its finest. This dish is a great way to use up leftovers. Have some leftover Drunken Mushrooms with Caramelized Onions (page 294)? Toss them in! Leftover Oven-Roasted Cabbage Steaks (page 300)? Reheat them in the oven and serve this ragout over the top. My favorite way to serve it is on top of Roasted Garlic and Chive Cauliflower Puree (page 284), as pictured.

INGREDIENTS

- 1 pound ground sirloin or ground beef
- 3 cloves garlic, minced
- 2 tablespoons Worcestershire sauce
- 1 teaspoon sea salt
- ½ teaspoon ground black pepper
- ½ teaspoon onion powder
- ½ cup beef stock or bone broth (page 370)
- 2 tablespoons reduced-sugar ketchup, store-bought or homemade (page 385)
- 1 (14.5-ounce) can diced tomatoes, drained
- 4 ounces cremini mushrooms, sliced
- 1 small zucchini, sliced lengthwise and quartered
- ½ cup pearl onions
- 2 sprigs fresh thyme
- 1 bay leaf

DIRECTIONS

1. Heat a large skillet over medium heat. When the pan is hot, add the ground sirloin, garlic, Worcestershire sauce, salt, pepper, and onion powder. Cook, breaking up the meat with a spatula, until the beef is completely browned, about 7 minutes.

2. Mix the stock and ketchup into the browned beef. Add the tomatoes, mushrooms, zucchini, pearl onions, thyme sprigs, and bay leaf. Reduce the heat to medium-low and let simmer for 30 minutes, or until the vegetables are tender. Remove the thyme sprigs and bay leaf before serving.

> *tip*: *You could also serve this dish over zucchini noodles or cauliflower rice.*

PER SERVING:

CALORIES: **315**	TOTAL CARBS: **7.7g**
FAT: **23g**	FIBER: **2g**
PROTEIN: **12.4g**	NET CARBS: **5.7g**

GINGERED PEPPER STEAK SKILLET

NET CARBS 3.8g

MAKES: 6 servings
PREP TIME: 15 minutes, plus 20 minutes to marinate · **COOK TIME:** 10 minutes

This is one of my favorite quick and easy meals for busy weeknights. It has minimal ingredients, maximum flavor, and comes together in less than thirty minutes of hands-on time. It is also a great option for weekly meal prep. It reheats really well, so you can even make a double batch and freeze half for later.

INGREDIENTS

- ⅓ cup gluten-free soy sauce or coconut aminos
- 1 tablespoon apple cider vinegar
- 2 cloves garlic, minced
- 1 teaspoon ground ginger
- 1½ pounds boneless top sirloin steak or other steak of choice, cut into ½-inch-thick strips
- 8 ounces cremini mushrooms, sliced
- 1 tablespoon avocado oil or olive oil
- 1 medium green bell pepper, seeded and cut into thin strips
- 1 medium red bell pepper, seeded and cut into thin strips

DIRECTIONS

1. Put the soy sauce, vinegar, garlic, and ginger in a large bowl and whisk to combine. Add the steak and mushrooms to the bowl and toss to coat. Let marinate for 20 minutes.

2. Heat the oil in a large skillet over medium-high heat. Add the bell peppers and stir-fry for 2 to 3 minutes, until they are crisp-tender. Remove the peppers from the pan and set aside.

3. Add the steak, mushrooms, and remaining marinade to the skillet and cook until the meat is browned and the mushrooms are tender, about 5 minutes.

4. Return the peppers to the pan and toss to heat before serving.

tip: For maximum flavor, marinate the meat the day before you cook it. This will also cut down on time in the kitchen on the day of preparation.

PER SERVING:
CALORIES: **380**   TOTAL CARBS: **5.1g**
FAT: **16.9g**   FIBER: **1.3g**
PROTEIN: **26.3g**   NET CARBS: **3.8g**

STEAK DAVID

NET CARBS
2.6g

🌰 🔪 🕐   **MAKES:** 4 servings
PREP TIME: 15 minutes (not including time to make hollandaise) · **COOK TIME:** 15 minutes

This recipe pays homage to all the years I worked at the iconic Seattle restaurant 13 Coins. Steak David was my absolute favorite dish on the menu, and I regularly tried to talk anyone and everyone into ordering it. It's been more than a decade since I worked there, but this dish still stays in high rotation in our home. My favorite thing about it is that you can use any vegetable as the base. It is also fantastic with asparagus, sautéed mushrooms, or even broccoli.

INGREDIENTS

- 4 (8-ounce) filet mignons
- Sea salt and ground black pepper
- 3 tablespoons avocado oil or olive oil, divided
- 4 cloves garlic, thinly sliced
- 1 pound fresh spinach leaves
- 1 batch Bacon Fat Hollandaise (page 372)
- 8 ounces lump crab meat, warmed

DIRECTIONS

1. Remove the filets from the fridge and allow to come to room temperature, about 30 minutes. Season the steaks generously on both sides with salt and pepper.

2. Heat 1 tablespoon of the oil in a grill pan or large skillet over medium-high heat. When the oil is hot, sear the steaks for 4 to 6 minutes on each side for medium-rare, or until the desired level of doneness is reached.

3. While the steaks are cooking, heat the remaining 2 tablespoons of oil in a very large skillet or Dutch oven over medium heat. Add the garlic and cook until it is tender and just starting to caramelize, but do not let it burn.

4. Add the spinach, 1½ teaspoons of salt, and 1 teaspoon of pepper to the pan and sauté until the spinach is wilted and tender, about 4 minutes.

5. Plate the spinach and top with the steak, hollandaise, and crab meat.

PER SERVING:
CALORIES: **899**   TOTAL CARBS: **5.1g**
FAT: **71g**   FIBER: **2.6g**
PROTEIN: **53.9g**   NET CARBS: **2.6g**

SWEET AND SPICY
BARBECUE RIBS

NET
CARBS
2.5g

 MAKES: 6 servings · **PREP TIME:** 20 minutes · **COOK TIME:** 2½ hours

What screams summer better than juicy, fall-off-the-bone barbecue ribs? Of course, they are amazing year-round, but there is something uniquely pleasing about a big ol' platter of messy ribs, enjoyed by friends around a picnic table in the warm summer sun. Serve them up with some Bourbon Onions (page 278), Cucumber Dill Broccoli Slaw (page 192), and Lemon-Lime Soda (page 349), and you've got yourself the perfect spread of food.

INGREDIENTS

- 3 pounds pork baby back ribs
- Sea salt and ground black pepper
- 1 batch Sweet and Spicy Barbecue Sauce (page 391)

DIRECTIONS

1. Preheat the oven to 300°F. Line a rimmed baking sheet with parchment paper or a silicone baking mat.

2. Remove the thin membrane from the back, or concave, side of the ribs. Start by slicing into the membrane with a sharp knife, then pull the skin away from the ribs. Put the ribs on the lined baking sheet. Season generously on both sides with salt and pepper.

3. Brush the barbecue sauce evenly over the ribs, covering both sides.

4. Bake until the ribs are tender and juicy on the inside and nice and crispy on the outside, about 2½ hours. Store leftovers in the refrigerator for up to a week.

> *tip: These ribs are also fantastic made with Blackening Seasoning (page 398) as a dry rub. To make dry-rubbed ribs, simply drizzle 2 tablespoons of olive oil over the ribs and then coat them generously with a full batch of the seasoning. Bake as directed above.*

PER SERVING: ─────────

CALORIES: **351**　　TOTAL CARBS: **2.5g**
FAT: **24.7g**　　　 FIBER: **0g**
PROTEIN: **28.8g**　 NET CARBS: **2.5g**

JALAPEÑO POPPER CHICKEN SALAD

NET CARBS 0.7g

MAKES: 8 servings · **PREP TIME:** 15 minutes (not including time to cook chicken and bacon)

With or without the buns, this chicken salad is amazing. It is one of my favorite recipes to meal prep because it tastes better and better as the days go on. If you don't want to make the buns or you don't have the ingredients on hand, you can serve this salad in lettuce wraps.

INGREDIENTS

- 2½ pounds boneless, skinless chicken breasts, cooked and chopped
- 6 slices bacon, cooked crisp and chopped
- ¼ cup chopped red onions
- 2 tablespoons sliced fresh chives
- 2 jalapeño peppers, charred and sliced
- ½ cup mayonnaise, store-bought or homemade (page 386)
- 1 tablespoon Dijon mustard
- 1 teaspoon apple cider vinegar
- 1 teaspoon hot sauce, or more to taste
- 1 teaspoon garlic powder
- ¼ teaspoon sea salt, or more to taste
- ¼ teaspoon ground black pepper
- 2 batches Everything Buns (page 360), or leaves from 1 head romaine lettuce, for serving (optional)

DIRECTIONS

1. Put the chicken, bacon, onions, chives, jalapeños, mayonnaise, mustard, vinegar, hot sauce, garlic powder, salt, and pepper in a large bowl and mix until the ingredients are well incorporated. Taste and add more hot sauce and/or salt, if desired.

2. Serve on Everything Buns, in lettuce wraps, or just as is.

3. Store leftovers in the refrigerator for up to a week.

> *tips*: *My favorite way to cook the chicken for this recipe is to pan-sear it in avocado oil. It gives the chicken excellent flavor and makes it incredibly juicy while giving it a crispy, golden brown outside.*
>
> *There are a couple of ways to roast the jalapeños. If you have a gas range, you can roast them directly over the flame, turning them frequently so they do not burn. They are done when they are charred and slightly blistered. Alternatively, you can lay them on a baking sheet and put them under the oven broiler for 3 to 4 minutes.*
>
> *If you aren't avoiding dairy, this salad is excellent with some shredded sharp cheddar cheese mixed in.*

PER SERVING:

CALORIES: **435**	TOTAL CARBS: **1g**
FAT: **21.8g**	FIBER: **0.3g**
PROTEIN: **55.2g**	NET CARBS: **0.7g**

GARLIC AND HERB SKILLET RIB-EYES

NET CARBS
2.1g

MAKES: 2 servings · **PREP TIME:** 5 minutes · **COOK TIME:** 12 minutes

There is nothing quite like a perfectly seared rib-eye that has been basted in butter—or, in this case, butter-flavored coconut oil. Generously seasoning the steak with salt and pepper and then cooking it in a ripping-hot pan creates a beautiful crust on the outside while locking in the juices. This is hands-down my favorite way to cook a steak.

INGREDIENTS

- 2 (10-ounce) boneless or (16-ounce) bone-in rib-eye steaks, about 1½ inches thick
- Sea salt and ground black pepper
- 2 tablespoons avocado oil or olive oil
- 2 tablespoons butter-flavored coconut oil (see page 64)
- 1 sprig fresh oregano
- 1 sprig fresh rosemary
- 1 sprig fresh thyme
- 4 cloves garlic, smashed with the side of a knife

DIRECTIONS

1. Remove the steaks from the refrigerator and allow to come to room temperature, about 30 minutes. Season generously on both sides with salt and pepper.

2. Heat the oil in a large cast-iron skillet over medium-high heat. Add the steaks and sear for 6 minutes, or until they have developed a nice crust.

3. Flip the steaks over and add the butter-flavored coconut oil, oregano, rosemary, thyme, and garlic to the pan. As the oil melts, coating the herbs and garlic, begin basting the steaks by continuously spooning the pan drippings over the top. Cook for an additional 5 minutes for medium-rare, or continue cooking to your desired level of doneness.

tip: If you do not have butter-flavored coconut oil, you can add more avocado oil to the pan.

PER SERVING:

CALORIES: **980**	TOTAL CARBS: **2.4g**
FAT: **83.7g**	FIBER: **0.4g**
PROTEIN: **53.7g**	NET CARBS: **2.1g**

CHICKEN FAJITA SHEET PAN MEAL

NET CARBS
5.5g

MAKES: 4 servings · PREP TIME: 15 minutes · COOK TIME: 30 minutes

There is nothing quite like perfectly crispy chicken skin. That is why I opted to use skin-on chicken thighs for this recipe instead of the boneless, skinless breasts that a typical chicken fajita recipe might call for. I have always been a fan of crispy poultry skin. In fact, crispy turkey skin is my favorite thing about Thanksgiving dinner. My mom was constantly shooing me out of the kitchen because I was always trying to get to the crispiest bits of the turkey before she could carve and serve it. For an extra kick of flavor, I love to serve this meal with Lime Sriracha Aioli (page 389).

INGREDIENTS

- 1 medium red bell pepper, seeded and sliced
- 1 medium yellow bell pepper, seeded and sliced
- 1 medium green bell pepper, seeded and sliced
- 1 small onion, sliced
- 4 cloves garlic, minced
- 3 tablespoons avocado oil or olive oil, divided
- 1 tablespoon fresh lime juice
- 3 tablespoons Fajita Seasoning (page 397), divided
- 8 bone-in, skin-on chicken thighs (2 pounds)
- 1 lime, cut into wedges, for serving (optional)
- Handful of torn fresh cilantro, or 2 green onions, sliced, for garnish (optional)

DIRECTIONS

1. Put the bell peppers, onion, garlic, 2 tablespoons of the oil, the lime juice, and 2 tablespoons of the fajita seasoning in a large mixing bowl. Toss the vegetables until they are evenly coated. Lay the vegetables in a thin layer across a rimmed baking sheet.

2. Preheat the oven to 400°F.

3. Heat the remaining tablespoon of oil in a large cast-iron skillet over medium-high heat. Season the chicken thighs on both sides with the remaining tablespoon of fajita seasoning. Add the chicken to the pan and sear on both sides until the skin is crispy and golden brown. (The chicken will not be fully cooked at this point.)

4. Transfer the chicken thighs to the sheet pan with the vegetables. Bake for 15 minutes, or until the chicken is cooked all the way through and the vegetables are tender. If desired, serve with lime wedges and garnish with cilantro or sliced green onions.

> tip: You can also use boneless chicken thighs or even chicken breasts for this recipe. Pan-sear them as directed above and then add them to the sheet pan, or simply slice or cube the raw chicken, toss it in the seasoning, and put it on the baking sheet with the vegetables. Adjust the cooking time as needed.

PER SERVING:

CALORIES: **489**	TOTAL CARBS: **7.6g**
FAT: **23g**	FIBER: **2.1g**
PROTEIN: **59.8g**	NET CARBS: **5.5g**

BEEF POT ROAST

NET CARBS 5g

MAKES: 8 servings · **PREP TIME:** 20 minutes · **COOK TIME:** 3 hours

A big, hearty roast is my favorite thing to cook low and slow. You can take an inexpensive cut of beef that would typically be far from tender and use time and heat to transform it into something that is fall-apart tender, juicy, and incredibly flavorful. Plus, few dishes are as warm and comforting in the winter as a well-made roast.

INGREDIENTS

- 2 teaspoons sea salt
- 2 teaspoons ground black pepper
- ½ teaspoon garlic powder
- ½ teaspoon onion powder
- ½ teaspoon smoked paprika
- 1 (3-pound) boneless chuck or bottom round roast
- 2 tablespoons olive oil
- 1 medium red onion, cut into large chunks
- 3 ribs celery, cut into large chunks
- 3 cloves garlic, minced
- 3 sprigs fresh thyme, plus more for garnish
- 2 bay leaves
- 1 cup dry red wine
- 2 cups beef stock or bone broth (page 370)
- 1 small head cauliflower, trimmed into florets
- 8 ounces cremini mushrooms, halved
- 1 large red bell pepper, seeded and cut into large chunks

DIRECTIONS

1. Preheat the oven to 350°F.

2. In a small bowl, combine the salt, pepper, garlic powder, onion powder, and paprika. Sprinkle the seasoning evenly over the entire roast, pressing it into the meat.

3. Heat the olive oil in a Dutch oven over medium-high heat. When the oil is hot, add the seasoned roast and cook for 6 to 8 minutes, browning it on all sides.

4. Remove the roast from the pot and set aside. Reduce the heat to medium and add the onion and celery. Sauté for 6 minutes, or until crisp-tender.

5. Add the garlic, thyme, and bay leaves and sauté for 1 additional minute.

6. Add the red wine to the pot and use a rubber spatula to scrape up and mix in any browned bits from the bottom of the pot.

7. Return the roast to the pot, then add the beef stock and bring to a simmer.

8. Cover and transfer to the oven. Cook for 1½ hours, or until the roast is almost tender.

9. Remove the pot from the oven, add the cauliflower, mushrooms, and bell pepper, and return to the oven for 1 additional hour, or until the vegetables are tender and the roast is fall-apart tender.

10. Remove the thyme sprigs and bay leaves and slice or shred the meat. Garnish with fresh thyme and serve with the vegetables and pot juices.

tip: You can also make this recipe with a pork roast.

PER SERVING:

CALORIES: **312**	TOTAL CARBS: **6.9g**
FAT: **10.9g**	FIBER: **1.9g**
PROTEIN: **41.6g**	NET CARBS: **5g**

EASY CUBAN PICADILLO

NET CARBS 3.2g

MAKES: 8 servings · PREP TIME: 10 minutes · COOK TIME: 25 minutes

Picadillo is one of those dishes that every person makes differently, but I have yet to try a version I didn't love. Many traditional versions of picadillo contain raisins. For that same subtle sweetness, you can always add some Sugar-Free Dried Cranberries (page 158). I love to serve this on top of "Goes with Everything" Garlicky Cauliflower Rice (page 288).

INGREDIENTS

- 2 tablespoons avocado oil or olive oil
- 1 small onion, chopped (about ½ cup)
- 4 cloves garlic, minced
- 1 small green bell pepper, seeded and chopped
- 2 pounds ground beef
- 1 tablespoon ground cumin
- 2 teaspoons dried oregano leaves
- 1 teaspoon sea salt
- ½ teaspoon ground black pepper
- 2 cups tomato sauce or crushed tomatoes
- 1 cup sliced pimiento-stuffed green olives
- 2 tablespoons capers

DIRECTIONS

1. Heat the oil in a large skillet over medium heat. When the oil is hot, add the onion, garlic, and bell pepper. Sauté until the vegetables are tender, about 5 minutes.

2. Add the ground beef, cumin, oregano, salt, and black pepper to the pan. Cook, breaking up the beef with a spatula, until completely browned, about 7 minutes.

3. Add the tomato sauce, olives, and capers. Reduce the heat to low and let simmer for 10 minutes to allow the flavors to come together before serving.

tip: You can substitute Mexican-style fresh chorizo or ground pork for the ground beef, or use any combination of the three meats.

PER SERVING:
CALORIES: **363**   TOTAL CARBS: **4.4g**
FAT: **28.8g**   FIBER: **1.2g**
PROTEIN: **20.4g**   NET CARBS: **3.2g**

BALSAMIC SHALLOT PORK CHOPS

NET CARBS 4.6g

🫒 🍅 🌰 🔪 🕐 **MAKES:** 4 servings · **PREP TIME:** 10 minutes · **COOK TIME:** 25 minutes

There is something so delicious about a sauce made right in the pan. It catches all the delicious flavors from every stage of cooking to create one bold explosion of flavor. This sauce is also amazing with a thick, juicy steak.

INGREDIENTS

- 4 thick-cut boneless pork chops (about 1½ pounds)
- Sea salt and ground black pepper
- 3 tablespoons avocado oil or olive oil, divided
- 1 shallot, finely chopped
- ½ cup beef stock or bone broth (page 370)
- ⅓ cup balsamic vinegar
- ¼ cup Dijon mustard
- 2 tablespoons chopped fresh flat-leaf parsley, for garnish

DIRECTIONS

1. Season the pork chops generously on both sides with salt and pepper.

2. Heat 2 tablespoons of the oil in a large skillet over medium-high heat. When the oil is hot, add the pork chops and sear for 3 to 4 minutes on each side, until they are almost cooked through. Move the chops to a plate and cover to keep warm.

3. Reduce the heat to medium and add the shallot and remaining tablespoon of oil to the skillet. Sauté until the shallot is soft and translucent.

4. Add the beef stock, vinegar, and mustard to the pan and whisk to combine. Use a rubber spatula to scrape up and mix in any bits that are stuck to the bottom of the pan.

5. Return the pork chops to the pan and let simmer until the sauce has thickened and the chops are golden brown and cooked all the way through.

6. Taste the sauce and add salt and pepper, if desired. Garnish with the parsley before serving.

PER SERVING: ─────────────

CALORIES: **317** TOTAL CARBS: **5.4g**

FAT: **15.8g** FIBER: **0.8g**

PROTEIN: **35.6g** NET CARBS: **4.6g**

BARBECUE PULLED PORK SANDWICHES

NET CARBS
8.5g

MAKES: 8 sandwiches (1 per serving) · **PREP TIME:** 20 minutes · **COOK TIME:** 7 hours

This is a recipe comprised of recipes, but I couldn't help myself. They complement each other so well that I would be doing you a great disservice if I didn't show you how to put them together into one harmonious symphony of flavor. The sandwich is a little higher in carbs than most of the recipes in the book, but it is definitely worth the splurge. I've included some tips for reducing the overall carb count.

INGREDIENTS

- 2½ pounds boneless pork shoulder or pork butt
- Sea salt and ground black pepper
- ½ cup chicken stock or bone broth (page 370)
- 1 batch Sweet and Spicy Barbecue Sauce (page 391)
- 2 batches Everything Buns (page 360)
- 1 batch Cucumber Dill Broccoli Slaw (page 192)
- Pickled Red Onions (page 368) (optional)

DIRECTIONS

1. Preheat a slow cooker on the low setting.

2. Season the pork generously with salt and pepper. Put the pork in the slow cooker, add the chicken stock, and cook for 6 hours, or until the meat is fall-apart tender.

3. Drain most of the juices from the slow cooker, retaining only about ¼ cup. Use two forks to shred the meat.

4. Mix the barbecue sauce into the meat and cook for 1 additional hour.

5. While the pork is in the final stage of cooking, prepare the buns and slaw.

6. Top each bun with pulled pork, slaw, and pickled red onions, if desired.

> *tips: If you don't want to make all 8 servings, you can scale all the recipes in half to make 4 servings. Alternatively, you can make a full batch of the pork and half batches of everything else and use the pork for leftovers.*
>
> *For a saucier meat, double the barbecue sauce recipe.*
>
> *Here are a few tips for lowering the carbs in this recipe: Instead of the coleslaw, toss some shredded lettuce in Ranch Dressing (page 376). Instead of the buns, eat it as a lettuce wrap or plate it as a salad.*

PER SERVING:

CALORIES: **683**   TOTAL CARBS: **23.2g**
FAT: **53.2g**   FIBER: **14.7g**
PROTEIN: **38.5g**   NET CARBS: **8.5g**

BEEF AND BROCCOLI STIR-FRY

NET CARBS 6.7g

MAKES: 4 servings · **PREP TIME:** 15 minutes, plus 1 hour to marinate · **COOK TIME:** 15 minutes

Beef and broccoli stir-fry is a favorite of many, but it is not a low-carb dish at most Chinese restaurants. Well, now you can make your own healthier, low-carb version at home. I love to serve this over "Goes with Everything" Garlicky Cauliflower Rice (page 288). Why? Because it goes with everything!

INGREDIENTS

- ¼ cup gluten-free oyster sauce
- ¼ cup beef stock or bone broth (page 370)
- 3 tablespoons fish sauce
- 1 tablespoon toasted sesame oil
- 4 cloves garlic, minced
- 1 teaspoon grated fresh ginger
- ¼ teaspoon red pepper flakes
- 1½ pounds boneless beef round steaks, sliced ¼ inch thick
- 3 tablespoons avocado oil or olive oil
- 1 pound broccoli florets
- 6 ounces cremini mushrooms, thinly sliced

DIRECTIONS

1. In a large mixing bowl, combine the oyster sauce, beef stock, fish sauce, sesame oil, garlic, ginger, and red pepper flakes.

2. Add the steak to the bowl and mix until all the pieces are coated. Place the bowl in the refrigerator and let the steak marinate for 1 hour or up to 24 hours.

3. When ready to cook the stir-fry, heat the oil in a wok or large sauté pan over high heat. When the oil is very hot, add the broccoli, coating it in the oil, and stir-fry for 2 to 3 minutes.

4. Remove the beef from the marinade and add it to the hot pan. Stir-fry 2 to 3 minutes.

5. Pour the marinade into the pan and add the mushrooms. Continue stir-frying over high heat until the meat is cooked through and the sauce has reduced and thickened. This will happen naturally with high heat and continuous stirring. If you lose too much of your sauce in the process, add a little stock or water to the pan.

PER SERVING: —————
CALORIES: **456**   TOTAL CARBS: **11g**
FAT: **27g**   FIBER: **4.3g**
PROTEIN: **44g**   NET CARBS: **6.7g**

BLACKENED SHRIMP FETTUCCINE ALFREDO

NET CARBS 2.1g

MAKES: 4 servings · PREP TIME: 15 minutes · COOK TIME: 20 minutes

If I had a dollar for every time I ordered fettuccine Alfredo at a restaurant in my twenties, I would have a truckload of dollars. It probably didn't help that I spent a lot of years working in Italian restaurants, and the pasta was free-flowing on the employee menu. While there is nothing quite like the real thing, this low-carb version sure does curb the craving. I love to serve it with Caesar Salad with Cumin-Spiced Pecans (page 180).

INGREDIENTS

- 1 pound large raw shrimp (25/30), peeled, deveined, and tails removed
- ¼ cup Blackening Seasoning (page 398)
- 3 tablespoons avocado oil, divided
- 1½ cups Dairy-Free Alfredo Sauce (page 380)
- 3 (8-ounce) packages fettuccine-style shirataki noodles (see tips)
- ½ teaspoon sea salt
- ¼ teaspoon ground black pepper
- 2 tablespoons chopped fresh flat-leaf parsley (optional)

DIRECTIONS

1. Put the shrimp, blackening seasoning, and 2 tablespoons of the avocado oil in a mixing bowl and toss to coat the shrimp evenly.

2. If using premade Alfredo sauce, heat the sauce in a large saucepan over medium heat until it is warmed through. Reduce the heat to low until you are ready to use it.

3. Heat the remaining tablespoon of avocado oil in a large skillet over medium heat. Add the shirataki noodles, salt, and pepper and cook for 5 minutes, or until the noodles are dry.

4. Remove the noodles from the skillet and add them to the saucepan with the Alfredo sauce. Toss the noodles in the sauce.

5. Add the shrimp to the skillet and cook until they are pink and cooked all way through, 2 to 3 minutes on each side.

6. Plate the noodles, then top with the shrimp. Garnish with the parsley, if desired.

> *tips: Shirataki noodles can give off a somewhat fishy odor. The key to preparing them is to rinse, soak, and drain them before using. This will improve the taste and texture and get rid of the smell.*
>
> *If you are not a fan of shirataki noodles, you can serve this sauce over zucchini noodles or spaghetti squash. Also, if you do not like seafood, you can make this recipe with chicken or beef instead of shrimp.*

PER SERVING:
CALORIES: 347   TOTAL CARBS: 7.4g
FAT: 11.4g   FIBER: 5.3g
PROTEIN: 29g   NET CARBS: 2.1g

BRAISED BRATWURST
AND CABBAGE

NET
CARBS
6.6g

MAKES: 6 servings · **PREP TIME:** 15 minutes · **COOK TIME:** 45 minutes

One of our favorite places to visit in our great state of Washington is Leavenworth. It is a Bavarian-themed town that instantly transports you to Oktoberfest. With authentic German food gracing every menu, there is deliciousness as far as the eye can see and the nose can smell. It is truly a gem tucked right in our own backyard. Well, with this one-pot brat and cabbage recipe, any night can be Oktoberfest.

INGREDIENTS

- 1 tablespoon avocado oil or olive oil
- 6 uncooked bratwurst sausages
- 4 slices bacon, chopped
- 1 small head purple cabbage, shredded
- 1 medium onion, sliced
- 2 cloves garlic, minced
- 2½ cups chicken stock or bone broth (page 370)
- 1 tablespoon apple cider vinegar
- 1 tablespoon Dijon mustard
- 1 teaspoon caraway seeds
- ¼ cup spicy brown mustard or Dijon mustard, for serving (optional)

DIRECTIONS

1. Heat the oil in a large heavy-bottomed sauté pan or Dutch oven over medium-high heat. Add the bratwurst and bacon and cook until the sausages are browned and the bacon is crispy, 6 to 8 minutes.

2. Add the cabbage, onion, garlic, chicken stock, vinegar, mustard, and caraway seeds. Stir to combine, reduce the heat to medium-low, cover, and braise for 30 minutes, or until all the liquid has evaporated, the brats are cooked through, and the cabbage is tender.

3. Serve with the mustard, if desired.

PER SERVING:
CALORIES: **421**   TOTAL CARBS: **9.1g**
FAT: **33.8g**   FIBER: **2.6g**
PROTEIN: **19g**   NET CARBS: **6.6g**

CHICKEN ADOBO

NET CARBS 3.9g

MAKES: 6 servings
PREP TIME: 20 minutes, plus 2 hours to marinate · **COOK TIME:** 1 hour 10 minutes

This recipe takes me back a couple of decades. My first serious boyfriend was Filipino, and he lived with his father and grandmother. His grandmother spent all day in the kitchen cooking the traditional dishes of the Philippines. There was not a single time of the day when you wouldn't find pans of food on the stove, rice in the rice cooker, and a fridge full of all the dishes she had made in the days prior. Her grown sons still stopped in to eat every day. It was then that I fell in love with dishes like chicken adobo, lumpia, and longaniza. There were so many other dishes I loved that I can't recall the names of. In fact, most of the time I had no idea what I was eating; I simply knew that it was delicious.

INGREDIENTS

- 3 pounds chicken drumsticks
- 1 cup unseasoned rice wine vinegar
- ⅔ cup gluten-free soy sauce or coconut aminos
- 1 medium onion, quartered and sliced
- 6 cloves garlic, smashed with the side of a knife
- 1 tablespoon black peppercorns
- 3 bay leaves
- 2 tablespoons avocado oil

DIRECTIONS

1. Combine the chicken drumsticks, vinegar, soy sauce, onion, garlic, peppercorns, and bay leaves in a large shallow bowl or resealable plastic bag. Place in the refrigerator to marinate for 2 hours or up to overnight.

2. When ready to cook the chicken, heat the avocado oil in a large skillet over medium-high heat. Take the drumsticks out of the marinade and put them in the pan; reserve the marinade. Cook until the drumsticks are browned on all sides, about 5 minutes. Transfer the chicken to a plate and set aside.

3. Pour the reserved marinade into the skillet and bring to a simmer. Use a rubber spatula to scrape up and mix in any browned bits from the bottom of the pan.

4. Reduce the heat to medium-low, maintaining a gentle simmer. Return the drumsticks to the pan, cover, and cook until the chicken is very tender, about 1 hour.

5. Transfer the chicken to a plate and cover loosely with foil. Bring the remaining liquid in the pan to a boil and cook, stirring frequently, until it is reduced by about one-third and has thickened, about 4 minutes.

6. Pour the sauce over the chicken before serving.

> *tips*: This recipe can also be made with a whole chicken, broken down, or half drumsticks and half thighs. I like to serve it with some sliced green onions and fried cauliflower rice.
>
> If you are using coconut aminos in place of gluten-free soy sauce in this recipe, it may be necessary to add salt to the marinade because coconut aminos has far less sodium than soy sauce.

PER SERVING:
CALORIES: **437**   TOTAL CARBS: **4.5g**
FAT: **25.6g**   FIBER: **0.6g**
PROTEIN: **44.7g**   NET CARBS: **3.9g**

CHILI LIME CHICKEN WITH AVOCADO SALSA

NET CARBS
5.5g

MAKES: 4 servings · PREP TIME: 20 minutes · COOK TIME: 20 minutes

Looking to add a bit of variety to your low-carb Taco Tuesday routine? Then this is the dish for you. It is the perfect fresh and light year-round meal. The chicken is tender and juicy while being perfectly balanced with spices and citrus. The avocado salsa is the ideal complement to the spice of the chicken. For the best flavor, I recommend that you marinate the chicken for a few hours and make the salsa about 1 hour ahead of time.

INGREDIENTS

FOR THE SALSA:

- 1 avocado, peeled, pitted, and cubed
- 1 Roma tomato, diced
- ¼ cup capers
- ¼ cup chopped red onions
- ¼ cup chopped canned artichoke hearts
- 1 tablespoon chopped fresh cilantro
- 3 cloves garlic, minced
- 3 tablespoons avocado oil
- Juice of ½ lime
- Sea salt and ground black pepper, to taste

FOR THE CHICKEN:

- Juice of ½ lime
- 2 tablespoons avocado oil or olive oil
- 3 cloves garlic, minced
- 1 teaspoon chopped fresh cilantro
- 1 tablespoon chili powder
- 1 tablespoon ground cumin
- ½ teaspoon garlic powder

- ½ teaspoon onion powder
- ½ teaspoon sea salt
- ¼ teaspoon ground black pepper

- 4 (6-ounce) boneless, skinless chicken breasts
- Lime wedges, for serving (optional)

DIRECTIONS

MAKE THE AVOCADO SALSA:

In a large bowl, lightly toss all the salsa ingredients until well combined. If time allows, refrigerate the salsa for at least 1 hour before serving. Doing so will allow all the vibrant flavors in this salsa to really come together.

MAKE THE CHICKEN:

1. In a large bowl, whisk the lime juice, oil, garlic, cilantro, chili powder, cumin, garlic powder, onion powder, salt, and pepper until combined.

2. Toss the chicken breasts in the marinade until evenly coated. If time allows, place the bowl in the refrigerator and let the chicken marinate in the sauce for a few hours.

3. When ready to cook the chicken, heat a large skillet or grill pan over medium-high heat. When the pan is hot, put the chicken breasts in the pan and pour in any remaining marinade. Sear the chicken until it is cooked all the way through, about 8 minutes on each side.

4. Top with the avocado salsa before serving. Serve with lime wedges, if desired.

PER SERVING:
CALORIES: **572**   TOTAL CARBS: **10.8g**
FAT: **30.1g**   FIBER: **5.3g**
PROTEIN: **40.8g**   NET CARBS: **5.5g**

CHORIZO AND CHICKEN CAULIFLOWER RICE PAELLA

NET CARBS 3.8g

🥚 🥥 🍤 **MAKES:** 10 servings · **PREP TIME:** 20 minutes · **COOK TIME:** 35 minutes

I love paella. It's like the Spanish version of jambalaya, which I also love. Paella is named for the type of pan it is cooked in, as shown in the photo. It comes in many different versions, but I think the two most commonly known are meat and seafood. You frequently see mixed freestyle combinations of meats, fish, and shellfish. I say, the more the merrier. I'll take it all!

INGREDIENTS

- 2 tablespoons avocado oil or olive oil
- 1 small onion, diced (about ½ cup)
- 4 cloves garlic, minced
- 1 teaspoon sea salt
- ½ teaspoon ground black pepper
- 1 pound boneless, skinless chicken breasts or thighs, cut into bite-sized pieces
- 3 Spanish-style dry-cured chorizo links (about 6 ounces), sliced
- 3 ounces pancetta, chopped
- 6 cups riced cauliflower
- 1 medium red bell pepper, seeded and diced
- 1 tomato, diced
- 2 cups chicken stock or bone broth (page 370)
- 2 bay leaves
- ½ teaspoon saffron threads
- ¼ teaspoon smoked paprika
- 2 tablespoons chopped fresh flat-leaf parsley, for garnish

DIRECTIONS

1. Heat the oil in a large skillet or paella pan over medium heat. Add the onion, garlic, salt, and pepper and cook until the onion is translucent and the garlic is fragrant.

2. Add the chicken, chorizo, and pancetta and cook until the chicken and chorizo have begun to brown and the pancetta is crisp, about 8 minutes.

3. Add the riced cauliflower, bell pepper, tomato, chicken stock, bay leaves, saffron, and paprika to the pan and bring to a boil. Reduce the heat to low and let simmer for 20 minutes.

4. Remove the bay leaves and garnish with the parsley before serving.

> *tip: If you do not have pancetta on hand, you can always substitute some good old-fashioned smoky bacon.*

PER SERVING:

CALORIES: **215**	TOTAL CARBS: **5.7g**
FAT: **13.1g**	FIBER: **1.9g**
PROTEIN: **17.5g**	NET CARBS: **3.8g**

CRISPY FIVE-SPICE CHICKEN THIGHS

NET CARBS 4.5g

MAKES: 4 servings · PREP TIME: 15 minutes · COOK TIME: 30 minutes

In my opinion, Chinese five-spice powder is one of the most underused spice blends in home kitchens. It is a mixture of star anise, cinnamon, cloves, fennel, and Szechwan pepper, and it adds such a depth of flavor with its unique taste and aroma. I love to pair this chicken dish with "Goes with Everything" Garlicky Cauliflower Rice (page 288) or sautéed shirataki noodles.

INGREDIENTS

- 2 tablespoons toasted sesame oil, divided
- 8 bone-in, skin-on chicken thighs (about 2 pounds)
- 1 tablespoon plus 2 teaspoons Chinese five-spice powder
- 2 teaspoons garlic powder
- 1 teaspoon sea salt
- ⅓ cup gluten-free soy sauce or coconut aminos
- 3 tablespoons unseasoned rice wine vinegar
- 1 tablespoon fresh lime juice
- 2 cloves garlic, minced
- 1 teaspoon grated fresh ginger
- Pinch of red pepper flakes, plus more for garnish
- 3 green onions, sliced on a bias, for garnish
- 2 tablespoons toasted sesame seeds, for garnish

DIRECTIONS

1. Preheat the oven to 400°F.

2. Brush 1 tablespoon of the sesame oil on both sides of the chicken thighs. In a small bowl, combine the Chinese five-spice powder, garlic powder, and salt.

3. Season the chicken thighs on both sides with the seasoning mix, pressing it into the skin.

4. In a mixing bowl, combine the soy sauce, vinegar, lime juice, garlic, ginger, and red pepper flakes. Set aside.

5. Heat the remaining tablespoon of sesame oil in a large ovenproof skillet over medium heat. Add the chicken to the skillet skin side down. Cook for 5 to 6 minutes, or until the skin is nice and crispy. Flip the chicken thighs and transfer the skillet to the oven. Bake for 15 to 20 minutes, until the chicken is cooked through.

6. Return the skillet to the stovetop. Remove the chicken from the pan and cover to keep warm.

7. Add the soy sauce mixture to the skillet and mix with the chicken juices. Use a rubber spatula to scrape up and mix in any browned bits that are stuck to the bottom of the pan. Bring the sauce to a boil, then reduce the heat to low. Simmer until the sauce is reduced by half and thickened. Return the chicken thighs to the pan to heat.

8. Plate the chicken thighs and pour the sauce over the top. Garnish with the green onions, sesame seeds, and red pepper flakes.

> tip: This is also a fantastic recipe for fresh salmon. Simply sear the salmon skin side down as you would the chicken thighs. After you flip the salmon and transfer the skillet to the oven, cook it for 6 to 8 minutes for medium-rare to medium-done salmon.

PER SERVING:

CALORIES: 332   TOTAL CARBS: 6.4g
FAT: 11.8g   FIBER: 1.8g
PROTEIN: 48.7g   NET CARBS: 4.5g

LOCO MOCO

NET CARBS 9.4g

MAKES: 6 servings · **PREP TIME:** 20 minutes · **COOK TIME:** 40 minutes

Maui is my favorite place on Earth. We go there every year, and it is where I find the most peace and joy. Enjoying that peace and joy over a hot bowl of loco moco never hurts, either. Loco moco is a staple on most Hawaiian menus. You will see many different variations, but traditional loco moco consists of white rice topped with a burger patty, gravy, and an egg. To keep this version traditional but lower in carbs, I used riced cauliflower instead. To thicken the gravy in this recipe, you puree some of the sautéed vegetables. This is a trick that I learned from Michelle Tam of Nom Nom Paleo. Not only is it a great way to thicken sauces and make gravies, but it is also an excellent trick for sneaking some extra vegetables into a meal.

INGREDIENTS

FOR THE BURGER PATTIES:

- 2 pounds ground beef
- 1 tablespoon Worcestershire sauce
- 1 tablespoon chopped fresh flat-leaf parsley
- 1 tablespoon garlic powder
- 1 tablespoon onion powder
- 1½ teaspoons sea salt
- ½ teaspoon ground black pepper
- 2 tablespoons avocado oil or olive oil

FOR THE GRAVY:

- 2 tablespoons avocado oil or olive oil
- 1 medium onion, chopped (about 1 cup)
- 2 cloves garlic, minced
- 8 ounces cremini mushrooms, thinly sliced
- ¼ cup gluten-free soy sauce or coconut aminos

- 2 tablespoons Worcestershire sauce
- 4 cups beef stock or bone broth (page 370)

FOR SERVING:

- 1 batch "Goes with Everything" Garlicky Cauliflower Rice (page 288)
- 6 eggs, cooked any way you like
- 4 green onions, sliced on a bias

DIRECTIONS

MAKE THE BURGER PATTIES:

1. Put the ground beef, Worcestershire sauce, parsley, garlic powder, onion powder, salt, and pepper in a large mixing bowl. Mix until the ingredients are well incorporated.

2. Divide the meat mixture into 6 equal portions and form into 1-inch-thick patties. Using your thumb, make a depression in the center of each patty. The burgers will plump as you cook them, and making this depression will help them stay flat and even.

3. In a large skillet, heat the oil over medium-high heat. When the oil is hot, add the patties to the pan. For medium-done burgers, sear until browned and slightly charred on the first side, 3 to 5 minutes. Flip the patties over and do the same on the second side. When the burgers are cooked, remove them from the pan and cover to keep warm.

PER SERVING: ——————
CALORIES: **602**   TOTAL CARBS: **12.2g**
FAT: **44.4g**   FIBER: **2.9g**
PROTEIN: **36.9g**   NET CARBS: **9.4g**

MAKE THE GRAVY:

1. In the same skillet, heat the oil over medium heat. Add the onion and garlic. Sauté until the onion is translucent and the garlic is fragrant.

2. Add the mushrooms, soy sauce, and Worcestershire sauce to the pan. Cook until the mushrooms are tender, about 10 minutes.

3. Add the beef stock to the skillet and, using a rubber spatula, scrape up and mix in any bits that are stuck to the bottom of the pan. Bring the sauce to a boil, then reduce the heat to medium and let simmer until the sauce is reduced by half, about 30 minutes.

4. Using a slotted spoon, remove half of the mushrooms and onion and set them aside. Transfer the remaining mushrooms and onion and all the sauce to a blender and puree until smooth.

5. Pour the mixture back into the skillet and add the reserved mushrooms and onion. Reduce the heat to low and keep warm.

BUILD THE BOWLS:

1. Put 1 cup of the cauliflower rice in a serving bowl and top with a burger patty.

2. Ladle some of the gravy over the top, then finish with a cooked egg.

3. Garnish with green onions.

MINI MEATLOAVES WITH BRUSSELS SPROUTS

NET CARBS
7.3g

 MAKES: 6 servings · PREP TIME: 20 minutes · COOK TIME: 30 minutes

I love the simplicity of sheet pan meals—no fuss, no muss, and, even better, very little cleanup. Now that's a winning combination. I also love how versatile they are. For example, if you aren't a fan of Brussels sprouts, you can easily throw some broccoli or cauliflower on the pan instead.

INGREDIENTS

FOR THE BRUSSELS SPROUTS:

- 1 pound Brussels sprouts, trimmed and halved
- ¼ cup avocado oil or olive oil
- 1 teaspoon grated lemon zest
- 2 tablespoons fresh lemon juice
- 1 teaspoon sea salt
- 1 teaspoon garlic powder
- ½ teaspoon ground black pepper

FOR THE MEATLOAVES:

- 1 pound ground beef
- 1 pound bulk mild Italian sausage
- 3 cloves garlic, minced
- 2 tablespoons Worcestershire sauce
- 3 tablespoons reduced-sugar ketchup, store-bought or homemade (page 385)
- ½ cup blanched almond flour
- 2 tablespoons dried minced onion
- 1½ teaspoons sea salt
- 1 teaspoon dried parsley
- ½ teaspoon ground black pepper

FOR THE TOPS (OPTIONAL):

- 3 tablespoons reduced-sugar ketchup, store-bought or homemade (page 385)

DIRECTIONS

1. Preheat the oven to 400°F.

2. Put the Brussels sprouts, oil, lemon zest, lemon juice, salt, garlic powder, and pepper in a bowl, then toss until the Brussels sprouts are evenly coated. Spread the Brussels sprouts in a single layer across a rimmed baking sheet.

3. Put the ground beef, sausage, garlic, Worcestershire sauce, ketchup, almond flour, dried minced onion, salt, parsley, and pepper in a separate large bowl and mix until the ingredients are well incorporated.

4. Form the meatloaf mixture into 6 mini loaves about 2½ inches by 4 inches.

5. Add the meatloaves to the baking sheet with the Brussels sprouts. Bake until the meatloaves are cooked all the way through and the Brussels sprouts are tender, about 30 minutes.

6. Remove the pan from the oven and brush the tops of the meatloaves with the ketchup, if desired. Return to the oven for 5 additional minutes.

---

tip: *To make a nut-free version, simply substitute crushed pork rinds for the blanched almond flour.*

PER SERVING:

CALORIES: **627**	TOTAL CARBS: **11.2g**
FAT: **52.8g**	FIBER: **3.8g**
PROTEIN: **28.3g**	NET CARBS: **7.3g**

PROSCIUTTO CHICKEN AND BROCCOLI SHEET PAN MEAL

NET CARBS 4.6g

MAKES: 5 servings · **PREP TIME:** 20 minutes · **COOK TIME:** 25 minutes

This is one of those dishes that leaves you scratching your head and wondering how such simple ingredients can develop such complex flavors. Plus, it has the added bonus of being a sheet pan meal, so it is very quick and easy!

INGREDIENTS

- 10 chicken tenders (about 2½ pounds)
- ¾ teaspoon ground black pepper, divided
- 10 fresh sage leaves
- 10 thin slices prosciutto (about 6 ounces)
- 2 tablespoons avocado oil
- 1 tablespoon balsamic vinegar
- ½ teaspoon garlic powder
- ½ teaspoon onion powder
- ½ teaspoon sea salt
- 1 pound broccoli florets

DIRECTIONS

1. Preheat the oven to 425°F.

2. Season the chicken tenders on both sides with ½ teaspoon of the pepper. Put a sage leaf on top of each piece of chicken. Wrap each piece tightly in a slice of prosciutto.

3. Arrange the chicken in a single, well-spaced layer across a rimmed baking sheet.

4. In a large mixing bowl, whisk the avocado oil, balsamic vinegar, garlic powder, onion powder, salt, and remaining ¼ teaspoon of pepper until combined. Add the broccoli to the bowl and toss until it is evenly coated in the oil mixture.

5. Arrange the broccoli in a single layer around the chicken. Bake for 20 to 25 minutes, or until the chicken is cooked through and the broccoli is slightly charred and crisp-tender.

PER SERVING:

CALORIES: **560**	TOTAL CARBS: **7.2g**
FAT: **31.5g**	FIBER: **2.6g**
PROTEIN: **60g**	NET CARBS: **4.6g**

DIJON PAPRIKA PORK TENDERLOIN

NET
CARBS
0.6g

MAKES: 6 servings · **PREP TIME:** 10 minutes · **COOK TIME:** 25 minutes

This pork tenderloin is seared in a skillet and then baked to perfection. Searing it first creates a wonderful crust on the outside, and finishing it in the oven ensures that it stays nice and juicy.

INGREDIENTS

- 3 tablespoons Dijon mustard
- 1½ teaspoons paprika
- 1 teaspoon sea salt
- ½ teaspoon dried oregano leaves
- ½ teaspoon garlic powder
- ½ teaspoon onion powder
- 2 (1-pound) pork tenderloins
- 2 tablespoons avocado oil or olive oil
- Maldon sea salt flakes, for finishing (optional)

DIRECTIONS

1. Preheat the oven to 425°F.

2. In a small bowl, whisk the mustard, paprika, salt, oregano, garlic powder, and onion powder until the ingredients are well incorporated. Spread the mixture all over both of the pork tenderloins.

3. Heat the oil in a large skillet over medium-high heat. When the oil is hot, add the pork tenderloins and cook until browned on both sides, about 4 minutes per side.

4. Transfer the tenderloins to a rimmed baking sheet and bake for 15 minutes, or until they are cooked all the way through (the juices will run clear when you cut into the meat).

5. Let the pork rest for 10 minutes before slicing it. This will help it retain its juices.

6. Sprinkle with salt flakes before serving, if desired.

PER SERVING: ———————
CALORIES: **314** TOTAL CARBS: **1.2g**
FAT: **8.3g** FIBER: **0.6g**
PROTEIN: **32.1g** NET CARBS: **0.6g**

GARLIC GINGER PORK NOODLE BOWL

NET CARBS 6.1g

MAKES: 4 servings · PREP TIME: 15 minutes · COOK TIME: 30 minutes

My favorite thing about whipping up a noodle bowl for lunch or dinner is that it is light enough for summer fare but substantial enough for when you want something a little heartier and more filling.

INGREDIENTS

- 4 (8-ounce) packages spaghetti-style shirataki noodles (see tips)
- 1 pound ground pork
- 4 ounces cremini mushrooms, sliced
- ½ small onion, grated
- 2 teaspoons grated fresh ginger
- 1 teaspoon garlic powder
- ½ teaspoon sea salt
- ¼ teaspoon ground black pepper
- 1 tablespoon avocado oil or olive oil
- 4 cloves garlic, peeled and sliced
- 3 tablespoons gluten-free soy sauce or coconut aminos
- 2 tablespoons fish sauce
- 1 cup broccoli slaw
- 1 small bell pepper, seeded and thinly sliced
- 3 cups beef stock or bone broth (page 370), divided
- 4 green onions, sliced on a bias

DIRECTIONS

1. Rinse the noodles, soak them in water for 10 minutes, and then drain and set aside.

2. Heat a large skillet over medium-high heat. When the pan is hot, add the ground pork, mushrooms, onion, ginger, garlic powder, salt, and black pepper. Sauté until the pork is browned and starting to get crispy. Using a slotted spoon, remove the pork and mushrooms from the pan and set aside. Leave any drippings in the pan.

3. Reduce the heat under the skillet to medium, then add the oil and garlic to the drippings and fry the garlic until it is crispy but not burned. Remove the garlic from the pan and set aside.

4. Add the soy sauce, fish sauce, and shirataki noodles to the pan and toss to coat the noodles in the sauce. Use a rubber spatula to scrape up and mix in any bits from the bottom of the pan. Sauté until the noodles are dry.

5. Divide the noodles among four large shallow bowls. Then divide the pork and mushrooms, broccoli slaw, and bell peppers among the bowls.

6. Add the beef stock to the skillet and bring to a boil. Again, use a rubber spatula to scrape up and mix in any browned bits from the bottom of the pan.

7. Pour some of the stock over each bowl. Top the bowls with the crispy garlic and green onions before serving.

> *tips: Shirataki noodles can give off a somewhat fishy odor. The key to preparing them is to rinse, soak, and drain them before using. This will improve the taste and texture and get rid of the smell.*
>
> *If you do not have broccoli slaw, you can use coleslaw or even zucchini noodles. This dish is also amazing served with a poached egg on top.*

PER SERVING:
CALORIES: **397**   TOTAL CARBS: **14.6g**
FAT: **28.7g**   FIBER: **8.5g**
PROTEIN: **25.4g**   NET CARBS: **6.1g**

CRISPY PORK
FRIED CAULIFLOWER RICE

NET
CARBS
3.2g

MAKES: 10 servings (1 cup per serving) · **PREP TIME:** 20 minutes · **COOK TIME:** 20 minutes

Cauliflower fried rice was one of the dishes that finally helped me turn a corner where cauliflower was concerned. I wasn't always a fan of this cruciferous low-carb staple. I figured if adding it to something as delicious as fried rice couldn't convince me, then nothing could. It was love at first bite, and I have been a fan ever since.

INGREDIENTS

- 1 pound pork tenderloin, diced
- ½ teaspoon sea salt
- ¼ teaspoon ground black pepper
- 2 tablespoons toasted sesame oil
- 4 green onions, sliced on a bias, white and green portions separated
- 3 cloves garlic, minced
- 6 cups riced cauliflower
- 1 small red bell pepper, seeded and diced
- 1 cup chopped broccoli florets
- ¼ cup gluten-free soy sauce or coconut aminos, or more to taste
- 1 tablespoon unseasoned rice wine vinegar
- ½ teaspoon ground ginger
- ¼ teaspoon red pepper flakes
- 3 large eggs
- 1 tablespoon toasted sesame seeds

DIRECTIONS

1. Heat a wok or large sauté pan over medium heat. When the pan is hot, add the pork, salt, and black pepper and cook until the pork is crispy. Use a slotted spoon to remove the pork from the pan, leaving the drippings in the pan.

2. To the wok, add the sesame oil, white portions of the green onions, and garlic. Cook until the onions are translucent and fragrant.

3. Increase the heat to medium-high. Add the riced cauliflower, bell pepper, broccoli, soy sauce, vinegar, ginger, and red pepper flakes to the skillet and stir-fry until the vegetables are tender, about 10 minutes.

4. Crack the eggs into a bowl and fork-whisk. Move the fried rice to one side of the pan and pour the eggs into the exposed side. Gently scramble the eggs as they cook, then mix them in with the rest of the ingredients in the pan.

5. Mix the cooked pork into the fried cauliflower rice. Garnish with the sesame seeds and the green portions of the green onions before serving. Refrigerate leftovers for up to a week.

tip: You don't have to use pork for this recipe; you can use any protein you prefer. Simply sub in your favorite meat, poultry, or seafood and cook it as directed above.

PER SERVING:

CALORIES: **104**   TOTAL CARBS: **5g**
FAT: **3.2g**   FIBER: **1.8g**
PROTEIN: **13.1g**   NET CARBS: **3.2g**

GRILLED STEAK WITH CHIMICHURRI

NET CARBS
2.9g

MAKES: 6 servings · PREP TIME: 10 minutes · COOK TIME: 5 minutes

The herbaceous flavors of the chimichurri elevate steak to a whole new level. When you add the fresh and light flavors of the strawberry salsa, the combination is over the top. Dare I say that the toppings are the real stars of the plate here?

INGREDIENTS

- 2 pounds flank steak, skirt steak, or thin top round steak
- Sea salt and ground black pepper
- 2 tablespoons avocado oil or olive oil
- 1 batch Balsamic Horseradish Chimichurri (page 392)
- Strawberry Cucumber Mint Salsa (page 134), for serving (optional)

DIRECTIONS

1. Season the steak generously on both sides with salt and pepper, then brush with the oil.

2. Heat a large grill pan or cast-iron skillet over medium-high heat. Sear the steak for 2 to 3 minutes on each side, or until it has reached your desired level of doneness. For medium-rare steak, 2 to 3 minutes should be about right.

3. Remove the steak from the pan and let rest for 5 to 10 minutes before slicing. This will help it retain its juices.

4. Thinly slice the steak and top with the chimichurri and salsa, if desired, before serving.

PER SERVING:

CALORIES: **401**	TOTAL CARBS: **3.9g**
FAT: **27.6g**	FIBER: **0.9g**
PROTEIN: **32.5g**	NET CARBS: **2.9g**

LEMON AND HERB CHICKEN KEBABS

NET CARBS
1g

MAKES: 8 kebabs (2 per serving) · PREP TIME: 15 minutes · COOK TIME: 10 minutes

These Greek-inspired lemon chicken kebabs are perfect for grilling indoors or out. They are one of my favorite dishes to bring to get-togethers because they are always a hit.

INGREDIENTS

- 2 cloves garlic, minced
- 2 tablespoons avocado oil or olive oil
- 1 teaspoon grated lemon zest
- 2 tablespoons fresh lemon juice
- 1 teaspoon chopped fresh oregano
- 1 teaspoon chopped fresh rosemary
- ½ teaspoon chopped fresh thyme
- 1 teaspoon sea salt
- ¼ teaspoon ground black pepper
- 1½ pounds boneless, skinless chicken breasts or thighs, cut into large chunks
- Lemon wedges, for serving
- Everything Bagel Aioli (page 388), for serving (optional)

SPECIAL EQUIPMENT:

8 skewers, about 12 inches long

DIRECTIONS

1. Put the garlic, oil, lemon zest, lemon juice, oregano, rosemary, thyme, salt, and pepper in a large bowl and whisk to combine.

2. Add the chicken to the bowl and toss to evenly coat in the oil mixture. Thread the chicken onto the skewers.

3. Heat a large grill pan over medium heat. Grill the skewers for 5 minutes on each side, or until the chicken is cooked all the way through.

4. Serve with lemon wedges and aioli, if desired.

PER SERVING:
CALORIES: **371**   TOTAL CARBS: **1.2g**
FAT: **11.5g**   FIBER: **0.2g**
PROTEIN: **38.4g**   NET CARBS: **1g**

MEATLOAF BURGERS

🕐 **MAKES:** 4 burgers (1 per serving) · **PREP TIME:** 20 minutes · **COOK TIME:** 10 minutes

I decided to call these Meatloaf Burgers because they have all the delicious flavors of my classic meatloaf recipe. In fact, meatloaf was a childhood favorite of mine. It's still a favorite to this day, well into my adulthood. Meatloaf is one of those foods that gets an unfairly bad rap. I can understand why, with some of the mushy lumps of meat that were passed off as meatloaf in the 1980s. If you are one of those people who has sworn off meatloaf altogether, this recipe (or the Mini Meatloaves with Brussels Sprouts on page 244) just might change your mind.

INGREDIENTS

- 1 pound ground beef
- 1 large egg
- 2 tablespoons reduced-sugar ketchup, store-bought or homemade (page 385)
- 2 tablespoons dried minced onion
- 2 tablespoons Worcestershire sauce
- 2 cloves garlic, minced
- ½ teaspoon sea salt
- ¼ teaspoon ground black pepper
- 2 tablespoons avocado oil or olive oil
- 1 batch Everything Buns (page 360)
- Low-carb condiments of choice
- 8 slices bacon, cooked crisp
- 1 tomato, sliced
- 1 small red onion, sliced
- 4 leaves romaine or iceberg lettuce
- Pickle spears, for serving (optional)

DIRECTIONS

1. In a large mixing bowl, mix the ground beef, egg, ketchup, dried minced onion, Worcestershire sauce, garlic, salt, and pepper until the ingredients are well incorporated.

2. Divide the mixture into 4 equal portions and form into patties about ¾ inch thick. Season both sides of the patties generously with the salt and pepper.

3. Using your thumb, make a depression in the center of each patty. The burgers will plump as you cook them, and making this depression will help them stay flat and even.

4. Heat the oil in a large skillet over medium-high heat. When the oil is hot, add the patties to the pan. Sear until browned and slightly charred on the first side, 3 to 5 minutes for medium-done burgers. Flip the patties over and do the same on the second side.

5. Put each burger patty on a bun and top with the low-carb condiments, 2 slices of bacon, a tomato slice, a few slices of red onion, and a lettuce leaf. Serve with pickles, if desired.

> *tip: These burgers are also fantastic made with ground chicken or turkey. In fact, you can substitute any ground meat you prefer.*

PER SERVING (without buns): —————

CALORIES: **561**	TOTAL CARBS: **5.7g**
FAT: **46g**	FIBER: **0.7g**
PROTEIN: **29.9g**	NET CARBS: **4.9g**

PER SERVING (with buns): —————

CALORIES: **803**	TOTAL CARBS: **24.6g**
FAT: **63.7g**	FIBER: **14.5g**
PROTEIN: **43.5g**	NET CARBS: **10.1g**

PEANUT CHICKEN ZOODLE BOWL

NET CARBS 6.2g

MAKES: 6 servings · PREP TIME: 20 minutes · COOK TIME: 15 minutes

There are few things I love more than a bright, colorful plate of food. All the flavors in this dish come together in perfect harmony, and the peanut sauce on top is just the icing on the zoodle bowl. If you are anything like me, you will find yourself looking for excuses to use this sauce.

INGREDIENTS

- 3 medium zucchini, spiral sliced
- Sea salt and ground black pepper
- 2 pounds boneless, skinless chicken breasts or thighs
- 2 tablespoons avocado oil or olive oil
- 1 medium red bell pepper, seeded and thinly sliced
- ½ cup shredded purple cabbage
- ¾ cup Peanut Sauce (page 394)
- 2 green onions, sliced on a bias
- 2 tablespoons toasted sesame seeds
- Fresh cilantro, for garnish
- Lime wedges, for serving

DIRECTIONS

1. Lay the zucchini noodles in a single layer on a bed of paper towels. Sprinkle the zucchini generously with salt and let rest for 10 to 15 minutes. The salt will help draw out the excess moisture so that the zucchini noodles do not become soupy. When the noodles have released their liquid, put a layer of fresh paper towels on top and dab away the excess moisture, then set the noodles aside.

2. Season the chicken generously on both sides with salt and pepper.

3. Heat the oil in a large skillet over medium-high heat. When the oil is hot, add the chicken and cook for 5 minutes on each side, or until browned and cooked all the way through. Remove from the pan and cover to keep warm while you prepare the rest of the ingredients.

4. In the same skillet, sauté the zucchini noodles over medium heat for 2 to 3 minutes, until they are tender but not mushy.

5. Put the zucchini noodles in a large serving bowl and arrange the bell pepper and cabbage on top.

6. Slice the chicken and put it on top of the noodle bowl. Drizzle with the peanut sauce (or serve the sauce on the side) and top with the green onions and sesame seeds.

7. Garnish with cilantro and serve with lime wedges.

> *tip*: This dish is also amazing as a cold salad with spiral-sliced cucumber noodles in place of the zucchini noodles.

PER SERVING: —————

CALORIES: **385**	TOTAL CARBS: **8.5g**
FAT: **12.8g**	FIBER: **2.3g**
PROTEIN: **25.1g**	NET CARBS: **6.2g**

PUTTANESCA PORK CHOPS

NET CARBS 6.2g

MAKES: 4 servings · PREP TIME: 10 minutes · COOK TIME: 20 minutes

Puttanesca sauce was a staple on the menu at both of the Italian restaurants I worked in over the years. In Italian, *puttanesca* literally translates to "whore." That was always a fun thing to explain to the guests. While the true origin is debatable, the fact that it tastes amazing is not. A traditional puttanesca is a robust tomato sauce made with light, fresh ingredients. It is typically briny and somewhat salty in nature, and it should always contain anchovies, capers, olives, and red pepper flakes.

INGREDIENTS

- 4 thick-cut boneless pork chops (about 1½ pounds)
- ½ teaspoon sea salt
- ¼ teaspoon ground black pepper
- 2 tablespoons avocado oil or olive oil, divided
- 4 cloves garlic, minced
- 2 anchovy fillets, minced
- 1 (14.5-ounce) can stewed tomatoes
- ¼ cup halved Kalamata olives
- 2 tablespoons capers
- ½ teaspoon dried oregano leaves
- ¼ teaspoon red pepper flakes

DIRECTIONS

1. Season the pork chops on both sides with the salt and pepper.

2. Heat 1 tablespoon of the oil in a large skillet over medium heat. Add the pork chops and cook until golden brown on both sides and cooked through, 4 to 5 minutes per side.

3. Remove the pork chops from the pan, place on a plate, and cover to keep warm.

4. Add the remaining tablespoon of oil, the garlic, and the anchovies to the skillet. Cook, stirring constantly, for 1 minute.

5. Reduce the heat to medium-low, then add the tomatoes, olives, capers, oregano, and red pepper flakes to the anchovy mixture. Gently smash the tomatoes to break them up. Simmer until the sauce has thickened, about 4 minutes.

6. Return the pork chops and any juices to the pan, then cover the chops in the sauce and cook for an additional 2 to 3 minutes to warm through.

tip: This recipe can also be made with chicken or shrimp.

PER SERVING:

CALORIES: **417**	TOTAL CARBS: **7.6g**
FAT: **25g**	FIBER: **1.5g**
PROTEIN: **39.7g**	NET CARBS: **6.2g**

QUICK BRAISED SAUSAGE AND PEPPERS

NET CARBS
3.9g

MAKES: 6 servings · PREP TIME: 15 minutes · COOK TIME: 30 minutes

The combination of a pan-fry followed by a quick braise gives these sausages a deeper flavor than either cooking method alone. This is one of my favorite recipes to make when we are low on groceries and want something fast and easy. Even when we are in need of a grocery shopping trip, I can usually find some sort of sausage and an array of vegetables between my fridge and freezer.

INGREDIENTS

- 2 tablespoons avocado oil or olive oil
- 6 large smoked sausages, sliced on a bias into 1-inch pieces
- 6 mini bell peppers (assorted colors), halved and seeded
- 4 large ribs celery, cut into fourths
- 1 small red onion, cut into large chunks
- 8 cloves garlic, peeled and smashed with the side of a knife
- 1 cup beef or chicken stock or bone broth (page 370)
- 3 sprigs fresh rosemary
- 2 sprigs fresh thyme

DIRECTIONS

1. Preheat the oven to 400°F.

2. Heat the oil in a large ovenproof skillet or sauté pan over medium-high heat. Add the sausages to the pan and brown on all sides.

3. Add the bell peppers, celery, onion, and garlic to the skillet and cook for 1 to 2 minutes, until the vegetables are lightly scorched.

4. Add the stock and rosemary and thyme sprigs to the pan, then cover and transfer to the oven. Braise for 12 minutes, or until the vegetables are tender and the stock is reduced by at least half.

PER SERVING: ——————
CALORIES: **167**   TOTAL CARBS: **5.2g**
FAT: **13.8g**   FIBER: **1.3g**
PROTEIN: **5g**   NET CARBS: **3.9g**

SLOW COOKER CRISPY PORK CARNITAS

NET CARBS
4.2g

MAKES: 10 servings (5 ounces per serving)
PREP TIME: 15 minutes · **COOK TIME:** 8 hours, plus 10 minutes to broil

There is something uniquely wonderful about pork carnitas. It is crispy while also being incredibly juicy and flavorful. That is a hard combination to come by. This is one of my favorite dishes to use for repurposing leftovers. I love to pile the carnitas on top of a salad with loads of vegetables or eat it in almond flour tortillas for pork carnitas tacos. But perhaps my favorite thing to make with the leftovers is Pork Carnitas Eggs Benedict (page 122).

INGREDIENTS

- 1 tablespoon dried oregano leaves
- 1 tablespoon sea salt
- 2 teaspoons ground cumin
- 1 teaspoon ground black pepper
- 4 pounds boneless pork shoulder
- 4 cloves garlic, peeled
- 1 medium onion, chopped (about 1 cup)
- 1 dried ancho chili pod, chopped
- Juice of 2 oranges
- Juice of 2 limes

DIRECTIONS

1. Preheat a slow cooker on the low setting.

2. In a small mixing bowl, combine the oregano, salt, cumin, and pepper. Rinse and pat dry the pork shoulder. Rub the seasoning mix over the entire pork shoulder.

3. Put the seasoned pork in the slow cooker, fat cap side up. Top with the garlic, onion, ancho chili, orange juice, and lime juice.

4. Cover and cook for 8 hours. When it is finished cooking, use two forks to shred the meat directly in the slow cooker.

5. Use a slotted spoon to transfer the shredded pork to a rimmed baking sheet. Broil until the meat starts to get crispy on the edges, about 5 minutes.

6. Ladle half of the juices from the slow cooker over the meat and broil for an additional 5 minutes, or until the meat is nice and crispy all over.

7. Ladle the remaining juices from the slow cooker over the top before serving.

8. Store leftovers in the refrigerator for up to a week. Alternatively, you can freeze them.

tip: *If you can't find dried ancho chili pods, you can substitute ancho chili powder or even chipotle chili powder. Simply season the meat to your desired level of spiciness.*

PER SERVING:
CALORIES: **257**   TOTAL CARBS: **5.1g**
FAT: **6.6g**   FIBER: **0.8g**
PROTEIN: **42.2g**   NET CARBS: **4.2g**

SOUTHWESTERN PORK SKILLET

NET CARBS 3.7g

MAKES: 6 servings · **PREP TIME:** 10 minutes · **COOK TIME:** 20 minutes

This is seriously one of the most versatile dishes ever. You can eat it just as it is, pile it on top of a taco salad, or put eggs in it and call it breakfast. The sky's the limit here. I love to buy almond flour tortillas and use this dish for soft tacos or burritos. If you aren't avoiding dairy, it is even more amazing with some shredded sharp cheddar cheese and sour cream on top.

INGREDIENTS

- 1 pound ground pork
- 1 medium onion, diced (about 1 cup)
- 2 cloves garlic, minced
- ¾ teaspoon sea salt, or more to taste
- ¼ teaspoon ground black pepper
- 3 cups riced cauliflower
- 1 (10-ounce) can diced tomatoes and green chilies, with juices
- 1 tablespoon Fajita Seasoning (page 397)
- Torn fresh cilantro, for garnish
- Lime wedges, for serving
- Sliced avocado, for serving (optional)

DIRECTIONS

1. Heat a large skillet over medium heat. When the pan is hot, add the ground pork and cook, using a spatula to break it up, until browned, about 8 minutes. Use a slotted spoon to remove the cooked pork from the pan, leaving the drippings in the pan.

2. Add the onion, garlic, salt, and pepper to the skillet and sauté until the onion is translucent and soft.

3. Add the riced cauliflower, tomatoes and green chilies, and fajita seasoning to the pan and mix until the ingredients are well combined. Cook for an additional 15 minutes, or until the cauliflower is tender.

4. Return the pork to the pan, mix with the vegetables, and cook for an additional 5 minutes to reheat the pork.

5. Garnish with cilantro and serve with lime wedges and avocado slices, if desired.

PER SERVING:

CALORIES: **233**   TOTAL CARBS: **6.5g**
FAT: **16.5g**   FIBER: **2.8g**
PROTEIN: **14.9g**   NET CARBS: **3.7g**

SPAGHETTI SQUASH WITH TOMATO MEAT SAUCE

NET CARBS 9.9g

MAKES: 6 servings · **PREP TIME:** 20 minutes · **COOK TIME:** 45 minutes

A batch of tomato sauce simmering on the stove has one of the most inviting aromas I can think of. We ate spaghetti almost weekly when I was growing up. In fact, it was in such high rotation that I would have sworn we were Italian. I'm so thankful that there are low-carb-friendly options out there so I can still enjoy the delicious flavors of a home-cooked spaghetti dinner. Now it just happens to be in the form of spaghetti squash.

INGREDIENTS

- 1½ cups Tomato Meat Sauce (page 378)
- 1 large spaghetti squash (about 4 pounds)
- 2 tablespoons avocado oil or olive oil
- Sea salt and ground black pepper
- Fresh basil, for garnish (optional)

DIRECTIONS

1. If you do not already have the sauce prepared, cook it while the spaghetti squash is roasting. If you prepared it in advance, warm the sauce over medium-low heat while the spaghetti squash is in the oven.

2. Preheat the oven to 400°F. Line a rimmed baking sheet with parchment paper or a silicone baking mat.

3. Cut the spaghetti squash in half lengthwise and, using a large spoon, scrape out the seeds. Put the squash cut side up on the lined baking sheet. Drizzle the squash with the oil and sprinkle with a little salt and pepper. Roast for 45 minutes, or until the squash is easily pierced with a fork.

4. Remove the squash from the oven and, once cool enough to handle, use a fork to scrape out the shreds of squash.

5. Divide the spaghetti squash among six plates. Top each serving with ¼ cup of the tomato meat sauce and garnish with basil, if desired.

PER SERVING:

CALORIES: **239**   TOTAL CARBS: **12.7g**
FAT: **18.1g**   FIBER: **2.8g**
PROTEIN: **8g**   NET CARBS: **9.9g**

SPICY CITRUS MEATBALLS

MAKES: 5 servings (4 meatballs per serving)
PREP TIME: 15 minutes · **COOK TIME:** 30 minutes

I just love adding avocado to meatballs. It makes them so tender and juicy. If you aren't avoiding dairy, be sure to check out the White Cheddar and Sun Dried Tomato Avocado Stuffed Meatballs on my site, peaceloveandlowcarb.com.

INGREDIENTS

FOR THE SAUCE:

- ½ cup beef stock or bone broth (page 370)
- 1 tablespoon Sriracha sauce or other hot sauce, or more to taste
- 1 tablespoon fresh lime juice
- 1 tablespoon fresh orange juice (see tips)
- ½ cup diced red onions
- 1 teaspoon garlic powder
- ½ teaspoon sea salt
- 1½ teaspoons sea salt
- 1 teaspoon ground ginger
- 2 tablespoons avocado oil or olive oil, for the pan

FOR THE MEATBALLS:

- 2 pounds ground beef
- 1 small avocado, peeled, pitted, and cubed
- 3 cloves garlic, minced
- 1 tablespoon plus 1 teaspoon Sriracha sauce or other hot sauce
- 1 tablespoon Worcestershire sauce
- 1 teaspoon grated orange zest
- 1 tablespoon fresh orange juice
- 1 teaspoon grated lime zest
- 1 tablespoon fresh lime juice
- 1 tablespoon dried minced onion

DIRECTIONS

1. Make the sauce: Put all the ingredients for the sauce in a small mixing bowl. Mix to combine and set aside.

2. Make the meatballs: In a large bowl, mix the ground beef, avocado, garlic, Sriracha, Worcestershire sauce, orange zest, orange juice, lime zest, lime juice, dried minced onion, salt, and ginger until the ingredients are well incorporated. Form the mixture into 20 meatballs, about 2 inches in diameter.

3. Preheat the oven to 400°F.

4. Heat the oil in a large skillet over medium heat. When the oil is hot, cook the meatballs in batches until browned all over. Transfer the browned meatballs to a rimmed baking sheet, leaving the drippings in the skillet.

5. Bake the meatballs for 10 minutes, or until cooked through. While the meatballs are baking, cook the sauce.

6. Add the sauce to the skillet with the pan drippings and use a rubber spatula to scrape up and mix in any browned bits that are stuck to the bottom of the pan. Reduce the heat to medium-low and let the sauce simmer until it has started to thicken.

7. Add the baked meatballs to the pan and toss to coat in the sauce.

PER SERVING:
CALORIES: **584**   TOTAL CARBS: **7.9g**
FAT: **46.2g**   FIBER: **2.5g**
PROTEIN: **32.9g**   NET CARBS: **5.4g**

tips: The trick to getting your meatballs to keep their shape and develop a nice brown crust is not to turn them too soon or too often. Once the meat has started to brown and develop a crust, it will release itself from the pan. Have you ever gone to flip a steak and had to practically rip it off the pan? That means it was not ready to be flipped. Use a pair of tongs to give the meat a gentle tug. If it is easily lifted, it is ready to be turned or flipped.

For this recipe, I recommend using freshly squeezed orange juice to avoid added sugar from store-bought orange juice. Juicing fresh oranges will also prevent you from having a leftover jug of orange juice in the fridge that you likely won't drink.

Side Dishes

"CHEESY" HERBED ROASTED CAULIFLOWER

NET CARBS 6g

MAKES: 6 servings · **PREP TIME:** 15 minutes · **COOK TIME:** 35 minutes

Would you believe me if I told you that I wasn't always a fan of cauliflower? I didn't come around to the whole cauliflower craze until I started living a low-carb lifestyle. Prior to that, it was just the vegetable that got left behind in the vegetable trays at parties. The things I love most about cauliflower are how versatile it is and how it takes on the taste and texture of so many of my favorite high-carb foods, like pasta, rice, and potatoes. If you are still not a fan of cauliflower, you can always make this recipe with any of your favorite low-carb vegetables. "Cheesy" Herbed Roasted Broccoli, anyone?

INGREDIENTS

- 1 large head cauliflower, trimmed into florets
- 2 tablespoons avocado oil or olive oil
- ¼ cup nutritional yeast
- 1 teaspoon dried chives
- 1 teaspoon garlic powder
- ½ teaspoon onion powder
- ½ teaspoon dried basil
- ½ teaspoon dried oregano leaves
- ½ teaspoon dried rosemary leaves
- ½ teaspoon sea salt
- ¼ teaspoon ground black pepper
- Chopped fresh flat-leaf parsley, for garnish (optional)

DIRECTIONS

1. Preheat the oven to 425°F.

2. Put the cauliflower florets in a large mixing bowl and drizzle the oil over them. Toss to coat, making sure that all the florets are evenly coated in the oil.

3. In a small mixing bowl, mix the nutritional yeast, chives, garlic powder, onion powder, basil, oregano, rosemary, salt, and pepper until the ingredients are well combined.

4. Sprinkle the spice mixture over the cauliflower, tossing to coat as you go.

5. Lay the seasoned cauliflower in a single layer across a rimmed baking sheet.

6. Roast for 35 minutes, or until the cauliflower is golden brown with crispy edges. Garnish with chopped parsley before serving, if desired.

> *tips: If you are not a fan of the nutty, cheesy flavor of nutritional yeast, you can omit it and still have a delicious roasted cauliflower side dish.*
>
> *If you aren't avoiding dairy, try replacing the nutritional yeast in this recipe with freshly grated Parmesan cheese. Delish!*

PER SERVING:

CALORIES: **109**   TOTAL CARBS: **11g**
FAT: **5.4g**   FIBER: **5g**
PROTEIN: **6.8g**   NET CARBS: **6g**

BOURBON ONIONS

NET CARBS
3.7g

 MAKES: 8 servings · **PREP TIME:** 10 minutes · **COOK TIME:** 20 minutes

Bourbon and brown sugar erythritol give these caramelized onions a rich, bold flavor that is almost dessert-like. It may sound weird to use *onions* and *dessert* in the same sentence, but you will know exactly what I mean as soon as you taste them. They are delicious on just about anything, especially a juicy steak.

INGREDIENTS

FOR THE ONIONS:

- 2 tablespoons avocado oil or olive oil
- 2 large onions, cut into ½-inch-thick slices
- ½ teaspoon garlic powder
- ½ teaspoon sea salt
- ¼ teaspoon ground black pepper

FOR THE SAUCE:

- ½ cup bourbon
- 2 tablespoons reduced-sugar ketchup, store-bought or homemade (page 385)
- 1 tablespoon brown sugar erythritol
- 1 tablespoon Worcestershire sauce
- 1 tablespoon balsamic vinegar
- 1 tablespoon cooking sherry
- 1 or 2 sprigs fresh thyme, for garnish (optional)

DIRECTIONS

1. Heat the oil in a large skillet over medium heat. Once hot, add the onions, garlic powder, salt, and pepper. Sauté until the onions are tender and slightly browned on the edges, about 10 minutes.

2. While the onions are cooking, make the sauce: Bring the bourbon, ketchup, erythritol, Worcestershire sauce, balsamic vinegar, and cooking sherry to a boil in a small saucepan over medium-high heat. Once it reaches a boil, reduce the heat to low and simmer until the sauce has started to thicken, about 10 minutes.

3. Pour the sauce over the onions and toss to coat. Cook for an additional 10 minutes, or until the onions are evenly coated in the sauce and the sauce is nice and thick. Garnish with fresh thyme before serving, if desired.

---

tips: Chop the onions instead of slicing them and mix in some chopped crispy bacon before serving to turn this into a delicious bacon jam.

If you don't want to use sweetener or don't have any on hand, you can make these onions without it. They will still be delicious.

PER SERVING: ———————————

CALORIES: **83** FIBER: **0.7g**

FAT: **3.5g** NET CARBS: **3.7g**

PROTEIN: **0.4g** ERYTHRITOL: **1.5g**

TOTAL CARBS: **4.4g**

CAULIFLOWER RICE PILAF

NET CARBS 2.8g

MAKES: 12 servings (½ cup per serving) · PREP TIME: 15 minutes · COOK TIME: 30 minutes

When I was growing up, rice pilaf was one of my favorite side dishes. Of course, back then it came straight from a box. You know, the all-too-familiar San Francisco treat. Rice is one of the things I've missed the most since I switched to a low-carb, ketogenic way of living, but I've found that, when cooked just right, cauliflower can really curb my cravings for rice. I've also found that the longer you cook riced cauliflower—low and slow—the more it takes on the taste and texture of real rice.

INGREDIENTS

- 2 tablespoons avocado oil or olive oil
- 1 small onion, diced (about ½ cup)
- 4 cloves garlic, minced
- ½ teaspoon sea salt, or more to taste
- ½ teaspoon ground black pepper, or more to taste
- 6 cups riced cauliflower
- 1 cup chicken stock or bone broth (page 370), divided
- 1 tablespoon chicken bouillon granules, or 3 chicken bouillon cubes, crushed
- ¼ cup slivered almonds
- 3 green onions, sliced

DIRECTIONS

1. Heat the oil in a large skillet over medium heat. Once hot, add the onion, garlic, salt, and pepper. Sauté until the onion is translucent and the garlic is fragrant.

2. Add the riced cauliflower, ¾ cup of the chicken stock, and the chicken bouillon granules to the skillet. Mix to combine the ingredients.

3. Cook, stirring frequently, until all the liquid has evaporated and the cauliflower is tender, about 20 minutes.

4. Add the remaining ¼ cup of chicken stock and use a rubber spatula to scrape any caramelized bits from the bottom of the pan and mix them into the rice pilaf.

5. Stir in the almonds, then taste and add more salt and pepper, if desired. Top with the green onions before serving.

---

tip: For a nightshade-free pilaf, be sure to check the ingredient list on the bouillon you use. Not all brands are free of nightshades.

PER SERVING:
CALORIES: 63   TOTAL CARBS: 4.7g
FAT: 4.3g   FIBER: 1.9g
PROTEIN: 2.6g   NET CARBS: 2.8g

ROASTED MUSHROOMS, ZUCCHINI, AND EGGPLANT

NET CARBS **3.1g**

MAKES: 6 servings · **PREP TIME:** 20 minutes · **COOK TIME:** 40 minutes

I love the tart, acidic taste of balsamic vinegar paired with savory ingredients like garlic and onion. Roasting these vegetables with the balsamic brings out the sweet component of the vinegar as well. I love to pair this dish with Sweet and Spicy Barbecue Ribs (page 212) or Blackened Shrimp Fettuccine Alfredo (page 230).

INGREDIENTS

- 1 medium eggplant, cubed
- 2 medium zucchini, halved lengthwise and sliced
- 8 ounces cremini mushrooms, quartered
- 6 cloves garlic, minced
- Leaves from 3 sprigs fresh rosemary, chopped
- ¼ cup avocado oil or olive oil
- 2 tablespoons balsamic vinegar
- 2 tablespoons dried minced onion
- 2 teaspoons sea salt
- 1 teaspoon ground black pepper

DIRECTIONS

1. Preheat the oven to 400°F. Line a rimmed baking sheet with parchment paper or a silicone baking mat.

2. Put all the ingredients in a large mixing bowl. Toss until the vegetables are evenly coated in the oil, vinegar, and spices.

3. Spread the mixture in a single layer across the prepared baking sheet. Bake for 40 minutes, tossing every 10 minutes, or until the vegetables are tender.

PER SERVING: ———————
CALORIES: **101**
FAT: **9g**
PROTEIN: **1.3g**

TOTAL CARBS: **4.6g**
FIBER: **1.5g**
NET CARBS: **3.1g**

ROASTED GARLIC AND CHIVE CAULIFLOWER PUREE

NET CARBS 3.9g

MAKES: 8 servings · **PREP TIME:** 15 minutes · **COOK TIME:** 30 minutes

I've tried a lot of different cauliflower mash and puree recipes in the fifteen years I've been living a low-carb lifestyle, and I can honestly tell you that I think I have finally figured out the perfect way to cook the cauliflower so that it more closely resembles mashed potatoes: oven roasting! It gives the cauliflower a greater depth of flavor. No more watery cauliflower mush masquerading as potatoes.

INGREDIENTS

- 1 large head cauliflower
- 6 cloves garlic, peeled
- 2 tablespoons avocado oil or olive oil
- Sea salt and ground black pepper
- ½ cup mayonnaise, store-bought or homemade (page 386)
- ½ cup unsweetened almond or coconut milk
- 2 tablespoons chopped fresh chives, plus more for garnish
- Garlic and Herb–Infused Olive Oil (page 365), for garnish (optional)

SPECIAL EQUIPMENT:

Food processor

DIRECTIONS

1. Preheat the oven to 425°F.

2. Core the head of cauliflower and cut it into florets. Spread the florets and the garlic cloves in a single layer across a rimmed baking sheet. Drizzle the oil over the top, toss to coat, and sprinkle generously with salt and pepper.

3. Roast for 25 to 30 minutes, until the cauliflower and garlic are tender and golden brown.

4. Put the roasted cauliflower and garlic, mayonnaise, almond milk, and chives in a food processor. Pulse until smooth and fluffy. Taste and add more salt and pepper, if desired.

5. Drizzle the puree with the infused olive oil before serving, if desired.

PER SERVING: ───────────
CALORIES: **153**   TOTAL CARBS: **6.1g**
FAT: **14g**   FIBER: **2.2g**
PROTEIN: **2.3g**   NET CARBS: **3.9g**

GREEN BEANS WITH TOASTED HAZELNUTS AND DRIED CRANBERRIES

NET CARBS 6g

MAKES: 6 servings · PREP TIME: 10 minutes · COOK TIME: 20 minutes

This is one of my favorite side dishes to prepare around the holidays. If you end up adding this dish to your keto holiday feast, you can blanch the green beans ahead of time and store them in the refrigerator until you are ready for them. Doing so will cut your hands-on prep time in half on the day of the feast.

INGREDIENTS

- ½ cup raw hazelnuts
- 1½ pounds fresh green beans, trimmed
- 2 tablespoons avocado oil or olive oil
- 3 cloves garlic, minced
- ½ cup sugar-free dried cranberries, store-bought or homemade (page 158)
- Sea salt and ground black pepper

DIRECTIONS

1. Preheat the oven to 350°F.

2. Lay the hazelnuts in a single layer across a rimmed baking sheet. Bake for 15 minutes. Remove the skins (see tip) and roughly chop the nuts.

3. Bring a large pot of water to a boil. Add the green beans and cook for 4 minutes. Drain the boiling water and fill the pot with ice water, covering the beans. This will shock the beans and stop the cooking process.

4. Drain the beans, pat dry, and set aside.

5. Heat the oil in a large skillet over medium heat. Add the garlic and blanched green beans and cook for 5 minutes, or until the beans are heated through.

6. Toss in the dried cranberries and toasted hazelnuts and season with salt and pepper to taste.

tip: To get the hazelnut skins off, after removing the nuts from the oven, wrap them in a kitchen towel and allow them to steam for 1 minute. Then rub the nuts against each other in the towel, and the skins will fall away. They may not come off entirely, but this is fine.

PER SERVING:
CALORIES: 139   TOTAL CARBS: 10g
FAT: 19.7g   FIBER: 4g
PROTEIN: 3.6g   NET CARBS: 6g

"GOES WITH EVERYTHING" GARLICKY CAULIFLOWER RICE

NET CARBS 4.5g

MAKES: 6 servings (1 cup per serving) · PREP TIME: 10 minutes · COOK TIME: 25 minutes

This is one of those side dishes that truly goes great with just about anything. Chicken? Check! Beef? Check! Seafood? Check! The flavors from the onion and garlic make this the perfect stand-alone side dish, but you can jazz it up in a variety of ways. Kick it up a notch by adding some Roasted Red Pepper Aioli (page 390), or give it a delightful creaminess by mixing in some Dairy-Free Alfredo Sauce (page 380). The possibilities really are endless.

INGREDIENTS

- 2 tablespoons avocado oil or olive oil
- 1 small onion, chopped (about ½ cup)
- 4 cloves garlic, minced
- 6 cups riced cauliflower
- 1½ teaspoons sea salt, or more to taste
- ¼ teaspoon ground black pepper
- ½ cup chicken stock or bone broth (page 370)
- 2 tablespoons chopped fresh flat-leaf parsley, for garnish

DIRECTIONS

1. Heat the oil in a large skillet over medium heat. Add the onion and garlic and sauté until the onion is translucent and the garlic is fragrant.

2. Add the riced cauliflower, salt, and pepper. Sauté until the cauliflower is tender, about 10 minutes.

3. Add the chicken stock and cook, stirring often, for an additional 10 minutes, or until all the stock has evaporated and the rice is tender but not mushy. Taste and add more salt, if desired.

4. Garnish with parsley before serving.

PER SERVING:
CALORIES: **93**   TOTAL CARBS: **7.8g**
FAT: **6g**   FIBER: **3.3g**
PROTEIN: **3.9g**   NET CARBS: **4.5g**

CHARRED LEMON PEPPER BROCCOLINI

MAKES: 4 servings · **PREP TIME:** 5 minutes · **COOK TIME:** 10 minutes

Broccoli was the one vegetable that I loved as a child. My parents never had to force me to eat it because it was always the first thing gone from my plate. However, it wasn't until I was much older that I realized broccoli isn't in fact supposed to be cooked until it is mushy. Broccoli is still my favorite vegetable, but now I serve it cooked perfectly crisp-tender. Broccolini is a cross between broccoli and Chinese broccoli. It has a mildly sweet, earthy taste. This charred broccolini has a deliciously smoky flavor that pairs perfectly with the fresh lemon.

INGREDIENTS

- 1 pound broccolini
- 2 tablespoons avocado oil, divided
- 2 tablespoons grated lemon zest
- Juice of 1 lemon
- 1 teaspoon sea salt
- 1 teaspoon ground black pepper
- ½ teaspoon garlic powder
- 1 lemon, halved

DIRECTIONS

1. Put the broccolini in a large shallow bowl.

2. Put 1 tablespoon of the avocado oil, the lemon zest, lemon juice, salt, pepper, and garlic powder in a small bowl. Mix to combine, then pour the mixture over the broccolini and toss to coat evenly.

3. Heat the remaining tablespoon of oil in a large cast-iron or other skillet over medium-high heat. Once hot, add the broccolini and cook until it is charred and crisp-tender, tossing every 20 seconds to keep it from burning.

4. Plate the broccolini and pour any remaining pan juices over the top.

5. Put the lemon halves cut side down in the hot pan and char just slightly. Serve alongside the broccolini.

> *tip: Because you are charring this broccolini over high heat, it will smoke quite a bit. Be sure to turn your vent fan on before cooking. Alternatively, you can roast the broccolini on a broiler pan in a 475°F oven until it has a nice char and is crisp-tender.*

PER SERVING:

CALORIES: **107**	TOTAL CARBS: **8.3g**
FAT: **7g**	FIBER: **5.7g**
PROTEIN: **4.2g**	NET CARBS: **2.5g**

OVEN-ROASTED VEGETABLES

NET CARBS 5.2g

MAKES: 10 servings · **PREP TIME:** 15 minutes · **COOK TIME:** 35 minutes

A perfectly roasted tray of mixed vegetables is one of my favorite things to make for weekly meal prep because the vegetables go well with just about anything. Pair them with your favorite protein for dinner or serve them up with some yolky fried eggs and crispy bacon for breakfast. And before you go saying, "Whoa, that is way too many carbs," I can assure you that it was never my love of roasted vegetables that contributed to my weight struggles over the years. I can honestly tell you that I've never uttered the words, "I'm overweight because I love broccoli so much." While a low-carb, keto approach works wonders for weight loss and wellness, it shouldn't come at the demonization of incredibly healthy foods like fresh vegetables.

INGREDIENTS

- 1 medium red bell pepper, seeded and cut into large chunks
- 1 medium orange bell pepper, seeded and cut into large chunks
- 1 medium yellow bell pepper, seeded and cut into large chunks
- 1 medium zucchini, sliced lengthwise and cut into half moons
- 10 ounces broccoli florets
- 10 ounces cauliflower florets
- 8 ounces cremini mushrooms, halved (quartered if large)
- ½ small red onion, cut into large chunks
- ¼ cup avocado oil
- 1½ teaspoons sea salt
- 1½ teaspoons garlic powder
- 1 teaspoon onion powder
- 1 teaspoon dried basil
- 1 teaspoon dried oregano leaves

- 1 teaspoon dried rosemary leaves
- ½ teaspoon dried thyme leaves
- ½ teaspoon ground black pepper

DIRECTIONS

1. Preheat the oven to 425°F.

2. Spread the vegetables in a single layer across a rimmed baking sheet. If your baking sheet is not large enough, divide the vegetables between two baking sheets and cook on separate racks in the oven, rotating the trays halfway through.

3. In a small mixing bowl, whisk the avocado oil, salt, garlic powder, onion powder, basil, oregano, rosemary, thyme, and black pepper until combined. Drizzle the oil mixture evenly over the vegetables.

4. Roast for 20 minutes, toss the vegetables gently, and then roast for an additional 15 minutes, or until the vegetables are slightly charred and perfectly tender.

> *tip:* *If you have a bottle of the Garlic and Herb–Infused Olive Oil (page 365) on hand, it is perfect for this recipe. Simply replace the oil and blend of seasonings listed in the recipe with ¼ cup of the infused oil.*

PER SERVING:

CALORIES: **89**	TOTAL CARBS: **7.9g**
FAT: **5.8g**	FIBER: **2.7g**
PROTEIN: **2.8g**	NET CARBS: **5.2g**

DRUNKEN MUSHROOMS WITH CARAMELIZED ONIONS

NET CARBS 4.5g

MAKES: 6 servings · **PREP TIME:** 10 minutes · **COOK TIME:** 30 minutes

Every time I make this recipe, it barely makes it out of the pan and into a serving dish because everyone has already plunged their forks into it while the pan is still on the stovetop. This is my favorite side dish to pile on my plate with a perfectly cooked, juicy medium-rare steak.

INGREDIENTS

- 1 tablespoon avocado oil or olive oil
- 1 medium onion, thinly sliced
- Sea salt and ground black pepper
- ¼ cup beef stock or bone broth (page 370)
- 1 pound cremini mushrooms, halved
- 5 cloves garlic, thinly sliced
- 1 bay leaf
- Pinch of red pepper flakes
- ¼ cup cooking sherry
- 2 tablespoons red wine vinegar
- Chopped fresh flat-leaf parsley, for garnish (optional)

DIRECTIONS

1. Heat the oil in a large skillet over medium heat. When the oil is hot, add the onion to the pan. Sprinkle generously with salt and pepper.

2. Cook, stirring every so often, until the onion is soft and nicely browned, about 20 minutes.

3. Add the stock to the skillet to deglaze the pan. Use a rubber spatula to scrape up and mix in any browned bits from the bottom of the pan.

4. Add the mushrooms, garlic, bay leaf, red pepper flakes, cooking sherry, and vinegar. Cook, tossing often, until the mushrooms are browned and the liquid has reduced, about 10 minutes.

5. Garnish with chopped parsley before serving, if desired.

> *tip*: This dish is also amazing with some chopped crispy bacon mixed in.

PER SERVING:

CALORIES: **52**	TOTAL CARBS: **5.7g**
FAT: **2.4g**	FIBER: **1.1g**
PROTEIN: **3.2g**	NET CARBS: **4.5g**

LEMON PESTO CAULIFLOWER RICE WITH ARTICHOKES

MAKES: 8 servings (1 cup per serving) · **PREP TIME:** 15 minutes · **COOK TIME:** 30 minutes

This recipe is reminiscent of a risotto dish that I ate while my husband and I were in Venice, Italy, a few years ago. I'm always amazed at how such simple ingredients can pack so much flavor. This is one of my favorite dishes to add to our weekly meal prep rotation because it goes well with just about any protein. My favorite foods to pair it with are chicken and seafood.

INGREDIENTS

- 2 tablespoons avocado oil or olive oil
- 1 small onion, diced (about ½ cup)
- 5 cloves garlic, minced
- 1 teaspoon sea salt
- ¼ teaspoon ground black pepper
- 6 cups riced cauliflower
- 1 tablespoon grated lemon zest
- 2 tablespoons fresh lemon juice
- 2 tablespoons chopped fresh flat-leaf parsley
- 1 cup chicken stock or bone broth (page 370)
- 1 cup chopped canned artichoke hearts
- 3 tablespoons dairy-free pesto, store-bought or homemade (page 395)

DIRECTIONS

1. Heat the oil in a large skillet over medium heat. Add the onion, garlic, salt, and pepper and sauté until the onion is translucent and the garlic is fragrant.

2. Add the riced cauliflower, lemon zest, and lemon juice. Sauté until the cauliflower is tender, about 10 minutes.

3. Add the chicken stock, artichoke hearts, and pesto and cook, stirring often, for an additional 15 minutes, or until all the stock has evaporated and the rice is tender but not mushy.

> *Tips*: *If you aren't avoiding dairy, this dish is fantastic with Parmesan cheese or even a creamy goat cheese. For those of you who can't have dairy but want to add a cheesy flavor to this dish, add 2 tablespoons of nutritional yeast.*
>
> *For this recipe and other recipes throughout the book that call for riced cauliflower, you are in luck: most grocery stores now carry fresh and frozen pre-riced cauliflower.*

PER SERVING:
CALORIES: **111**   TOTAL CARBS: **7.9g**
FAT: **8.2g**   FIBER: **3.2g**
PROTEIN: **3.5g**   NET CARBS: **4.7g**

MAPLE BACON BRUSSELS SPROUTS

NET CARBS
5.8g

MAKES: 6 servings · **PREP TIME:** 15 minutes · **COOK TIME:** 30 minutes

Maple syrup with Brussels sprouts? Now that's an idea I can get behind. These are salty and sweet and will even have your kids asking for seconds.

INGREDIENTS

- 2 pounds Brussels sprouts, trimmed and halved
- 8 slices bacon, chopped
- ¼ cup sugar-free maple syrup
- 2 tablespoons avocado oil or olive oil
- ½ teaspoon sea salt
- ½ teaspoon ground black pepper

DIRECTIONS

1. Preheat the oven to 400°F.

2. Put all the ingredients in a large mixing bowl and toss to coat.

3. Arrange everything in a single layer across a rimmed baking sheet. Bake for 15 minutes, toss, and then bake for an additional 10 to 15 minutes, until the Brussels sprouts are caramelized and tender and the bacon is crispy.

tip: If you do not have sugar-free maple syrup on hand, you can also use a maple smoked bacon.

PER SERVING:
CALORIES: **202**   FIBER: **4.3g**
FAT: **15g**   NET CARBS: **5.8g**
PROTEIN: **9.3g**   ERYTHRITOL: **4g**
TOTAL CARBS: **10.1g**

OVEN-ROASTED CABBAGE STEAKS

NET CARBS 3.8g

MAKES: 6 servings (1 slice per serving)
PREP TIME: 10 minutes · COOK TIME: 45 minutes

Not only are these roasted cabbage steaks a good side dish on their own, but they are amazing with Barbecue Pulled Pork (page 226) or Slow Cooker Crispy Pork Carnitas (page 266) served on top.

INGREDIENTS

- 1 medium head green cabbage (about 2 pounds)
- ¼ cup avocado oil or olive oil
- 1 teaspoon garlic powder
- 1 teaspoon onion powder
- 1 teaspoon fennel seeds
- 1 teaspoon sea salt
- ½ teaspoon ground black pepper

DIRECTIONS

1. Put an oven rack in the middle position. Preheat the oven to 400°F.

2. Cut the cabbage into six equal slices (about 1 inch thick) from the top through the stem on the bottom.

3. Lay the cabbage slices in a single layer across a rimmed baking sheet. Brush the slices with the oil.

4. In a small bowl, combine the garlic powder, onion powder, fennel seeds, salt, and pepper. Sprinkle the seasoning over the slices.

5. Bake for 45 minutes, flipping halfway through, or until the cabbage is golden brown and the leaves are slightly charred on the edges.

> *tip*: This dish is amazing brushed with Lemon Basil Vinaigrette (page 377) before serving.

PER SERVING:

CALORIES: **105**	TOTAL CARBS: **6.6g**
FAT: **9.2g**	FIBER: **2.7g**
PROTEIN: **1.2g**	NET CARBS: **3.8g**

ROASTED ASPARAGUS WITH PANCETTA

NET CARBS
2.8g

MAKES: 6 servings · **PREP TIME:** 10 minutes · **COOK TIME:** 10 minutes

In case you aren't familiar with pancetta, it is just Italian bacon. So if you can't find it at your local grocery store, you can simply substitute regular bacon. This dish will still taste fantastic. I love to serve this asparagus with Bacon Fat Hollandaise. The bright and fresh citrusy flavor of hollandaise complements the salty fat of the pancetta perfectly, making this a deliciously balanced side dish. If you don't have time to make the hollandaise, a squeeze of lemon juice over the top before serving will do the job.

INGREDIENTS

- 2 large bunches asparagus (about 50 spears), trimmed
- 2 tablespoons avocado oil or olive oil
- 1 tablespoon balsamic vinegar
- ½ teaspoon sea salt
- ¼ teaspoon ground black pepper
- Pinch of red pepper flakes
- 4 ounces pancetta, diced
- Bacon Fat Hollandaise (page 372), for serving (optional)

DIRECTIONS

1. Preheat the oven to broil-high.

2. Lay the asparagus in a single layer across a broiling pan. Drizzle with the oil and balsamic vinegar. Sprinkle with the salt, black pepper, and red pepper flakes. Top the asparagus with the pancetta.

3. Broil for 8 to 10 minutes, until the asparagus is tender and the pancetta is crispy.

4. Serve with hollandaise, if desired.

PER SERVING:

CALORIES: **132**   TOTAL CARBS: **5.6g**
FAT: **10.1g**   FIBER: **2.8g**
PROTEIN: **6.3g**   NET CARBS: **2.8g**

SALT AND VINEGAR ROASTED RADISHES AND GREEN BEANS

NET CARBS
5.3g

MAKES: 6 servings · PREP TIME: 15 minutes · COOK TIME: 25 minutes

I bet the first thing that comes to mind when you see the words *salt* and *vinegar* together is potato chips. I know it is for me. I was never into that whole salt and vinegar chip craze. It wasn't until just a few years ago that I realized just how much I love the tart, acidic flavor of vinegar paired with a generous amount of salt. Those flavors come together perfectly in these roasted radishes and green beans.

INGREDIENTS

- 1½ pounds radishes (without greens), halved (quartered if large)
- 1 pound fresh green beans, cleaned and trimmed
- 2 tablespoons avocado oil
- 3 tablespoons malt vinegar, divided
- 1½ teaspoons Maldon sea salt flakes, divided
- ½ teaspoon ground black pepper

DIRECTIONS

1. Preheat the oven to 400°F.

2. Put the radishes, green beans, avocado oil, 2 tablespoons of the vinegar, 1 teaspoon of the salt, and the pepper in a large mixing bowl and toss to coat.

3. Spread the vegetables in a single layer across a rimmed baking sheet.

4. Roast for 25 minutes, tossing halfway through, or until the vegetables are tender.

5. Remove from the oven. Drizzle with the remaining vinegar and sprinkle with the remaining salt before serving.

> *tip: For an even easier version of this recipe, pick up a jar of malt salt and use that instead of the vinegar and sea salt flakes, seasoning the vegetables to your liking.*

PER SERVING:
CALORIES: **83**
FAT: **4.9g**
PROTEIN: **2.2g**
TOTAL CARBS: **9.1g**
FIBER: **3.9g**
NET CARBS: **5.3g**

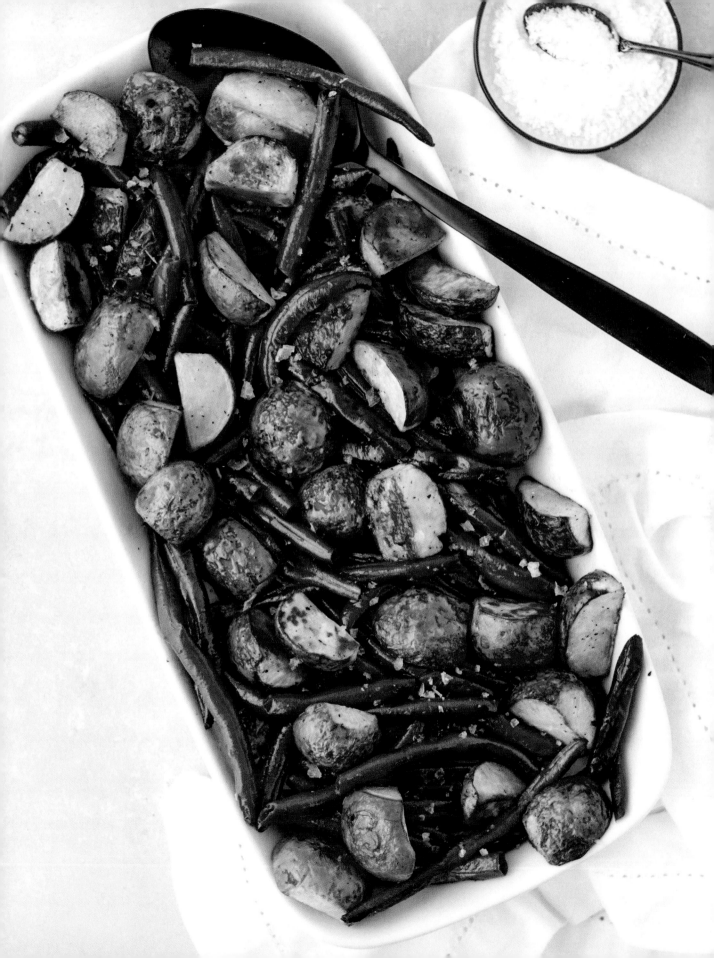

Sweet Treats

FRUIT AND NUT CHOCOLATES

NET CARBS 2.9g

MAKES: 10 chocolates (1 per serving) · PREP TIME: 10 minutes · COOK TIME: 5 minutes

I love this recipe because it is like combining a sweet treat with a trail mix. With so many different textures and flavors, this dessert has a little something for everyone.

INGREDIENTS

- 1 cup sugar-free dark chocolate chips
- 2 tablespoons coconut oil
- 1 tablespoon sugar-free dried cranberries, store-bought or homemade (page 158)
- 1 tablespoon pepitas (pumpkin seeds)
- 1 tablespoon shelled pistachio pieces
- 1 tablespoon slivered almonds
- 1 teaspoon unsweetened coconut flakes
- 2 teaspoons hulled hemp seeds
- 1 teaspoon chia seeds

DIRECTIONS

1. Line a rimmed baking sheet with parchment paper or a silicone baking mat.

2. In a microwave-safe bowl, microwave the chocolate chips and coconut oil on 50% power until the chocolate is melted. Alternatively, the chocolate can be melted in a double boiler. (See tip below.) Use a rubber spatula to mix until smooth. Let cool just slightly before using.

3. Drop 10 large spoonfuls of the melted chocolate onto the prepared baking sheet. Be sure to space them out enough that they do not run together.

4. Top each one with dried cranberries, pepitas, pistachios, almonds, coconut, hemp seeds, and chia seeds.

5. Refrigerate until solid. Store in an airtight container in the refrigerator for up to 3 weeks. Alternatively, you can store them in the freezer.

tip: Set up a double boiler by placing a heatproof bowl on top of a saucepan filled with about 1 inch of water. Make sure that the bowl is not touching the water and is suspended above the waterline by the rim of the pan.

PER SERVING: ─────────

CALORIES: **120**	TOTAL CARBS: **8.6g**
FAT: **10g**	FIBER: **5.7g**
PROTEIN: **2.2g**	NET CARBS: **2.9g**

BEGNETS

NET CARBS 1.1g

🍅 🌿 🕐 **MAKES:** 16 beignets (2 per serving) · **PREP TIME:** 15 minutes · **COOK TIME:** 30 minutes

If you have followed me on social media over the years, then you likely have seen my family's many trips to New Orleans. It is one of our favorite places in the world, and we go every year. No trip to NOLA would be complete without popping into Café du Monde for beignets and chicory coffee. This is a special treat and something we never deprive ourselves of. However, we always come home wishing that we could somehow work beignets into our keto lifestyle. I am happy to say that after lots of trial and error and countless batches, I have finally created a delicious low-carb beignet recipe that we can enjoy at home between trips to the city. I hope you enjoy them as much as we do.

INGREDIENTS

- 1¼ cups blanched almond flour
- ¼ cup plus 2 teaspoons psyllium husk powder
- 2 tablespoons powdered erythritol, plus more for dusting
- 2 teaspoons baking powder
- ½ teaspoon sea salt
- 3 large egg whites
- 2 teaspoons apple cider vinegar
- 1 cup hot water
- Oil, for frying

DIRECTIONS

1. Put an oven rack in the lower third position. Preheat the oven to 350°F. Line a cookie sheet with parchment paper or a silicone baking mat.

2. In a large mixing bowl, mix the almond flour, psyllium husk powder, erythritol, baking powder, and salt until well combined and there are no visible clumps.

3. Add the vinegar and eggs to the bowl and, using a rubber spatula, continue to mix while slowly adding the hot water. You want to mix just enough that the ingredients are well combined, but that the dough is not overmixed.

4. Transfer the dough to the prepared baking sheet and, using your hands, shape it into an 8-inch square. Cut the dough into 16 equal squares, then pull them apart and spread them out across the baking sheet. Bake for 20 minutes, or until puffed and golden brown.

5. Heat 1 to 2 inches of oil in a large 4-inch-deep (or deeper) skillet or Dutch oven over medium-high heat. When the oil is hot (370°F) and begins to bubble slightly, gently drop the par-cooked dough, in batches, into the oil and fry until golden brown and crispy, 2 to 3 minutes on each side.

6. Remove the beignets from the oil and put them on paper towels to absorb the excess oil. Dust with powdered erythritol while still hot.

tips: Some brands of psyllium husk powder will cause these beignets to turn purple. I recommend using Now Foods brand.

To get the temperature of the oil exactly where you need it, I recommend using a candy thermometer. Correct temperature is crucial to the success of this recipe.

PER SERVING:
CALORIES: **58**   FIBER: **4.5g**
FAT: **4.2g**   NET CARBS: **1.1g**
PROTEIN: **3.3g**   ERYTHRITOL: **1.5g**
TOTAL CARBS: **5.6g**

CHOCOLATE PEANUT BUTTER COCONUT FAT BOMBS

NET CARBS 3.5g

MAKES: 24 fat bombs (1 per serving) · **PREP TIME:** 10 minutes · **COOK TIME:** 15 minutes

These are the perfect sweet treats, with the added boost of healthy fats. If you are not a fan of coconut, you can top them with chopped nuts, chocolate chips, peanut butter, or even some Sugar-Free Dried Cranberries (page 158).

INGREDIENTS

- 6 ounces unsweetened baking chocolate
- ½ cup coconut butter
- ½ cup reduced-sugar creamy peanut butter
- 1½ teaspoons pure vanilla extract
- ½ cup powdered erythritol
- 1 cup unsweetened shredded coconut

SPECIAL EQUIPMENT:

24-well silicone mini muffin pan or candy molds

DIRECTIONS

1. Set up a double boiler by placing a heatproof bowl on top of a saucepan filled with about 1 inch of water. Make sure that the bowl is not touching the water and is suspended above the waterline by the rim of the pan. Bring the water to a simmer.

2. Put the chocolate, coconut butter, and peanut butter in the bowl. Whisk until the mixture is melted and smooth.

3. Mix in the vanilla extract and erythritol. Remove the bowl from the pan.

4. Divide the chocolate mixture evenly among the wells of a silicone mini muffin pan, filling them nearly to the top. Refrigerate until the tops have just begun to set, about 10 minutes.

5. Sprinkle the shredded coconut over the fat bombs and return the pan to the fridge until they are completely solid. Store in an airtight container in the refrigerator for up to a month.

> *tips: Coconut butter differs from coconut oil in that it includes all the fat, fiber, and nutrients from the coconut flesh. It is ground into a spreadable paste and can be found in large jars and as meltable wafers.*
>
> *This recipe is marked as nut-free because, technically speaking, a peanut is a legume, not a nut. However, if you have a peanut allergy, feel free to substitute almond butter for the peanut butter.*

PER SERVING:

CALORIES: **105** FIBER: **2.6g**
FAT: **8.6g** NET CARBS: **3.5g**
PROTEIN: **3g** ERYTHRITOL: **4g**
TOTAL CARBS: **6.1g**

FAT-BOOSTED
CHOCOLATE NUT BUTTER

NET CARBS
3.5g

🥚 🍅 🌿 ⏱ **MAKES:** 2 cups (2 tablespoons per serving) · **PREP TIME:** 15 minutes

Warning: This nut butter is highly addictive. Proceed with caution. I love trying out different flavored nut butters, but they are always so expensive and they rarely live up to the hype. Once I decided to start making my own, I never bought another overpriced designer nut butter again. The thing I love most about this recipe is that you can make it with any type of nut that you prefer, and it turns out perfect every time. Another of my favorite combinations is macadamia nuts and cashews.

INGREDIENTS

- 1 cup raw almonds
- 1 cup raw cashews
- 1 scoop dairy-free keto vanilla protein powder
- ¼ cup MCT oil or melted coconut oil
- 3 tablespoons granular erythritol
- 2 tablespoons unsweetened cocoa powder
- ¼ teaspoon sea salt

SPECIAL EQUIPMENT:

Food processor or high-powered blender

DIRECTIONS

1. Put the almonds and cashews in a food processor with a large capacity and a strong motor. Let the food processor run for 2 to 3 minutes. As the mixture starts to build up on the side of the bowl, scrape it down with a rubber spatula.

2. To the food processor, add the protein powder, oil, erythritol, cocoa powder, and salt. Continue processing for 10 minutes, or until the nut butter has reached your desired consistency. The time can vary greatly depending on the power of your food processor. Just keep processing and it will get there, I promise. Store in the refrigerator for up to a month.

> *tip*: If you have a high-powered blender like a Vitamix or a Blendtec, this can also be made in a blender, following the same steps.

PER SERVING: ─────────────
CALORIES: **140**   FIBER: **1.7g**
FAT: **12.1g**   NET CARBS: **3.5g**
PROTEIN: **4.8g**   ERYTHRITOL: **2.3g**
TOTAL CARBS: **5.2g**

CHEWY DOUBLE CHOCOLATE CHIP COOKIES

NET CARBS 1.4g

MAKES: 18 cookies (1 per serving) · PREP TIME: 15 minutes · COOK TIME: 10 minutes

I'm pretty sure this will become your all-time favorite low-carb cookie recipe. Think low-carb brownie meets the perfect keto cookie. It's a marriage made in chocolate heaven.

INGREDIENTS

- 1 cup natural creamy almond butter
- ⅔ cup powdered erythritol
- 2 tablespoons unsweetened cocoa powder
- 2 tablespoons peanut butter powder
- 2 large eggs
- 2 tablespoons water
- 1 tablespoon melted coconut oil
- 1½ teaspoons pure vanilla extract
- 1 teaspoon baking soda
- ¼ cup sugar-free dark chocolate chips

DIRECTIONS

1. Preheat the oven to 350°F. Line a cookie sheet with parchment paper or a silicone baking mat.

2. Put the almond butter, erythritol, cocoa powder, peanut butter powder, eggs, water, coconut oil, vanilla extract, and baking soda in a large mixing bowl. Using an electric hand mixer, mix until the ingredients are well combined. The dough will be very thick. Fold in the chocolate chips.

3. Form the cookie dough into eighteen 1½-inch balls. Put the cookie dough balls on the prepared baking sheet, spacing them about 2 inches apart. Bake for 8 to 11 minutes, until the tops are golden brown and the edges are crispy (begin checking on them at the 8-minute mark).

4. Remove from the oven and place the cookie sheet on a cooling rack to allow the cookies to cool before eating. Store leftovers in an airtight container for up to a week. Alternatively, you can freeze them for up to 4 months.

> *tip*: I like to pull the cookies out of the oven at the 8-minute mark and lightly press on them to flatten them. This makes for a deliciously fudgy, brownie-like texture.

PER SERVING:
CALORIES: **115**   FIBER: **2.4g**
FAT: **10g**   NET CARBS: **1.4g**
PROTEIN: **4g**   ERYTHRITOL: **6.7g**
TOTAL CARBS: **3.8g**

JUMBO CHOCOLATE PEANUT BUTTER CUPS

NET CARBS
5.1g

MAKES: 12 peanut butter cups (1 per serving)
PREP TIME: 20 minutes, plus time to refrigerate · **COOK TIME:** 5 minutes

I'm not sure a greater pairing ever existed than chocolate and peanut butter. It is the stuff keto dreams are made of. Speaking of dreams, these jumbo peanut butter cups will have you dreaming about them after the first delicious bite. And when I say jumbo, I mean JUMBO. These are not your average-sized peanut butter cups. They are a super indulgent treat that just might leave you saying, "I can't possibly finish this." You can also make these in a silicone mini muffin pan to yield 24 peanut butter cups of a more typical size. This will lower the carb count even further.

INGREDIENTS

- 2 cups sugar-free dark chocolate chips
- ¼ cup coconut oil
- ¾ cup reduced-sugar creamy peanut butter

SPECIAL EQUIPMENT:

12-well standard-sized silicone muffin pan, or 12 silicone or paper muffin liners, or 1 candy mold

DIRECTIONS

1. Set a 12-well standard-sized silicone muffin pan or 12 silicone muffin liners on a tray or rimmed baking sheet. You can also use a candy mold or paper muffin liners.

2. Put the chocolate chips and coconut oil in a microwave-safe bowl and microwave on 50% power until the chocolate is melted. Alternatively, the chocolate can be melted in a double boiler (see tip below). Use a rubber spatula to mix until smooth. Let cool just slightly before using.

3. Pour 1½ tablespoons of the melted chocolate into each muffin well. Transfer the tray to the refrigerator to allow the chocolate to harden.

4. When the chocolate has solidified, remove the tray from the refrigerator and spoon 1 tablespoon of peanut butter onto the center of each piece of chocolate.

5. Pour an additional 1½ tablespoons of the melted chocolate over the peanut butter in each well. It may be necessary to reheat the chocolate so that it is pourable again.

6. Refrigerate the peanut butter cups until solid. Store in an airtight container in the refrigerator for up to 3 weeks. Alternatively, you can store them in the freezer.

> *tips: Set up a double boiler by placing a heatproof bowl on top of a saucepan filled with about 1 inch of water. Make sure that the bowl is not touching the water and is suspended above the waterline by the rim of the pan.*
>
> *This recipe is marked as nut-free because, technically speaking, a peanut is a legume, not a nut. However, if you have a peanut allergy, feel free to substitute almond butter for the peanut butter.*

PER SERVING:

CALORIES: **123**	TOTAL CARBS: **9.9g**
FAT: **9.3g**	FIBER: **4.7g**
PROTEIN: **2.7g**	NET CARBS: **5.1g**

LEMON BLUEBERRY ACCIDENTS

NET CARBS 3.2g

MAKES: 8 muffins (1 per serving) · **PREP TIME:** 10 minutes · **COOK TIME:** 20 minutes

I named this dessert Lemon Blueberry Accidents because I set out to make a perfectly light and moist low-carb muffin, but that is not what I ended up with. I thought the entire recipe was a fail until I tasted them. One bite and I was in love! It turned out to be the happiest accident I have ever had in the kitchen. Think muffin meets bread pudding. I hope you enjoy these happy accidents as much as we do.

INGREDIENTS

- 1 cup blanched almond flour
- ¼ cup plus 2 tablespoons coconut flour
- ¾ cup granular erythritol
- 2 teaspoons baking powder
- ¼ teaspoon sea salt
- 3 large eggs
- ⅓ cup water
- 1½ teaspoons pure lemon extract
- 1½ teaspoons pure vanilla extract
- 1 cup frozen blueberries

FOR THE GLAZE:

- ¼ cup plus 2 tablespoons powdered erythritol
- 1 tablespoon plus 1½ teaspoons fresh lemon juice

DIRECTIONS

1. Preheat the oven to 350°F. Lightly oil 8 wells of a standard-sized muffin pan. Alternatively, you can line the wells with silicone or paper muffin liners or use a standard-sized silicone muffin pan.

2. Put all the dry ingredients in a large bowl and mix to combine.

3. In a separate bowl, whisk the eggs, water, and extracts until the ingredients are well incorporated.

4. Pour the wet ingredients into the dry ingredients, using a rubber spatula to mix as you pour. Continue mixing until the ingredients are well incorporated.

5. Gently fold in the blueberries.

6. Divide the mixture among the prepared wells of the muffin pan, filling each about three-quarters of the way full.

7. Bake for 20 minutes, or until the tops are golden brown and the centers are set.

8. While the accidents are baking, make the glaze: Put the erythritol and lemon juice in a small bowl and mix until there are no visible clumps of sweetener.

9. When the accidents are done baking, place the pan on a cooling rack and allow to cool for 10 minutes before removing the accidents from the pan. Drizzle the glaze over the tops before serving. Store in the refrigerator for up to a week.

PER SERVING:

CALORIES: **131**   FIBER: **2.6g**
FAT: **9.3g**   NET CARBS: **3.2g**
PROTEIN: **6.2g**   ERYTHRITOL: **18g**
TOTAL CARBS: **5.8g**

FLOURLESS CHOCOLATE LAVA CAKES

NET CARBS 3.1g

MAKES: 2 cakes (1 per serving) · **PREP TIME:** 5 minutes · **COOK TIME:** 15 minutes

These chocolate lava cakes are my go-to treat for when that raging sweet tooth strikes. With simple ingredients and only five minutes of hands-on prep time, I always have a healthier option at my fingertips—so much better than diving face-first into a sugary, gluten-filled cake.

INGREDIENTS

- ¼ cup unsweetened cocoa powder
- ¼ cup granular erythritol
- 2 large eggs
- 2 tablespoons unsweetened coconut milk
- 1 teaspoon pure vanilla extract
- ½ teaspoon baking powder
- 2 tablespoons reduced-sugar creamy peanut butter, warmed, for drizzling (optional)

DIRECTIONS

1. Preheat the oven to 350°F. Lightly grease two 6-ounce ramekins. Put the ramekins on a rimmed baking sheet.

2. Put all the ingredients, except the peanut butter, in a mixing bowl and whisk until smooth. Divide the mixture evenly between the ramekins.

3. Bake for 15 minutes, or until the edges are set and the centers are still jiggly, but not raw.

4. Remove from the oven and drizzle with the warmed peanut butter before serving, if desired.

tips: *To make a peanut butter drizzle, heat the peanut butter in the microwave for 20 seconds at a time until it is warm enough to drizzle over the cakes.*

Although they are much better when baked in the oven, these cakes can also be cooked in the microwave. Cook them one at a time for 1 minute each.

PER SERVING:
CALORIES: **131**   FIBER: **4g**
FAT: **9.4g**   NET CARBS: **3.1g**
PROTEIN: **8.7g**   ERYTHRITOL: **24g**
TOTAL CARBS: **7.1g**

SALTED CARAMEL CHOCOLATE CHIP COOKIES

NET CARBS 1.9g

MAKES: 18 cookies (1 per serving) · **PREP TIME:** 10 minutes · **COOK TIME:** 12 minutes

Have you ever had keto chocolate chip cookies that just got better and better days after you made them? Me neither . . . until I made these. I thought they were great straight off the cookie sheet, scorching my mouth because I refused to let them cool first, but boy, oh boy, they were even more amazing when I grabbed one from the pantry the next day. Rich and chewy, with a texture similar to that of a high-carb cookie made with real flour and conventional sugar. In fact, if I hadn't made them myself and someone else had served me one, I never would have been able to tell that they were low-carb cookies at all.

INGREDIENTS

- 3 cups blanched almond flour
- 1 tablespoon grass-fed gelatin
- 1 teaspoon baking soda
- ½ teaspoon sea salt
- 2 large eggs
- 1 teaspoon caramel extract
- 1 teaspoon pure vanilla extract
- ½ cup sugar-free maple syrup
- ½ cup coconut oil, melted but not hot
- 1 cup sugar-free dark chocolate chips
- Maldon sea salt flakes, for sprinkling

DIRECTIONS

1. Preheat the oven to 375°F. Line a cookie sheet with parchment paper or a silicone baking mat.

2. In a large mixing bowl, whisk together the almond flour, gelatin, baking soda, and salt.

3. Crack the eggs into a medium mixing bowl. Add the extracts and whisk to combine. Add the maple syrup and melted coconut oil to the egg mixture, whisking as you pour.

4. Pour the wet ingredients into the dry ingredients and beat with an electric hand mixer until the ingredients are well incorporated.

5. Using a rubber spatula, fold the chocolate chips into the dough.

6. Using a 2-tablespoon cookie scoop, drop balls of the dough onto the prepared cookie sheet, spacing them about 2 inches apart. Bake for 10 to 12 minutes, until the tops are golden brown and the edges are crispy.

7. Sprinkle with sea salt flakes and let cool for 10 minutes before eating. Store in an airtight container for up to a week.

> *tip: I like to pull these cookies out of the oven at the 10-minute mark and lightly press on them to flatten. This makes for a deliciously dense and chewy cookie.*

PER SERVING:

CALORIES: **189**   FIBER: **2.8g**
FAT: **17g**   NET CARBS: **1.9g**
PROTEIN: **6g**   ERYTHRITOL: **1.3g**
TOTAL CARBS: **4.7g**

VANILLA BEAN CUSTARD

NET CARBS 1.2g

MAKES: 4 servings · PREP TIME: 20 minutes · COOK TIME: 35 minutes, plus 3 hours to refrigerate

This light and delicate custard has maximum vanilla flavor. It is the perfect treat for when your sweet tooth comes calling but you don't want something too heavy.

INGREDIENTS

- 5 large egg yolks
- ⅓ cup granular erythritol
- 1 teaspoon pure vanilla extract
- Pinch of sea salt
- 1 vanilla bean
- 1¾ cups unsweetened almond or coconut milk

DIRECTIONS

1. Preheat the oven to 325°F. Bring a large pot of water to a boil.

2. Put the egg yolks, erythritol, vanilla extract, and salt in a medium mixing bowl and whisk to combine.

3. Split the vanilla bean down the middle and use the tip of a sharp knife to scrape all the vanilla bean paste into a medium saucepan. Add the bean pod and the almond milk to the pan. Bring the milk to a gentle simmer over medium heat.

4. Very slowly whisk the hot almond milk into the egg yolk mixture. Adding the milk too fast or without whisking will leave you with scrambled eggs.

5. Put a fine-mesh sieve over a large bowl and strain the custard into the bowl. Discard the vanilla bean pod.

6. Put four 6-ounce ovenproof baking dishes or ramekins in a large roasting pan that is at least 2 inches deep. Divide the custard evenly among the dishes. Pour boiling water around the baking dishes until it reaches about halfway up the sides.

7. Cover the roasting pan loosely with foil and bake the custard for 30 to 35 minutes, until it is set around the sides but still a little jiggly in the center.

8. Transfer the baking dishes to a cooling rack and allow to cool to room temperature.

9. Cover and refrigerate for a minimum of 3 hours before serving, but preferably 24 hours or more.

PER SERVING: —————————
CALORIES: 83   FIBER: 0.3g
FAT: 6.9g   NET CARBS: 1.2g
PROTEIN: 3.9g   ERYTHRITOL: 15g
TOTAL CARBS: 1.5g

MOCHA CHOCOLATE CHIP MUFFINS

NET CARBS 3.2g

MAKES: 8 muffins (1 per serving) · **PREP TIME:** 10 minutes · **COOK TIME:** 20 minutes

These warm and delicious chocolate muffins taste a lot like cupcakes. But calling them muffins means we can eat them for breakfast, right?

INGREDIENTS

- 1 cup blanched almond flour
- ¼ cup coconut flour
- ¼ cup unsweetened cocoa powder
- ¼ cup granular erythritol
- 2 teaspoons baking powder
- ¼ teaspoon sea salt
- 3 large eggs
- ½ cup unsweetened coconut milk
- 2 teaspoons pure coffee extract
- 1 teaspoon pure vanilla extract
- ¼ cup coconut oil, melted but not hot
- ¼ cup sugar-free dark chocolate chips

DIRECTIONS

1. Preheat the oven to 350°F. Line 8 wells of a standard-sized 12-well muffin pan with paper liners. (Alternatively, use a 12-well standard-sized silicone muffin pan or 8 silicone muffin liners placed on a rimmed baking sheet.)

2. Put the almond flour, coconut flour, cocoa powder, erythritol, baking powder, and salt in a large mixing bowl and whisk to combine.

3. In a separate mixing bowl, whisk the eggs, coconut milk, extracts, and melted coconut oil until well combined.

4. Pour the wet ingredients into the dry ingredients, mixing as you pour. Continue mixing until the ingredients are well incorporated and there are no visible clumps.

5. Using a rubber spatula, fold in the chocolate chips, reserving some to sprinkle on top of the muffins.

6. Spoon the batter into the 8 lined wells of the muffin pan, filling each about three-quarters of the way full. Top with the reserved chocolate chips.

7. Bake for 20 minutes, or until the tops are firm. Set the pan on a cooling rack and allow the muffins to cool in the pan before serving. Store in an airtight container for up to a week.

PER SERVING:
CALORIES: **217**   FIBER: **4.5g**
FAT: **19.1g**   NET CARBS: **3.2g**
PROTEIN: **6.8g**   ERYTHRITOL: **6g**
TOTAL CARBS: **7.7g**

PEANUT BUTTER CHOCOLATE CHIP NO-BAKE GRANOLA SQUARES

NET CARBS 3.1g

MAKES: 25 squares (1 per serving) · **PREP TIME:** 15 minutes, plus 2 hours to refrigerate

These no-bake granola bars are the perfect sweet treat for an added boost of energy during the day. But they are so good, I dare you to try and just eat one!

INGREDIENTS

- 1 cup reduced-sugar creamy peanut butter
- ½ cup sugar-free maple syrup
- 2 cups unsweetened coconut flakes
- ½ cup sugar-free dark chocolate chips
- ¼ cup hulled sunflower seeds
- ¼ cup crushed almonds
- ½ teaspoon sea salt

DIRECTIONS

1. Put the peanut butter and maple syrup in a large bowl and, using a rubber spatula, mix to combine.

2. Combine the coconut flakes, chocolate chips, sunflower seeds, crushed almonds, and sea salt in another large bowl.

3. Pour the nut mixture into the peanut butter mixture and use the spatula to mix until all the ingredients are evenly dispersed and there are no dry patches of coconut flakes.

4. Line a 10-inch square baking pan with parchment paper. Press the mixture into the pan until it forms a nice even layer. Alternatively, you can free-form it by placing the mixture on a parchment paper–lined baking sheet and shaping it by hand into a 10-inch square, approximately ¾ inch tall.

5. Refrigerate for 2 hours before serving. Cut into 25 even squares when ready to serve. Store in an airtight container in the refrigerator for up to 2 weeks.

> *tip:* Switch up this recipe by using any keto-friendly nuts and seeds you prefer. From time to time, I also like to add some Sugar-Free Dried Cranberries (page 158).

PER SERVING:

CALORIES: **123**   FIBER: **2.8g**
FAT: **10.7g**   NET CARBS: **3.1g**
PROTEIN: **3.4g**   ERYTHRITOL: **1g**
TOTAL CARBS: **5.8g**

PUMPKIN SPICE CHOCOLATE CHIP COOKIES

NET CARBS 3g

MAKES: 18 cookies (1 per serving) · PREP TIME: 10 minutes · COOK TIME: 12 minutes

These cookies are soft and chewy and full of fall flavors.

INGREDIENTS

- 3 cups blanched almond flour
- 2 teaspoons pumpkin pie spice, store-bought or homemade (page 396)
- 1 teaspoon baking soda
- ½ teaspoon sea salt
- 2 large eggs
- 1 teaspoon pure vanilla extract
- ½ cup sugar-free maple syrup
- ½ cup coconut oil, melted but not hot
- 1 cup sugar-free dark chocolate chips

DIRECTIONS

1. Preheat the oven to 375°F. Line a cookie sheet with parchment paper or a silicone baking mat.

2. In a large mixing bowl, whisk together the almond flour, pumpkin pie spice, baking soda, and salt.

3. Crack the eggs into a medium mixing bowl. Add the vanilla extract and whisk to combine. Add the maple syrup and melted coconut oil, whisking as you pour.

4. Pour the wet ingredients into the dry ingredients, then beat with an electric hand mixer until the ingredients are well incorporated.

5. Using a rubber spatula, fold the chocolate chips into the dough.

6. Using a 2-tablespoon cookie scoop, drop balls of the dough onto the prepared cookie sheet, spacing them about 2 inches apart. Bake for 10 to 12 minutes, until the tops are golden brown and the edges are crispy. Start checking at the 10-minute mark.

7. Remove from the oven and set the cookie sheet on a cooling rack. Let the cookies cool for 10 minutes before serving. Store in an airtight container for up to a week.

> *tip*: I like to pull these cookies out of the oven at the 10-minute mark and lightly press on them to flatten. This makes for a deliciously dense and chewy cookie.

PER SERVING:
CALORIES: **205**   FIBER: **4.6g**
FAT: **18.1g**   NET CARBS: **3g**
PROTEIN: **5g**   ERYTHRITOL: **1.3g**
TOTAL CARBS: **7.6g**

SNICKERDOODLES

NET CARBS 1.2g

MAKES: 15 cookies (1 per serving) · **PREP TIME:** 10 minutes · **COOK TIME:** 15 minutes

When it comes to cookies, I love them soft and chewy and warm right out of the oven. These fit the bill perfectly. When it comes to the great cookie debate, which side are you on—chewy or crunchy?

INGREDIENTS

FOR THE DOUGH:

- 2 cups blanched almond flour
- ½ cup granular erythritol
- ½ cup coconut oil, room temperature
- 1 teaspoon baking powder
- 1 teaspoon pure vanilla extract
- ½ teaspoon ground cinnamon
- Pinch of sea salt

FOR THE TOPPING:

- 2 tablespoons granular erythritol
- 1 teaspoon ground cinnamon

DIRECTIONS

1. Preheat the oven to 350°F. Line a cookie sheet with parchment paper or a silicone baking mat.

2. In a large mixing bowl, using a rubber spatula, mix together all the ingredients for the dough until they are well incorporated.

3. Roll the dough into fifteen 1½-inch balls.

4. In a small bowl, mix together the erythritol and cinnamon for the topping. Roll each dough ball in the topping and put on the prepared cookie sheet, spacing them about 2 inches apart. Flatten slightly.

5. Bake for 15 minutes, or until the edges are golden brown but the centers are still soft and slightly doughy.

6. Remove from the oven and set the cookie sheet on a cooling rack. Let the cookies cool for 10 minutes before serving. Store in an airtight container for up to a week.

PER SERVING:
CALORIES: **144**   FIBER: **1.5g**
FAT: **14.2g**   NET CARBS: **1.2g**
PROTEIN: **2.9g**   ERYTHRITOL: **6.4g**
TOTAL CARBS: **2.7g**

VANILLA CHIA PUDDING

NET CARBS 1.1g

MAKES: 4 puddings (1 per serving) · PREP TIME: 4 minutes, plus 2 hours to refrigerate

This thick and creamy pudding is super easy to make and packs a wonderful nutritional punch from the chia seeds. It's loaded with fiber, healthy fats, and protein. Garnish it with your favorite low-carb nuts, seeds, berries, or even chocolate chips.

INGREDIENTS

- 2 cups unsweetened almond or coconut milk
- ¼ cup powdered erythritol
- 2 teaspoons pure vanilla extract
- ⅓ cup chia seeds

TOPPINGS (OPTIONAL):

- Unsweetened coconut flakes
- Fresh blueberries
- Sugar-free dark chocolate chips

DIRECTIONS

1. In a large mixing bowl, whisk together the almond milk, erythritol, and vanilla extract until well combined.

2. Add the chia seeds and whisk vigorously for 1 to 2 minutes.

3. Transfer the pudding to 4 individual serving bowls or cups and refrigerate for 1 to 2 hours.

4. Top with coconut flakes, blueberries, and/or chocolate chips, if desired, before serving.

PER SERVING: ─────────
CALORIES: **81**   FIBER: **4.8g**
FAT: **5.5g**   NET CARBS: **1.1g**
PROTEIN: **3.1g**   ERYTHRITOL: **12g**
TOTAL CARBS: **5.9g**

Drinks and Cocktails

BOOSTED KETO COFFEE

NET CARBS 0.4g

MAKES: 1 serving · PREP TIME: 5 minutes (not including time to brew coffee)

By now, you have undoubtedly seen a lot of fatty coffee recipes. They go by different names, such as boosted coffee, bulletproof coffee, fat-fueled coffee, and butter coffee. I like to call my own personal version keto coffee, or just boosted coffee. Why? Well, because it gives me the fatty boost that I need in the morning.

INGREDIENTS

- 8 ounces freshly brewed dark roast coffee
- 1 tablespoon butter-flavored coconut oil or coconut oil
- 1 scoop vanilla MCT oil powder
- 1 scoop collagen peptides
- 2 teaspoons monk fruit–sweetened caramel syrup or vanilla syrup, or more to taste (optional)
- Splash of unsweetened coconut or almond milk

DIRECTIONS

Put all the ingredients in a blender or milk frother and blend until smooth and creamy. Pour into a 12-ounce coffee cup to serve.

tip: For specific brand suggestions for the ingredients used in this recipe and why I chose them, see "Ingredients Used in This Book" (pages 64 to 66).

PER SERVING:
CALORIES: **321**
FAT: **31.2g**
PROTEIN: **3g**
TOTAL CARBS: **0.4g**
FIBER: **0g**
NET CARBS: **0.4g**

GOLDEN MILK TWO WAYS

NET CARBS
2.6g

MAKES: 1 serving · **PREP TIME:** 10 minutes

All the healthy benefits of immune-boosting, anti-inflammatory turmeric in a rich and delicious dairy-free, creamy fat-burning coffee. You can make this drink in two ways: the first version makes a true latte using espresso and steamed milk; the second is a more traditional take on the drink, often called golden milk or turmeric tea, and requires no special equipment.

INGREDIENTS

- 1½ cups unsweetened coconut milk
- ½ teaspoon pure vanilla extract
- ½ teaspoon turmeric powder
- ¼ teaspoon ground cinnamon, plus more for garnish
- ¼ teaspoon ground ginger
- Pinch of Himalayan pink salt
- Pinch of ground black pepper
- 2 shots espresso (optional)
- 1 teaspoon granular erythritol, or more to taste (optional)

SPECIAL EQUIPMENT:

Espresso machine plus milk steaming pitcher and frother (optional)

DIRECTIONS

AS A LATTE:

1. Put the coconut milk in the milk steaming pitcher. Add the vanilla extract, turmeric, cinnamon, ginger, salt, and pepper. Stir to mix and use the steamer wand to heat and froth the milk. This will fully incorporate the spices into the milk.

2. Pull 2 shots of espresso from the machine and pour them into a 16-ounce mug. Top with the golden milk and sprinkle cinnamon and turmeric on top. Stir in the erythritol, if desired.

MORE TRADITIONAL:

1. Put the coconut milk, vanilla extract, turmeric, cinnamon, ginger, salt, pepper, and erythritol, if using, in a medium saucepan over medium heat.

2. Whisk to combine the ingredients. Heat until the golden milk is hot but not boiling.

3. Pour into a 16-ounce mug. Garnish with a sprinkle of cinnamon and turmeric before serving.

PER SERVING: ————

CALORIES: **86**   TOTAL CARBS: **4.5g**
FAT: **4.4g**   FIBER: **1.8g**
PROTEIN: **2g**   NET CARBS: **2.6g**

HOT COCOA

NET CARBS 2.2g

🥥 🍅 🥜 🌿 🕐 MAKES: **2 servings** · PREP TIME: **5 minutes** · COOK TIME: **5 minutes**

Hot cocoa is one of those things that is adored by children and adults alike. It is so warm and comforting, especially on a chilly winter day.

INGREDIENTS

- 2 cups unsweetened coconut or almond milk
- 3 tablespoons powdered erythritol
- 2 tablespoons unsweetened cocoa powder
- ½ teaspoon pure vanilla extract
- ¼ teaspoon ground cinnamon
- Coconut Milk Whipped Cream (page 367), for serving (optional)
- 1 teaspoon unsweetened cacao nibs or sugar-free dark chocolate chips, for garnish (optional)

DIRECTIONS

1. Put the coconut milk, erythritol, cocoa powder, vanilla extract, and cinnamon in a small saucepan over medium heat and whisk to combine. Heat until it reaches a comfortable drinking temperature.

2. Divide between two 12-ounce mugs. Top with whipped cream and cacao nibs, if desired.

PER SERVING: ——————
CALORIES: **47**   FIBER: **2.9g**
FAT: **3.6g**   NET CARBS: **2.2g**
PROTEIN: **2.3g**   ERYTHRITOL: **18g**
TOTAL CARBS: **5.1g**

ALMOND COCONUT MILK

NET CARBS 1.4g

🥥 🍅 🔪 🌿 🕐 **MAKES:** 1 quart (¼ cup per serving) · **PREP TIME:** 15 minutes, plus time to soak overnight

Finding a good low-carb almond or coconut milk can be tricky. Then, once you find a brand you like, you practically need a second job just to keep it stocked. I have no idea why I waited so long to make my own nut milk. Once I finally gave it a try and realized how easy it is, there was no going back. Not only does it save money, but it is the healthiest, cleanest version you can find.

INGREDIENTS

- 2 cups raw almonds
- 2 cups filtered water
- 1 (14.5-ounce) can coconut cream
- 2 teaspoons pure vanilla extract

SPECIAL EQUIPMENT:

High-powered blender

Nut milk bag

DIRECTIONS

1. Cover the almonds with water and let soak overnight. They will soften and plump. Discard the soaking water.

2. Put the almonds in a high-powered blender with 2 cups fresh filtered water, the coconut cream, and vanilla extract. Blend on high for 2 minutes, or until it is creamy and the almonds are ground.

3. Put a fine-mesh sieve over a bowl or large measuring cup. Put a large nut milk bag over the sieve. Pour the almond mixture into the bag and let it strain through into the bowl.

4. Close the bag, twist it around the almond pulp, and squeeze. Press firmly into the sieve to extract as much milk as possible.

5. Store in the fridge for up to 2 weeks.

> *tip: This milk is perfect for any of the recipes in this book that call for almond or coconut milk. It is also great as a coffee creamer, or just to drink when you are craving a creamy glass of milk.*

PER SERVING:

CALORIES: **91**	TOTAL CARBS: **2.7g**
FAT: **8.4g**	FIBER: **1.3g**
PROTEIN: **2.3g**	NET CARBS: **1.4g**

COLD BREW PROTEIN SHAKE

MAKES: 1 serving · **PREP TIME:** 10 minutes

If there is something I love more than writing low-carb, keto recipes, it is coffee. So naturally, I will try to sneak coffee in wherever I can. I am a huge fan of cold brew coffee, so I figured why not combine a delicious keto protein powder with my beloved coffee addiction? It is so simple, but it tastes so good.

INGREDIENTS

- 8 ounces cold brew coffee
- ⅓ cup unsweetened coconut or almond milk
- 1 scoop dairy-free keto vanilla protein powder
- Handful of ice cubes

DIRECTIONS

Put all the ingredients in a milk frother or shaker bottle and mix or shake until well combined. Pour into a 16-ounce glass to serve.

tip: If you prefer chocolate over vanilla, simply substitute a keto-friendly dairy-free chocolate protein powder.

PER SERVING:

CALORIES: **268**
FAT: **18.1g**
PROTEIN: **25.5g**
TOTAL CARBS: **3.1g**
FIBER: **1g**
NET CARBS: **2.1g**

LEMON-LIME SODA

MAKES: 2 quarts (1 cup per serving) · PREP TIME: 10 minutes

Who needs store-bought lemon-lime soda when it is so easy to make your own? Not to mention that this version is a lot healthier for you.

INGREDIENTS

- 1 cup powdered erythritol
- ½ cup fresh lemon juice
- ½ cup fresh lime juice
- 1 lemon, cut into slices
- 2 limes, cut into slices
- 6 cups club soda, chilled
- Ice, for serving (optional)
- Fresh mint sprigs, for garnish (optional)

DIRECTIONS

1. In a large pitcher, stir together the erythritol, lemon juice, and lime juice. Mix until well incorporated and the erythritol is dissolved. Mix in the lemon and lime slices.

2. Add the club soda to the pitcher, stirring gently so as not to lose the carbonation.

3. Serve in chilled glasses or over ice. Garnish with fresh mint, if desired.

PER SERVING:
CALORIES: 13
FAT: 0.1g
PROTEIN: 0.3g
TOTAL CARBS: 4.2g
FIBER: 0.6g
NET CARBS: 3.5g
ERYTHRITOL: 24g

PB&J SMOOTHIE

NET CARBS
6g

 MAKES: 2 servings · PREP TIME: 10 minutes

When I switched to a low-carb lifestyle, smoothies were one of the things I missed the most. There is something so comforting and refreshing about drinking a smoothie. Back in my high-carb days, I used to order a 32-ounce peanut butter and jelly smoothie at our local smoothie shop. Looking back on it, I don't even want to know how many grams of carbs and sugar those smoothies had. Thankfully, I've got a much healthier alternative these days.

INGREDIENTS

- 1 cup frozen mixed berries
- 2 tablespoons peanut butter powder
- 1 scoop dairy-free keto vanilla protein powder
- 1½ cups unsweetened coconut or almond milk
- Fresh berries, for garnish (optional)

tip: This recipe is marked as nut-free because, technically speaking, a peanut is a legume, not a nut. However, if you have a peanut allergy, feel free to substitute almond butter, to taste, for the peanut butter powder.

DIRECTIONS

Put all the ingredients in a blender and pulse until smooth and creamy. Divide between two 10-ounce glasses to serve. Garnish with fresh berries, if desired.

PER SERVING:

CALORIES: **140**	TOTAL CARBS: **11g**
FAT: **4g**	FIBER: **5g**
PROTEIN: **5g**	NET CARBS: **6g**

SHAMROCK SHAKE

MAKES: 1 serving · **PREP TIME:** 10 minutes

The perfect sugar-free, low-carb St. Patty's Day treat. Skip the high-carb, sugar-loaded version and go for this dairy-free keto shamrock shake instead.

INGREDIENTS

- ½ medium avocado, peeled and pitted
- 1 scoop dairy-free keto vanilla protein powder
- ½ cup unsweetened coconut or almond milk
- 8 ice cubes
- ⅛ teaspoon pure peppermint extract
- 5 drops natural green food coloring (optional)
- 2 tablespoons Coconut Milk Whipped Cream (page 367), for garnish (optional)
- 1 tablespoon sugar-free dark chocolate chips, for garnish (optional)

DIRECTIONS

1. Put the avocado, protein powder, coconut milk, ice, peppermint extract, and food coloring, if using, in a blender and pulse until blended and creamy.

2. Pour into a 12-ounce glass. Top with the whipped cream and chocolate chips, if desired.

tip: If using food coloring for this recipe, opt for a natural food coloring that is free of artificial dyes. You can also tint this drink green by using a little organic matcha powder or even chlorophyll. It is deep green in color and already has a fresh minty taste.

PER SERVING: ───────

CALORIES: **259**   TOTAL CARBS: **7g**
FAT: **14g**   FIBER: **5g**
PROTEIN: **26g**   NET CARBS: **2g**

STRAWBERRY BASIL BOURBON SMASH

NET CARBS
2.2g

MAKES: 1 serving · PREP TIME: 5 minutes

I have been asked time and time again if it is okay to drink alcohol on a low-carb diet. While I don't think there is necessarily a one-size-fits-all approach, I think that with a little creativity and some moderation, you can easily work the occasional low-carb cocktail into your keto lifestyle. This is the perfect recipe for such an occasion.

INGREDIENTS

- 3 strawberries, hulled and sliced, plus more for garnish
- 3 fresh basil leaves, plus more for garnish
- 1 teaspoon powdered erythritol
- 2 ounces bourbon
- 1 ounce fresh lemon juice
- Pinch of ground black pepper

tip: If you are not a fan of bourbon, this drink is also great with vodka or rum.

DIRECTIONS

1. Put the strawberries, basil, erythritol, and bourbon in a cocktail shaker. Muddle until the strawberries and basil are crushed and have released their juices.

2. Add the lemon juice and pepper and fill the shaker with ice. Cap and shake.

3. Pour the contents of the cocktail shaker into a large rocks glass.

4. Garnish with a strawberry and a sprig of basil.

PER SERVING: ─────────
CALORIES: 139   FIBER: 0.6g
FAT: 0.1g   NET CARBS: 2.2g
PROTEIN: 0.4g   ERYTHRITOL: 4g
TOTAL CARBS: 2.8g

STRAWBERRY MOJITO

NET CARBS 4.4g

MAKES: 1 serving · **PREP TIME:** 5 minutes

Mojitos just scream summer to me. My husband and I love to entertain at home, especially during the summer months. We quadruple this recipe and mix up a pitcher to enjoy with friends out on our back patio. These mojitos are incredibly refreshing, not to mention delicious.

INGREDIENTS

- 2 strawberries, hulled and sliced, plus more for garnish
- 8 fresh mint leaves, plus more for garnish
- ½ lime, cut into 4 wedges
- 1 tablespoon fresh lime juice
- 2 teaspoons powdered erythritol
- 2 ounces white rum
- 5 ounces club soda

DIRECTIONS

1. Fill a 16-ounce highball glass with ice.

2. Put the strawberries, mint leaves, lime wedges, lime juice, and erythritol in a cocktail shaker and muddle.

3. Add the rum to the cocktail shaker, then cap and shake.

4. Pour the mixture over the ice. Top with the club soda.

5. Garnish with a strawberry and a sprig of mint.

PER SERVING:
CALORIES: **147**   FIBER: **1.3g**
FAT: **0.1g**   NET CARBS: **4.4g**
PROTEIN: **0.4g**   ERYTHRITOL: **8g**
TOTAL CARBS: **5.7g**

TART CRANBERRY COOLER

NET CARBS 3g

MAKES: 1 serving · **PREP TIME:** 5 minutes

This cocktail is so crisp and refreshing. Best of all, it is quick and easy to make, with only simple ingredients. If you are not a fan of gin, it is also great with vodka or rum. If you prefer a sweeter drink, simply add a little more erythritol.

INGREDIENTS

- 10 fresh cranberries, plus more for garnish
- 2 teaspoons powdered erythritol
- 2 ounces dry gin
- 2 lime wedges, plus more for garnish
- 1 tablespoon fresh lime juice
- 2 ounces prosecco

DIRECTIONS

1. Fill a large rocks glass with ice.

2. Put the cranberries, erythritol, gin, lime wedges, and lime juice in a cocktail shaker. Muddle until the cranberries and lime wedges are crushed and have released their juices.

3. Strain the contents of the cocktail shaker into the ice-filled glass.

4. Top with the prosecco and garnish with cranberries and a lime wedge.

PER SERVING: ————
CALORIES: **203**   FIBER: **1g**
FAT: **0g**   NET CARBS: **3g**
PROTEIN: **0g**   ERYTHRITOL: **8g**
TOTAL CARBS: **4g**

BLACK BEAUTY

MAKES: 1 serving · **PREP TIME:** 5 minutes

This black pepper, blackberry, and vodka cocktail, or "Black Beauty," as I like to call it, is simple to make but complex in flavor. The hint of black pepper really makes this drink. Trust me, don't skip this ingredient; it pairs so perfectly with the blackberries and fresh mint. This drink is sure to become a new summertime favorite.

INGREDIENTS

- 2 ounces vodka
- 5 blackberries, plus more for garnish
- 1½ tablespoons fresh lemon juice
- 2 teaspoons powdered erythritol
- ¼ teaspoon ground black pepper
- 5 fresh mint leaves, plus more for garnish
- Club soda

DIRECTIONS

1. Fill a large rocks glass with ice.

2. Put the vodka, blackberries, lemon juice, erythritol, pepper, and mint leaves in a cocktail shaker. Muddle until the fruit and mint are crushed and have released their juices.

3. Strain the contents of the cocktail shaker into the ice-filled glass.

4. Top with club soda and garnish with blackberries and mint leaves.

PER SERVING:
CALORIES: **180**
FAT: **0g**
PROTEIN: **1g**
TOTAL CARBS: **5g**
FIBER: **2g**
NET CARBS: **3g**
ERYTHRITOL: **8g**

CUCUMBER LIME LAVENDER SPRITZER

NET CARBS
5.3g

MAKES: 1 serving · PREP TIME: 5 minutes

The floral notes of the lavender pair perfectly with the lime to make an aromatic and fresh cocktail. This drink is also fantastic with gin or rum.

INGREDIENTS

- 4 lime wedges, plus more for garnish
- 4 slices English cucumber, plus more for garnish
- 1 teaspoon fresh lavender buds, plus more for garnish
- 2 ounces vodka
- 1 ounce fresh lime juice
- 2 teaspoons powdered erythritol
- 5 ounces club soda

DIRECTIONS

1. Fill a 16-ounce highball glass with ice.

2. Put the lime wedges, cucumber slices, and lavender buds in a cocktail shaker. Muddle until the limes and cucumbers are crushed and have released their liquids.

3. Add the vodka, lime juice, and erythritol to the shaker, then cap and shake.

4. Strain the mixture into the ice-filled glass. Top with the club soda and garnish with lime wedges and lavender buds.

PER SERVING:
CALORIES: 149   FIBER: 1.2g
FAT: 0.1g   NET CARBS: 5.3g
PROTEIN: 0.5g   ERYTHRITOL: 8g
TOTAL CARBS: 6.5g

Basics

EVERYTHING BUNS

NET CARBS 5.1g

MAKES: 4 buns (1 per serving) · PREP TIME: 10 minutes · COOK TIME: 1 hour

This recipe was inspired by the famous Diet Doctor dinner roll recipe. My take on these buns is so appropriately named, not only for the use of Everything Bagel Seasoning, but also for the fact that I use these buns for everything. They are great for burgers and sandwiches. I like to use them in the morning for breakfast sandwiches with sausage, egg, avocado, and mayo. They are also fantastic as a base for Pork Carnitas Eggs Benedict (page 122). Delicious! If you aren't avoiding dairy, you can use them to make a mean grilled cheese sandwich, too.

INGREDIENTS

- 1¼ cups blanched almond flour
- ¼ cup plus 2 teaspoons psyllium husk powder
- 2 tablespoons nutritional yeast
- 2 teaspoons baking powder
- ½ teaspoon sea salt
- 3 large egg whites
- 2 teaspoons apple cider vinegar
- 1 cup hot water
- 2 tablespoons Everything Bagel Seasoning (page 399)

DIRECTIONS

1. Put an oven rack in the lower third position. Preheat the oven to 350°F. Line a rimmed baking sheet with parchment paper or a silicone baking mat.

2. In a large bowl, mix the almond flour, psyllium husk powder, nutritional yeast, baking powder, and salt until there are no visible clumps.

3. Add the egg whites and vinegar to the bowl and, using a rubber spatula, mix while slowly pouring in the hot water. Continue to mix just until the ingredients are well combined; be careful not to overmix the dough.

4. Moisten your hands and divide the dough into 4 equal parts, then shape them into hamburger-sized buns. Put the buns on the lined baking sheet. Sprinkle the bagel seasoning over the tops of the buns.

5. Bake for 1 hour, until the buns have doubled in size, are crisp on top, and make a hollow sound when you thump them. Allow to cool before slicing.

258   214   226

Meatloaf Burgers   Jalapeño Popper Chicken Salad Sandwiches   Barbecue Pulled Pork Sandwiches

PER SERVING:
CALORIES: **242**   TOTAL CARBS: **18.9g**
FAT: **17.7g**   FIBER: **13.8g**
PROTEIN: **13.6g**   NET CARBS: **5.1g**

tips: *Some brands of psyllium husk powder will cause these buns to turn purple. I recommend Now Foods brand.*

The leftover egg yolks from this recipe are perfect for making Bacon Fat Hollandaise (page 372).

GARLIC AND HERB CROUTONS

NET CARBS 1.3g

MAKES: 4 cups (¼ cup per serving) · PREP TIME: 20 minutes · COOK TIME: 1 hour 15 minutes

Like any good homemade crouton recipe, this one is best made with day-old bread. You can make the whole recipe the day you wish to serve the croutons, but they truly are best if you make the bread the day before, cube it, and let it sit out on the counter. But I feel I must warn you, these croutons are highly addictive. I end up eating them as snacks, and they rarely make it to my salads. They are also amazing on top of soups to add that crunchy element that you would normally get from crackers.

INGREDIENTS

FOR THE CROUTONS:

- 1¼ cups blanched almond flour
- ¼ cup plus 2 teaspoons psyllium husk powder
- 2 tablespoons nutritional yeast
- 2 teaspoons baking powder
- ½ teaspoon sea salt
- 3 large egg whites
- 2 teaspoons apple cider vinegar
- 1 cup hot water

FOR THE HERBED OIL COATING:

- ¼ cup olive oil or avocado oil
- ½ teaspoon sea salt
- ½ teaspoon garlic powder
- ½ teaspoon dried basil
- ¼ teaspoon dried oregano leaves
- ¼ teaspoon dried thyme leaves
- ¼ teaspoon ground black pepper

DIRECTIONS

1. Put an oven rack in the lower third position. Preheat the oven to 350°F. Line a rimmed baking sheet with parchment paper or a silicone baking mat.

2. In a large mixing bowl, whisk together the almond flour, psyllium husk powder, nutritional yeast, baking powder, and salt until well combined with no visible clumps.

3. Add the egg whites and vinegar to the bowl and, using a rubber spatula, mix while slowly pouring in the hot water. Continue to mix just until the ingredients are well combined; be careful not to overmix the dough.

4. Scoop the dough onto the lined baking sheet. Moisten your hands and form the dough into a large ½-inch-thick rectangle.

5. Bake for 1 hour. Allow to cool on the baking sheet, then slice into ¾-inch cubes. Transfer to a large mixing bowl.

6. Combine all the ingredients for the herbed oil coating in a small mixing bowl.

7. Drizzle over the bread cubes, tossing as you pour. Toss until the oil is well distributed and all the bread cubes are evenly coated.

8. Spread the croutons in a single layer across the rimmed baking sheet and bake for 12 minutes, or until crunchy.

> *tips*: Some brands of psyllium husk powder will cause this bread to turn purple. I recommend Now Foods brand.
>
> If you have Garlic and Herb–Infused Olive Oil (page 365) on hand, coat the croutons in ⅓ cup of that and adjust the salt as needed.

PER SERVING:
CALORIES: **90**   TOTAL CARBS: **4.7g**
FAT: **7.8g**   FIBER: **3.5g**
PROTEIN: **3.4g**   NET CARBS: **1.3g**

SAVORY NUT-FREE BREADING MIX

NET CARBS 0.7g

MAKES: 1½ cups (2 tablespoons per serving) · PREP TIME: 10 minutes

Whether you want to make Crispy Oven-Fried Pickles (page 152) or you just want to make some breaded chicken tenders or crispy fried shrimp, this is your go-to breading. It is incredibly versatile and will work for just about any deep-fried or oven-"fried" food.

INGREDIENTS

- ¾ cup crushed pork rinds
- ¾ cup golden flaxseed meal
- ½ teaspoon Italian seasoning
- ½ teaspoon garlic powder
- ½ teaspoon onion powder

DIRECTIONS

Combine all the ingredients and store in an airtight container in the pantry for up to 2 weeks.

tips: If you don't have golden flaxseed meal on hand, you can substitute blanched almond flour. If you aren't avoiding dairy, you can also substitute freshly grated Parmesan cheese. If using cheese, I recommend using the breading the same day you make it.

PER SERVING:

CALORIES: **54**	TOTAL CARBS: **2.4g**
FAT: **2.8g**	FIBER: **1.7g**
PROTEIN: **3.7g**	NET CARBS: **0.7g**

GARLIC AND HERB–INFUSED OLIVE OIL

NET CARBS 0.6g

MAKES: 1¼ cups (2 tablespoons per serving) · **PREP TIME:** 5 minutes

I love making infused olive oils. In fact, they are one of my favorite homemade gifts to give at the holidays. Not only are infused oils great for cooking, but they are also great for use as salad dressings or for dipping Everything Buns (page 360).

INGREDIENTS

- 1 cup extra-virgin olive oil
- 4 cloves garlic, minced
- 1 teaspoon grated lemon zest
- 1 teaspoon dried chives
- 1 teaspoon dried minced onion
- 1 teaspoon dried oregano leaves
- 1 teaspoon dried parsley
- 1 teaspoon dried rosemary leaves
- ½ teaspoon dried basil
- ¼ teaspoon dried thyme leaves
- ¼ teaspoon red pepper flakes
- ¼ teaspoon coarse sea salt
- ¼ teaspoon ground black pepper

DIRECTIONS

1. Put all the ingredients in a mixing bowl and whisk to combine. Use a funnel to transfer the oil mixture to a glass bottle.

2. Store in the refrigerator for up to a month. Remove from the refrigerator before use to allow the infused oil to return to a liquid state.

PER SERVING:

CALORIES: **194**	TOTAL CARBS: **0.8g**
FAT: **21.6g**	FIBER: **0.2g**
PROTEIN: **0.1g**	NET CARBS: **0.6g**

WHOLE ROASTED GARLIC

NET CARBS 5.6g

MAKES: 4 bulbs (½ bulb per serving) · **PREP TIME:** 5 minutes · **COOK TIME:** 45 minutes

Before I started writing cookbooks and food blogging, I worked in the restaurant industry for 15 years. A lot of those years were spent working in Italian restaurants. One of the restaurants I worked in served its house breads with whole roasted garlic. The garlic was roasted in giant batches in the wood-fired pizza oven, and the aroma permeated every inch of the restaurant. By the end of a shift, it permeated every inch of me also. But I never minded, because it was out-of-this-world delicious. I think this is where my love affair with garlic truly began. Not only is this roasted garlic amazing in Roasted Garlic Mayo (page 387), but it is also delicious served with Dinner Rolls (page 146), olive oil, and balsamic vinegar.

INGREDIENTS

- 4 large bulbs garlic
- ¼ cup avocado oil or olive oil
- 1 teaspoon sea salt
- ¼ teaspoon ground black pepper
- 4 sprigs fresh thyme

tip: If you do not want to roast the garlic in foil, you can roast the bulbs in a small covered baking dish.

DIRECTIONS

1. Preheat the oven to 400°F.

2. Cut the top ¼ inch off of each bulb of garlic, exposing the cloves.

3. Put each bulb of garlic on a sheet of aluminum foil that is large enough to wrap the entire bulb.

4. Drizzle the bulbs of garlic with the oil, then sprinkle them with the salt and pepper. Top each bulb with a sprig of thyme.

5. Wrap each bulb tightly in the foil. Put the foil packets on a rimmed baking sheet and bake for 45 minutes, or until the garlic is fragrant and the cloves are tender and caramelized.

PER SERVING:

CALORIES: **87**   TOTAL CARBS: **6g**
FAT: **6.8g**   FIBER: **0.4g**
PROTEIN: **1.2g**   NET CARBS: **5.6g**

COCONUT MILK WHIPPED CREAM

MAKES: about 1½ cups (2 tablespoons per serving)
PREP TIME: 10 minutes, plus time to chill coconut milk, mixing bowl, and beaters

This quick and healthy dairy-free whipped cream is just as silky and delectable as any dairy-based version. I love to serve it on top of an ice-cold Shamrock Shake (page 351). It is best made fresh and served immediately.

INGREDIENTS

- 1 (14.5-ounce) can unsweetened full-fat coconut milk or coconut cream, refrigerated overnight
- 2 tablespoons powdered erythritol
- 1 teaspoon pure vanilla extract

tip: For this whipped cream to get thick and creamy, it is imperative to use full-fat canned coconut milk. Using the brands that come in shelf-stable cartons will not do the trick.

DIRECTIONS

1. Put a metal mixing bowl and the beaters for a hand mixer or the whisk attachment for a stand mixer in the freezer for 1 hour before making the whipped cream.

2. Open the can of coconut milk from the bottom. This will make it easier to discard the watery liquid that has separated from the fat. Pour out the liquid. Scoop the coconut cream into the chilled mixing bowl. If using coconut cream, it will already be solid.

3. Using an electric mixer, beat the coconut cream on medium speed. Gradually increase the speed to high and beat until stiff peaks form, about 6 minutes.

4. Add the erythritol and vanilla extract and beat for 1 additional minute.

PER SERVING:
CALORIES: **69**
FAT: **7.5g**
PROTEIN: **0.7g**
TOTAL CARBS: **1g**
FIBER: **0g**
NET CARBS: **1g**
ERYTHRITOL: **2g**

PICKLED RED ONIONS

NET CARBS 1.3g

MAKES: 4 cups (¼ cup per serving)
PREP TIME: 15 minutes, plus 1 hour to sit · **COOK TIME:** 5 minutes

The perfect blend of sweet, sour, and salty. I love to put these onions on everything from my morning eggs to my lunchtime salad to my steak for dinner. They are also amazing on sandwiches, tacos, and burgers. Should I keep going?

INGREDIENTS

- 1 cup apple cider vinegar
- 1 cup red wine vinegar
- 2 tablespoons granular erythritol, or more to taste
- 1 teaspoon sea salt
- 2 medium red onions, sliced
- 6 cloves garlic, halved
- 1 teaspoon dried oregano leaves
- Pinch of red pepper flakes

DIRECTIONS

1. In a saucepan over medium heat, bring the apple cider vinegar, red wine vinegar, erythritol, and salt to a light boil, stirring until the erythritol and salt have dissolved.

2. Put the onions, garlic, oregano, and red pepper flakes in a 32-ounce mason jar. Pour the vinegar mixture over the top, submerging the onions and mixing in the oregano and red pepper flakes.

3. Let the jar sit on the counter for 1 hour, or until completely cool, then cap and refrigerate. You can eat the pickled onions as soon as the next day, but the longer they are in the fridge, the better they taste.

4. Store in the refrigerator for up to a month.

PER SERVING:
CALORIES: **10**   FIBER: **0.2g**
FAT: **0g**   NET CARBS: **1.3g**
PROTEIN: **0.2g**   ERYTHRITOL: **00g**
TOTAL CARBS: **1.5g**

BONE BROTH

MAKES: about 3 quarts (1 cup per serving) · **PREP TIME:** 20 minutes · **COOK TIME:** 24 hours

While the process of making your own bone broth can seem a little daunting and can even get a little messy, the health benefits alone make it so worth the effort. Bone broth is amazing for gut health and digestion. It also helps inhibit infection and fight inflammation. You can use this broth in any recipe in the book that calls for beef or chicken stock.

INGREDIENTS

- 3 pounds beef or chicken bones
- 5 cloves garlic, peeled
- 2 medium carrots, cut into large chunks
- 2 ribs celery, cut into large chunks
- 2 bay leaves
- 1 medium red onion, cut into large chunks
- ¼ cup fresh herbs (parsley, dill, thyme, oregano, rosemary)
- 2 tablespoons apple cider vinegar
- 1 tablespoon sea salt
- 2 teaspoons black peppercorns

DIRECTIONS

1. Preheat the oven to 375°F. Lay the bones in a single layer on a rimmed baking sheet and roast until browned, about 20 minutes.

2. Preheat a slow cooker on the low setting. Put the garlic, carrots, celery, bay leaves, onion, herbs, vinegar, salt, and peppercorns in the slow cooker.

3. Put the roasted bones on top of the vegetables and fill the slow cooker with water. Cover and cook for 24 to 48 hours. The longer you cook it, the more minerals and nutrients will be drawn out of the bones.

4. Pour the broth through a fine-mesh sieve and discard the bones and vegetables.

5. Transfer to jars and store in the refrigerator for up to a week, or freeze for later use.

> *tips: For chicken bone broth, I use whole chicken carcasses from rotisserie chickens and leave any remaining bits of meat on the bones. For beef bone broth, I like to use a combination of oxtail, knuckles, and short ribs. You can usually find large packs of soup bones in the butcher's section of the grocery store. If you do not see them, ask someone at the deli counter.*
>
> *A good bone broth will develop a gel-like consistency in the fridge and have a thick layer of hardened fat on top. Scrape the fat off and discard, or use it for cooking. When you heat the broth, it will return to a liquid state.*

PER SERVING:

CALORIES: **33**	TOTAL CARBS: **0g**
FAT: **0.9g**	FIBER: **0g**
PROTEIN: **6.5g**	NET CARBS: **0g**

BACON FAT HOLLANDAISE

NET CARBS
0.3g

MAKES: about 1½ cups (2 tablespoons per serving)
PREP TIME: 10 minutes · **COOK TIME:** 10 minutes

Fresh hollandaise is one of my absolute favorite sauces. Many people think of it as a breakfast sauce, but it goes far beyond that. Not only is it amazing on eggs, but it is also fantastic on top of vegetables, seafood, and steak. Don't believe me? Check out my recipes for Steak David (page 210) and Roasted Asparagus with Pancetta (page 302).

INGREDIENTS

- ¼ cup bacon drippings
- ¼ cup avocado oil
- 6 egg yolks
- 2 tablespoons plus 2 teaspoons fresh lemon juice
- Dash of hot sauce
- Pinch of cayenne pepper
- ¼ teaspoon sea salt

DIRECTIONS

1. Heat the bacon drippings and avocado oil until warmed and liquefied, about 120°F. This can be done on the stovetop or in the microwave at 50% power. If you do not have a thermometer, the goal here is to make sure that the mixture is warm but not hot so that it scrambles the eggs.

2. In a stainless-steel mixing bowl, whisk together the egg yolks and lemon juice. Continue whisking until the mixture thickens and increases in volume.

3. Heat a saucepan with 1 to 2 inches of water in it over medium heat until the water is simmering. Reduce the heat to medium-low. Put the bowl with the eggs and lemon juice on top of the saucepan, making sure that the water is not touching the bottom of the bowl or the eggs will begin to scramble. Continue whisking rapidly.

4. Little by little, whisk in the warm bacon drippings and avocado oil until the sauce has thickened and is light and fluffy.

5. Remove from the heat and gently whisk in the hot sauce, cayenne pepper, and salt.

6. Serve immediately.

> *tip*: I love cooking with bacon fat, so I always save my drippings. No need to put them in the refrigerator—you can store them in an airtight container in the pantry with the rest of your cooking oils.

PER SERVING:
CALORIES: **114**   TOTAL CARBS: **0.3g**
FAT: **11.9g**   FIBER: **0g**
PROTEIN: **1.4g**   NET CARBS: **0.3g**

CREAMY AVOCADO DRESSING

NET CARBS 0.6g

MAKES: 1¾ cups (2 tablespoons per serving) · PREP TIME: 5 minutes

Using avocados is one of my favorite ways to develop a rich, creamy texture without adding dairy to a recipe. With their mild taste and buttery texture, they bring a silkiness to whatever you add them to—not to mention the added benefit of healthy fats. The sesame oil in this recipe imparts a toasted nuttiness to the flavor. However, it is not required; you can omit it for a lighter, more citrusy vibe.

INGREDIENTS

- 1 medium-sized ripe avocado, peeled and pitted
- 3 cloves garlic, minced
- ¾ cup avocado oil
- ¼ cup white vinegar
- 1 tablespoon plus 2 teaspoons fresh lemon juice
- 1 tablespoon Dijon mustard
- 1 teaspoon toasted sesame oil (optional)
- 1 teaspoon sea salt
- ¼ teaspoon ground black pepper
- ¼ teaspoon ground cumin

DIRECTIONS

Put all the ingredients in a food processor or blender and pulse until smooth and creamy. Store in the refrigerator for up to a week.

PER SERVING:

CALORIES: **129**   TOTAL CARBS: **1.6g**
FAT: **13.9g**   FIBER: **1g**
PROTEIN: **0.4g**   NET CARBS: **0.6g**

CAESAR DRESSING

NET CARBS 0.8g

MAKES: 1¼ cups (2 tablespoons per serving) · **PREP TIME:** 10 minutes

Extra creamy and bursting with savory flavors, this homemade Caesar dressing tastes far better than any variety you might find at your local grocery store, and it is a lot healthier for you, too. Have you ever read the ingredient list on a bottle of store-bought salad dressing? It can be pretty scary.

INGREDIENTS

- 1 cup mayonnaise, store-bought or homemade (page 386)
- 2 tablespoons fresh lemon juice
- 4 cloves garlic, minced
- 3 anchovy fillets, minced
- 1 tablespoon Worcestershire sauce
- 1 teaspoon Dijon mustard
- ½ teaspoon sea salt
- ½ teaspoon ground black pepper

tips: For a cheesier taste, add 2 teaspoons of nutritional yeast.

If you aren't avoiding dairy, add ¼ cup of freshly grated Parmesan cheese to this dressing to elevate it to the next level.

DIRECTIONS

Put all the ingredients in a small mixing bowl and whisk to combine. Store in the refrigerator for up to 2 weeks.

PER SERVING:
CALORIES: **150**   TOTAL CARBS: **0.9g**
FAT: **16.1g**   FIBER: **0.1g**
PROTEIN: **0.5g**   NET CARBS: **0.8g**

RANCH DRESSING

MAKES: 1¼ cups (2 tablespoons per serving) · **PREP TIME:** 5 minutes

In my world, ranch dressing is one of the greatest things ever invented. Yes, I am one of those people. I will literally put ranch on just about anything. Once I started making my own, I never bought it again. Making your own means way cleaner ingredients, and you get to control all the herbs and spices so that it tastes exactly how you like it.

INGREDIENTS

- 1 cup mayonnaise, store-bought or homemade (page 386)
- ¼ cup water
- 2 teaspoons chopped fresh chives
- 1½ teaspoons apple cider vinegar
- 1 teaspoon Dijon mustard
- 1 teaspoon chopped fresh dill
- 1 teaspoon chopped fresh flat-leaf parsley
- 1 teaspoon garlic powder
- ½ teaspoon onion powder
- ½ teaspoon sea salt
- ½ teaspoon ground black pepper

DIRECTIONS

Put all the ingredients in a small mixing bowl and whisk to combine. Store in the refrigerator for up to 2 weeks.

PER SERVING:
CALORIES: **146**   TOTAL CARBS: **0.4g**
FAT: **16g**   FIBER: **0.1g**
PROTEIN: **0.1g**   NET CARBS: **0.3g**

LEMON BASIL VINAIGRETTE

NET CARBS 0.5g

MAKES: 1½ cups (2 tablespoons per serving) · PREP TIME: 10 minutes

This lemony vinaigrette is fresh and bright and perfect for pairing with heartier greens like kale, cabbage, or Brussels sprouts. It also makes an excellent marinade for chicken or fish.

INGREDIENTS

- 1 cup avocado oil
- ¼ cup fresh lemon juice
- 2 tablespoons minced shallots
- 1 tablespoon chopped fresh basil
- 1 tablespoon white balsamic vinegar
- 2 teaspoons Dijon mustard
- ¾ teaspoon sea salt
- ½ teaspoon ground black pepper
- ¼ teaspoon red pepper flakes (optional)

tip: Omit the red pepper flakes to make this dressing nightshade-free.

DIRECTIONS

Put all the ingredients in a small mixing bowl and whisk to combine. Store in the refrigerator for up to 2 weeks.

PER SERVING:
CALORIES: 0.3   TOTAL CARBS: 0.7g
FAT: 18.2g   FIBER: 0.1g
PROTEIN: 0.1g   NET CARBS: 0.5g

TOMATO MEAT SAUCE

NET CARBS 3.4g

MAKES: 5 cups (¼ cup per serving) · **PREP TIME:** 10 minutes · **COOK TIME:** 40 minutes

When I was a kid, we ate a lot of spaghetti. It was easy, cheap, and on the table in less than 30 minutes. But that also meant that the sauce went straight from the jar, to a pan, to my plate. My mom would always say that she was making homemade spaghetti sauce, and I would joke that the only thing homemade about it was the fact that it was cooked in a home. These days, our family spaghetti nights look a little different. Few things can stir up the warm, fuzzy feelings of home quite like a scratch-made batch of meat sauce. It's amazing to me what a few simple ingredients and a little slow simmering can do. My favorite thing about making sauces from scratch (aside from how much healthier they are) is that you can customize them to your liking. If you are anything like me, then each batch is sure to include extra garlic.

INGREDIENTS

- 1 pound ground beef
- 1 small onion, diced (about ½ cup)
- 3 cloves garlic, minced
- 1½ teaspoons sea salt
- 1 (28-ounce) can San Marzano tomatoes
- 1 (6-ounce) can tomato paste
- 1 bay leaf
- 1 teaspoon dried basil
- 1 teaspoon dried oregano leaves
- 1 teaspoon dried parsley
- ½ teaspoon garlic powder
- ½ teaspoon onion powder
- ¼ teaspoon red pepper flakes

DIRECTIONS

1. Heat a large sauté pan over medium-high heat. When the pan is hot, add the ground beef, onion, garlic, and salt. Cook, breaking up the ground beef with a spatula, until it is browned, about 8 minutes. Drain the excess grease.

2. Add the tomatoes to the pan and mash them until they are crushed and broken up.

3. Mix in the tomato paste, bay leaf, basil, oregano, parsley, garlic powder, onion powder, and red pepper flakes.

4. Reduce the heat to low and simmer, uncovered, for 30 minutes to allow the flavors to come together.

5. Store leftovers in the refrigerator for up to a week. Alternatively, you can freeze it.

tips: You can use fresh herbs in this sauce if you prefer. When substituting fresh herbs for dried herbs in a recipe, a good rule of thumb is that 1 tablespoon of fresh herbs is equal to 1 teaspoon of dried herbs.

This recipe makes a large amount of sauce, making it perfect for meal prep. I like to make a batch and then portion it out and freeze it for later use. It reheats beautifully.

PER SERVING:
CALORIES: **76**   TOTAL CARBS: **4.1g**
FAT: **4.5g**   FIBER: **0.7g**
PROTEIN: **4.6g**   NET CARBS: **3.4g**

DAIRY-FREE ALFREDO SAUCE TWO WAYS

NET CARBS
5g

Rich, creamy, and sinfully delicious: those are the three descriptions that come to mind when I think of Alfredo sauce. You would never believe that these versions do not contain some sort of dairy. The first version has a slightly nutty flavor from the cashews, while the second adds an extra serving or two of vegetables to your day. Either way, Alfredo sauce is back on your dairy-free table. These sauces are amazing over zoodles, shirataki noodles, or spaghetti squash for a pastalike dish, or even just ladled over roasted chicken or grilled seafood. You can use them as a base for casseroles or soups or even as a dipping sauce for Dinner Rolls (page 146). If you are feeling really saucy, you can even mix them with Pistachio Pesto (page 395) to make a pesto Alfredo sauce.

VERSION 1 (CASHEW)

 MAKES: 4 cups (¼ cup per serving) · **PREP TIME:** 15 minutes, plus 30 minutes to soak cashews
COOK TIME: 15 minutes

INGREDIENTS

- 3 cups chicken stock or bone broth (page 370), divided, plus more if needed
- 2 cups raw cashews
- 4 cloves garlic, peeled
- ½ cup unsweetened almond milk
- 3 tablespoons nutritional yeast
- 2 tablespoons Worcestershire sauce
- 1 tablespoon chopped fresh flat-leaf parsley
- 2 teaspoons sea salt
- 1 teaspoon ground black pepper

SPECIAL EQUIPMENT:

High-powered blender or food processor

DIRECTIONS

1. Heat the stock in a medium saucepan over high heat. Once it comes to a boil, add the cashews and garlic and let boil for 5 minutes. Remove from the heat and let the cashews continue to soak for 30 minutes.

2. Pour the stock with the soaked cashews and garlic into a high-powered blender or food processor. Add the rest of the ingredients and pulse until smooth and creamy.

3. Return the sauce mixture to the saucepan and cook over medium heat, stirring frequently, to allow the flavors to continue to come together, about 5 minutes. If the sauce is too thick, add some additional stock.

4. Store leftovers in the refrigerator for up to a week. Alternatively, you can freeze it.

VERSION 1 (cashew)
PER SERVING:
CALORIES: **101**   TOTAL CARBS: **5.3g**
FAT: **7.9g**   FIBER: **0.3g**
PROTEIN: **3.6g**   NET CARBS: **5g**

VERSION 2 (CAULIFLOWER)

MAKES: 3½ cups (¼ cup per serving) · **PREP TIME:** 15 minutes · **COOK TIME:** 20 minutes

INGREDIENTS

- 1½ pounds fresh cauliflower florets
- 2 cups chicken stock or bone broth (page 370)
- 4 cloves garlic, peeled
- ½ cup unsweetened almond or coconut milk
- 2 tablespoons bacon drippings
- 1 tablespoon nutritional yeast
- 1 tablespoon chopped fresh flat-leaf parsley
- 1½ teaspoons sea salt
- ½ teaspoon ground black pepper
- 1 tablespoon fish sauce or gluten-free soy sauce

SPECIAL EQUIPMENT:

Food processor or high-powered blender

DIRECTIONS

1. Put the cauliflower florets, stock, and garlic in a large saucepan. Cover and bring to a boil over medium-high heat. Once it comes to a boil, reduce the heat to medium and let simmer until the cauliflower is fork-tender, about 10 minutes.

2. Transfer the cauliflower, with any remaining stock, to a high-powered blender or food processor. Add the rest of the ingredients and pulse until smooth and creamy.

3. Pour the sauce mixture back into the saucepan and cook over medium heat, stirring occasionally, to allow the flavors to continue to come together, about 5 minutes. Store leftovers in the refrigerator for up to a week. Alternatively, you can freeze the sauce.

> *tip*: *Reheat leftovers on the stovetop and add extra chicken stock or bone broth to thin the sauce, if needed.*

VERSION 2 (cauliflower)
PER SERVING:
CALORIES: **40** TOTAL CARBS: **3.2g**
FAT: **2.6g** FIBER: **1.2g**
PROTEIN: **2g** NET CARBS: **2g**

CLASSIC MARINARA SAUCE

MAKES: 4 cups (¼ cup per serving) · **PREP TIME:** 10 minutes · **COOK TIME:** 30 minutes

Keto-friendly sauces, dips, and dressings are some of my favorite recipes to make. They allow me to play around with different fresh herbs and flavor profiles. Not only are sauces made from scratch a lot healthier for you, but the homemade versions are significantly lower in carbs—not to mention that you get to skip all the nasty, unnecessary additives. This low-carb marinara sauce is perfect to make a large batch of and freeze in individual smaller portions. You can even freeze it in ice cube trays for individual portions.

INGREDIENTS

- 1 (28-ounce) can crushed tomatoes
- 1 (6-ounce) can tomato paste
- 5 cloves garlic, minced
- 1½ teaspoons dried basil
- 1 teaspoon sea salt
- 1 teaspoon dried oregano leaves
- 1 teaspoon dried parsley
- ½ teaspoon garlic powder
- ½ teaspoon onion powder
- ¼ teaspoon red pepper flakes

DIRECTIONS

Put all the ingredients in a large saucepan and mix until well combined. Simmer over medium-low heat, stirring frequently, for 30 minutes to allow the flavors to come together.

PER SERVING:

CALORIES: **22**	TOTAL CARBS: **5.1g**
FAT: **0.2g**	FIBER: **1.2g**
PROTEIN: **1.1g**	NET CARBS: **3.9g**

KETCHUP

NET CARBS 2.1g

MAKES: 2 cups (2 tablespoons per serving) · **PREP TIME:** 5 minutes

Store-bought ketchup is loaded with added sugars. Making your own ketchup is so much easier, and the ingredients are much cleaner. I have a sneaking suspicion that once you make your own, you won't be buying it any longer. I'll also let you in on a little secret: I have an amazing dry rub barbecue seasoning on my website, peaceloveandlowcarb.com, that mixes perfectly with this ketchup to make an amazing smoky barbecue sauce.

INGREDIENTS

- 1 (6-ounce) can tomato paste
- ¾ cup water
- ¼ cup white vinegar
- 1 tablespoon granular erythritol
- 1 teaspoon brown sugar erythritol
- 1 teaspoon sea salt
- ½ teaspoon garlic powder
- ½ teaspoon onion powder
- ⅛ teaspoon ground cinnamon
- ⅛ teaspoon ground cloves
- ⅛ teaspoon ground nutmeg

DIRECTIONS

Put all the ingredients in a mixing bowl and whisk to combine. Store in the refrigerator for up to 3 weeks.

> **tips:** *For less of a molasses taste, omit the brown sugar erythritol.*
>
> *If the ketchup is too thick after you pull it out of the refrigerator, simply let it come to room temperature before using. Alternatively, you can thin it out by adding a little water. It won't water down the flavor.*

PER SERVING: ———————

CALORIES: **10**   FIBER: **0.3g**
FAT: **0g**   NET CARBS: **2.1g**
PROTEIN: **0.3g**   ERYTHRITOL: **1g**
TOTAL CARBS: **2.4g**

MAYO TEN WAYS

MAKES: 1½ cups basic mayo (2 tablespoons per serving) · PREP TIME: 2 minutes

I love a good basic mayonnaise, but sometimes you want some variety. The mayonnaise variations that follow are great for dips, dressings, sauces, and marinades. From using them in place of salad dressing to tossing them with zucchini noodles like a pasta sauce, the sky is the limit. All you need to do is make the basic mayo recipe and then stir in the additional ingredients for the variation of your choice. Of course, you can use a store-bought mayonnaise and flavor it using the recipes below, but it doesn't take much longer to make your own mayo from scratch, and it will likely have a much cleaner ingredient list.

INGREDIENTS

BASIC MAYO:

- 2 teaspoons fresh lemon juice
- 1 large egg
- ½ teaspoon mustard powder
- 1 teaspoon sea salt
- Pinch of ground black pepper
- 1 cup avocado oil

SPECIAL EQUIPMENT:

Immersion blender (see tip)

tip: For me, getting this mayonnaise to set up as it should is highly dependent upon using an immersion blender. I have not been able to achieve the same thick consistency when using a countertop blender or food processor.

DIRECTIONS

1. Starting with the lemon juice and ending with the avocado oil, put the ingredients, one at a time and in the order listed, in a wide-mouth pint-sized mason jar. Let the ingredients rest for 20 seconds or so.

2. Insert an immersion blender into the jar, placing it all the way at the bottom. Turn it on high speed and leave it at the bottom of the jar for about 20 seconds. The mayonnaise will immediately begin to set up and fill the jar.

3. When the mayonnaise is almost all the way set, slowly lift the immersion blender toward the top of the jar without taking the blades out of the mayonnaise. Then slowly push it back toward the bottom of the jar. Repeat this up-and-down motion a couple of times until the ingredients are well incorporated. Store in the refrigerator for up to 2 weeks.

PER SERVING:

CALORIES: **172**	TOTAL CARBS: **0g**
FAT: **19g**	FIBER: **0g**
PROTEIN: **0.5g**	NET CARBS: **0g**

CINCO DE MAYO

- 1 cup mayonnaise, store-bought or homemade (Basic Mayo)
- ¼ cup restaurant-style salsa, store-bought or homemade (page 142)

DIJON MAYO

- 1 cup mayonnaise, store-bought or homemade (Basic Mayo)
- 2 tablespoons Dijon mustard

HONEY MUSTARD MAYO

- 1 cup mayonnaise, store-bought or homemade (Basic Mayo)
- ¼ cup Dijon mustard
- 1 tablespoon plus 1 teaspoon powdered erythritol

PESTO MAYO

- 1 cup mayonnaise, store-bought or homemade (Basic Mayo)
- 2 tablespoons dairy-free pesto, store-bought or homemade (page 395)

ROASTED GARLIC MAYO

- 1 cup mayonnaise, store-bought or homemade (Basic Mayo)
- Cloves from 1 whole bulb roasted garlic (page 366), mashed to a paste

SUN-DRIED TOMATO MAYO

- 1 cup Roasted Garlic Mayo (above)
- ¼ cup finely chopped sun-dried tomatoes
- 2 teaspoons fresh lemon juice

DILLY MAYO

- 1 cup Roasted Garlic Mayo (above)
- ¼ cup chopped fresh dill
- 1 teaspoon fresh lemon juice

BALSAMIC MAYO

- 1 cup Roasted Garlic Mayo (above)
- 2 tablespoons balsamic vinegar

BUFFALO MAYO

- 1 cup Roasted Garlic Mayo (above)
- 2 tablespoons Buffalo wing sauce

EVERYTHING BAGEL AIOLI

MAKES: 1¼ cups (2 tablespoons per serving) · **PREP TIME:** 5 minutes, plus 1 hour to chill

Aioli is one of my favorite condiments ever. It is so fresh and bright tasting. The punch of raw garlic is what gives aioli its signature flavor. But the reason I love it so much is that it is incredibly versatile. It is so good with seafood, as a sandwich spread, with eggs, on steak, on roasted vegetables—you name it! Better yet, it uses such simple ingredients that you likely already have everything that you need to make it. For this version, I take things to the next level by adding Everything Bagel Seasoning.

INGREDIENTS

- 1 cup mayonnaise, store-bought or homemade (page 386)
- 4 cloves garlic, minced
- 2 tablespoons fresh lemon juice
- 2 tablespoons Everything Bagel Seasoning (page 399)

tip: If you do not want to make your own bagel seasoning, most stores now carry a premade version in the spice aisle.

DIRECTIONS

Put all the ingredients in a bowl and mix until well combined. Refrigerate for at least 1 hour before serving to allow the flavors to come together. Store in the refrigerator for up to 2 weeks.

PER SERVING:

CALORIES: **149**	TOTAL CARBS: **0.8g**
FAT: **16.2g**	FIBER: **0.1g**
PROTEIN: **0.2g**	NET CARBS: **0.7g**

LIME SRIRACHA AIOLI

MAKES: about 1½ cups (2 tablespoons per serving) · PREP TIME: 5 minutes

I love the vibrant flavors of this aioli. The heat of the Sriracha is perfectly balanced by the acidity of the lime juice. It is an excellent dipping sauce for recipes like Crispy Oven-Fried Pickles (page 152) and Bacon-Wrapped Avocado Fries (page 130), or even as a spread for Meatloaf Burgers (page 258). Despite its simplicity, this is an incredibly versatile and flavor-packed sauce.

INGREDIENTS

- 1 cup mayonnaise, store-bought or homemade (page 386)
- ¼ cup Sriracha sauce
- 4 cloves garlic, minced
- Juice of 1 small lime

DIRECTIONS

Put all the ingredients in a small mixing bowl and whisk to combine. Store in the refrigerator for up to 2 weeks.

PER SERVING: ─────────
CALORIES: **126**   TOTAL CARBS: **1.5g**
FAT: **13.4g**   FIBER: **0.1g**
PROTEIN: **0.1g**   NET CARBS: **1.4g**

ROASTED RED PEPPER AIOLI

MAKES: 1¼ cups (2 tablespoons per serving) · **PREP TIME:** 15 minutes, plus 30 minutes to chill

This aioli is such a delicious and versatile sauce. The mayonnaise makes it creamy while keeping it dairy-free. It is so easy to make, too. I use this aioli for a wide variety of things. It is delicious served as a dip for fresh vegetables or pork rinds. It is also amazing as a low-carb sauce for chicken, fish, or even pork.

INGREDIENTS

- ¾ cup mayonnaise, store-bought or homemade (page 386)
- ½ cup chopped roasted red peppers
- 6 cloves garlic, minced
- 2 tablespoons fresh lemon juice
- A few sprigs of fresh flat-leaf parsley
- ¼ teaspoon sea salt, or more to taste
- Pinch of ground black pepper, or more to taste

SPECIAL EQUIPMENT:

Food processor or high-powered blender

DIRECTIONS

Put all the ingredients in a food processor or high-powered blender and pulse until well blended and smooth. Taste and add more salt and/or pepper, if desired. Refrigerate for at least 30 minutes before serving.

PER SERVING:

CALORIES: **124**   TOTAL CARBS: **1.3g**
FAT: **13.1g**   FIBER: **0.1g**
PROTEIN: **0.2g**   NET CARBS: **1.2g**

SWEET AND SPICY BARBECUE SAUCE

MAKES: 1¼ cups (1 tablespoon per serving) · **PREP TIME:** 5 minutes · **COOK TIME:** 15 minutes

I've made several different low-carb barbecue sauce recipes over the years, but this one is hands-down my favorite. It comes together quickly. While you certainly can simmer it on the stovetop as directed, I have found that cooking it really isn't necessary. I love to keep a batch on hand for quick and easy meal prep options like barbecue grilled chicken or even a juicy barbecue pork tenderloin. With the sauce already in the fridge, all I need is the protein and I am just 30 minutes away from a delicious meal.

INGREDIENTS

- ½ cup reduced-sugar ketchup, store-bought or homemade (page 385)
- 1 tablespoon Sriracha sauce, or more to taste
- 1 tablespoon apple cider vinegar
- 1 tablespoon Worcestershire sauce
- 2 teaspoons dried minced onion
- 1 teaspoon brown sugar erythritol (optional)
- 1 teaspoon garlic powder
- ½ teaspoon chili powder
- ½ teaspoon ground cumin

DIRECTIONS

Put all the ingredients in a small saucepan and whisk to combine. Simmer over medium-low heat, stirring frequently, for 15 minutes. Store in the refrigerator for up to 3 weeks.

PER SERVING:
CALORIES: **5**
FAT: **0g**
PROTEIN: **0.1g**
TOTAL CARBS: **1.1g**
FIBER: **0.2g**
NET CARBS: **0.9g**

BALSAMIC HORSERADISH CHIMICHURRI

NET CARBS 2.2g

 MAKES: 1 cup (2 tablespoons per serving) · PREP TIME: 5 minutes

Chimichurri is an uncooked, oil-based sauce that originated in Argentina. It is typically served over meats or used as a marinade. I decided to kick things up a notch in my version by adding balsamic vinegar and horseradish. It is wonderful on grilled meats, as a salad dressing, or on Everything Chimichurri Eggs (page 110).

INGREDIENTS

- ⅓ cup olive oil
- 5 cloves garlic, minced
- 3 tablespoons balsamic vinegar
- 3 tablespoons chopped fresh chives
- 3 tablespoons chopped fresh flat-leaf parsley
- 3 tablespoons chopped fresh oregano leaves
- 2 teaspoons prepared horseradish
- 1 teaspoon chili powder
- ¾ teaspoon sea salt
- ¼ teaspoon ground cumin

tip: This chimichurri is best made a day ahead so that the flavors have time to come together.

DIRECTIONS

Put all the ingredients in a small bowl and whisk to combine. Store in the refrigerator for up to 2 weeks.

PER SERVING:

CALORIES: **94**	TOTAL CARBS: **2.9g**
FAT: **9.1g**	FIBER: **0.7g**
PROTEIN: **0.3g**	NET CARBS: **2.2g**

CRACK SAUCE

NET CARBS 1.1g

MAKES: ¾ cup (1 tablespoon per serving) · PREP TIME: 5 minutes

I called this recipe Crack Sauce because it has such an addictive flavor. It's the kind of flavor that calls you back for more—sweet, salty, and spicy all in one. I can't get enough of it. My favorite thing to put it on is the Sesame Chicken Egg Roll in a Bowl (page 204).

INGREDIENTS

- ½ cup reduced-sugar ketchup, store-bought or homemade (page 385)
- 3 tablespoons gluten-free soy sauce or coconut aminos
- 1 tablespoon plus 2 teaspoons Sriracha sauce, or more to taste

DIRECTIONS

Put all the ingredients in a mixing bowl and whisk to combine. Store in the refrigerator for up to 2 weeks.

PER SERVING:
CALORIES: 8
FAT: 0g
PROTEIN: 0.6g
TOTAL CARBS: 1.3g
FIBER: 0.2g
NET CARBS: 1.1g

PEANUT SAUCE

 MAKES: 1¼ cups (1 tablespoon per serving) · **PREP TIME:** 10 minutes

I'm not even remotely embarrassed to tell you that I would drink this sauce. Okay, maybe that is a little embarrassing, but it is that good. It's perfect as a salad dressing or to pour over grilled chicken, but it is especially good on a Peanut Chicken Zoodle Bowl (page 260).

INGREDIENTS

- ½ cup reduced-sugar creamy peanut butter
- ¼ cup water
- 3 tablespoons gluten-free soy sauce or coconut aminos
- 2 tablespoons unseasoned rice wine vinegar
- 2 tablespoons fresh lime juice
- 1 teaspoon toasted sesame oil
- 1 teaspoon grated fresh ginger
- 1 clove garlic, minced
- ¼ teaspoon red pepper flakes (optional)

DIRECTIONS

Put all the ingredients in a small mixing bowl and whisk to combine. Store in the refrigerator for up to 2 weeks.

> *tip*: *Peanuts are legumes, not nuts, so this recipe is marked as being nut-free. If you cannot tolerate peanuts, you can substitute almond butter for the peanut butter.*

PER SERVING:

CALORIES: **59** TOTAL CARBS: **2g**
FAT: **4.5g** FIBER: **0.6g**
PROTEIN: **2.2g** NET CARBS: **1.4g**

PISTACHIO PESTO

MAKES: 1½ cups (2 tablespoons per serving) · **PREP TIME:** 10 minutes

Homemade pesto is so easy to make that you will wonder why you ever used store-bought pesto in the first place. For this variation, I chose pistachios for their buttery, earthy flavor, but it is equally delicious made with pine nuts, which are more traditional. You can also use walnuts, pecans, almonds, or a combination of nuts.

INGREDIENTS

- 2 cups loosely packed fresh basil leaves
- 2 cups loosely packed fresh flat-leaf parsley leaves
- 4 cloves garlic, peeled
- ⅔ cup shelled pistachios
- ½ teaspoon sea salt, or more to taste
- ¼ teaspoon ground black pepper
- Juice of ½ lemon
- ½ cup plus 2 tablespoons olive oil
- 2 tablespoons water, if needed

SPECIAL EQUIPMENT:

Food processor or high-powered blender

 tip: If you aren't avoiding dairy, add ⅓ cup freshly grated Parmesan cheese to take this pesto to the next level.

DIRECTIONS

1. Put all the ingredients, except the olive oil and water, in a food processor or high-powered blender. Pulse until everything is finely chopped and a paste begins to form.

2. With the food processor running, slowly pour in the oil. Continue to pulse until smooth.

3. If the pesto is thicker than you like, with the food processor running, add the water 1 tablespoon at a time until the desired consistency is reached.

4. Store in the refrigerator for up to 2 weeks.

PER SERVING:

CALORIES: **142**	TOTAL CARBS: **2.8g**
FAT: **14.1g**	FIBER: **1.1g**
PROTEIN: **1.8g**	NET CARBS: **1.7g**

PUMPKIN PIE SPICE

 MAKES: about ½ cup (1 tablespoon per serving) · **PREP TIME:** 5 minutes

It is so easy to make your own low-carb and gluten-free pumpkin pie spice, and it is a lot more affordable, too. When fall rolls around, it turns into the season of pumpkin everything, and you can end up paying a premium for the store-bought blends.

INGREDIENTS

- ¼ cup ground cinnamon
- 2 tablespoons ground ginger
- 1 tablespoon ground nutmeg
- 2 teaspoons ground cloves

DIRECTIONS

Combine all the ingredients and store in an airtight container or spice jar. Shake well before using.

PER SERVING:
CALORIES: **20**   TOTAL CARBS: **4.8g**
FAT: **0.5g**   FIBER: **2.6g**
PROTEIN: **0.4g**   NET CARBS: **2.2g**

FAJITA SEASONING

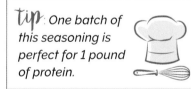 **MAKES:** 3 tablespoons plus 2 teaspoons (1 teaspoon per serving) · **PREP TIME:** 5 minutes

This fajita seasoning is so quick and easy to throw together. It's also much healthier than the store-bought seasoning packets. I like to make a triple or quadruple batch so I always have some on hand for simple weeknight dinners like a Chicken Fajita Sheet Pan Meal (page 218).

INGREDIENTS

- 1 tablespoon chili powder
- 1½ teaspoons ground cumin
- 1¼ teaspoons sea salt
- 1 teaspoon chicken bouillon granules, or 1 chicken bouillon cube, crushed
- 1 teaspoon smoked paprika
- 1 teaspoon garlic powder
- 1 teaspoon onion powder
- ½ teaspoon dried oregano leaves
- ½ teaspoon granular erythritol (optional)
- ¼ teaspoon cayenne pepper

tip: One batch of this seasoning is perfect for 1 pound of protein.

DIRECTIONS

Combine all the ingredients and store in an airtight container or spice jar.

PER SERVING:

CALORIES: **6**	TOTAL CARBS: **1.1g**
FAT: **0.2g**	FIBER: **0.4g**
PROTEIN: **0.3g**	NET CARBS: **0.7g**

BLACKENING SEASONING

MAKES: 6½ tablespoons (1 teaspoon per serving)
PREP TIME: 5 minutes

I love to keep a batch of this seasoning in the pantry at all times for quick and easy weeknight meals. It pairs perfectly with just about any protein—beef, chicken, seafood, you name it. In less than thirty minutes, you could be eating a piece of blackened salmon, a Blackened Chicken Salad (page 182), or even Blackened Shrimp Fettuccine Alfredo (page 230).

INGREDIENTS

- 1 tablespoon plus 1½ teaspoons smoked paprika
- 1 tablespoon garlic powder
- 1 tablespoon onion powder
- 1 tablespoon dried thyme leaves
- 1 teaspoon cayenne pepper, or more for a spicier blend
- 1 teaspoon dried basil
- 1 teaspoon ground cumin
- 1 teaspoon celery salt
- 1 teaspoon sea salt
- ½ teaspoon ground black pepper
- ½ teaspoon dried oregano leaves

DIRECTIONS

Mix all the ingredients together and store in an airtight container or spice jar. Shake well before using.

tip: Mix 3 tablespoons of this seasoning with 1 cup of Roasted Garlic Mayo (page 387) to make a deliciously versatile sauce. I like to use it as a sandwich spread, as a dip for veggies, or to make deviled eggs.

PER SERVING:
CALORIES: **5**   TOTAL CARBS: **0.7g**
FAT: **0g**   FIBER: **0.2g**
PROTEIN: **0.2g**   NET CARBS: **0.5g**

EVERYTHING BAGEL SEASONING

MAKES: 1 cup (2 tablespoons per serving) · **PREP TIME:** 5 minutes

Am I going too far if I say that this Everything Bagel Seasoning is everything? I have been putting it on just about everything, so I'd say it's a fair assessment—Everything Chimichurri Eggs (page 110), Everything Buns (page 360), and Everything Bagel Aioli (page 388), just to name a few.

INGREDIENTS

- ¼ cup black and/or white sesame seeds
- 3 tablespoons plus 1 teaspoon poppy seeds
- 3 tablespoons plus 1 teaspoon dried minced garlic
- 3 tablespoons plus 1 teaspoon dried minced onion
- 2 tablespoons coarse sea salt

DIRECTIONS

Mix all the ingredients together and store in an airtight container or spice jar. Shake well before using.

PER SERVING:

CALORIES: **29**	TOTAL CARBS: **2.4g**
FAT: **1.9g**	FIBER: **0.8g**
PROTEIN: **1g**	NET CARBS: **1.6g**

EVERYDAY SEASONING BLEND

MAKES: 6 tablespoons (½ teaspoon per serving) · **PREP TIME:** 5 minutes

I keep a batch of this blend on hand at all times. It is my go-to seasoning for everything from seafood to beef. I remember growing up, we always had a jar of Johnny's Seasoning Salt in the pantry. I seasoned everything with it. These days, I prefer to make my own blends. This one is perfect for those hectic weeknights when you want to cook something flavorful but are short on time. Just pick your protein and season away.

INGREDIENTS

- 2 tablespoons garlic powder
- 2 tablespoons onion powder
- 1 tablespoon sea salt
- 2 teaspoons ground black pepper
- 1 teaspoon Italian seasoning

DIRECTIONS

Mix all the ingredients together and store in an airtight container or spice jar. Shake well before using.

PER SERVING:
CALORIES: **3**   TOTAL CARBS: **0.7g**
FAT: **0g**   FIBER: **0.1g**
PROTEIN: **0.1g**   NET CARBS: **0.6g**

ACKNOWLEDGMENTS

To my husband, Jon: Thank you for being everything that is good and pure about this world, all wrapped up into one human. I love doing this crazy thing called life with you.

To my sister, Pamela: Thanks for being the best big sister a girl could ask for. I love you to the moon and back.

To Erin: Thanks for being my lifelong best friend and for always knowing exactly what to do and say. Also, thanks for not disowning me for being so absent while I was writing this book. I love you super-duper.

To Cristina, my internet bestie turned real-life forever friend: Thanks for always being a loyal friend, a shoulder to lean on, and the Thelma to my Louise. There is no one I would rather spend hours on the phone talking to. I love you!

To the whole crew at Victory Belt: Thank you for believing in me and continuing to allow me to live my dreams of creating and writing. There isn't a publisher out there that I would rather work with. Pam and Holly, thank you for helping to make my work better, without changing my voice. Without the both of you, my books would be full of large paragraphs strung together with commas.

To Bill Staley and Haley Mason: Thank you for the stunning cover photography on all my books. You always nail my vision and bring it to life. I truly appreciate you.

RECOMMENDED RESOURCES

Low-Carb, Keto, and Paleo Food Blogs

All Day I Dream About Food (alldayidreamaboutfood.com)

Beauty and the Bench Press (beautyandthebenchpress.com)

The Castaway Kitchen (thecastawaykitchen.com)

Ditch the Carbs (ditchthecarbs.com)

Gnom Gnom (gnom-gnom.com)

I Breathe I'm Hungry (ibreatheimhungry.com)

KetoDiet App (ketodietapp.com/blog)

Low Carb Maven (lowcarbmaven.com)

Peace, Love and Low Carb (peaceloveandlowcarb.com)

Sugar Free Mom (sugarfreemom.com)

Tasty Yummies (tasty-yummies.com)

Whole Kitchen Sink (wholekitchensink.com)

Resource Websites and Online Support

Balanced Bites (balancedbites.com)

Diet Doctor (dietdoctor.com)

Dr. Becky Campbell (drbeckycampbell.com)

Healthful Pursuit (healthfulpursuit.com)

Ketogenic Girl (ketogenicgirl.com)

Maria Mind Body Health (mariamindbodyhealth.com)

Peace Love and Low Carb Friends Support Group
(facebook.com/groups/peaceloveandlowcarbfriends)

Low-Carb and Keto Cookbooks

30-Minute Ketogenic Cooking by Kyndra D. Holley

Against All Grain by Danielle Walker

Craveable Keto by Kyndra D. Holley

The Everyday Ketogenic Kitchen by Carolyn Ketchum

The Keto Diet by Leanne Vogel

Keto Essentials by Vanessa Spina

Keto Happy Hour by Kyndra D. Holley

Keto for Life by Mellissa Sevigny

Keto Quick Start by Diane Sanfilippo

Made Whole by Cristina Curp

Simply Keto by Suzanne Ryan

Nutrition and Wellness Books

The 30-Day Thyroid Reset Plan by Dr. Becky Campbell

The Anti-Anxiety Diet by Ali Miller, RD

The Big Fat Surprise by Nina Teicholz

It Starts With Food by Dallas Hartwig and Mellissa Hartwig

Nutritional and Physical Degeneration by Weston A. Price, DDS

Paleo Principles by Sarah Ballantyne, PhD

Unconventional Medicine by Chris Kresser

Wired to Eat by Robb Wolf

Real-Food, Nutrition, and Keto Recipe Instagram Accounts

@alimillerrd

@dannyvega.ms

@dasrobbwolf

@dianesanfilippo

@doctor_health_ed

@dominic.dagostino.kt

@drbeckycampbell

@drmarkhyman

@foundmyfitness

@gnomgnom.yum

@grassfedgirl

@healthfulpursuit

@ibreatheimhungry

@ketodiet_app

@ketogenicgirl

@killinitketo

@lowcarbdashian

@mickeytrescott

@peaceloveandlowcarb

@realfoodwithdana

@ryanplowery

@steph_gaudreau

@sugarfreemom

@tastyyummies

@thecastawaykitchen

@thefittrainerswife

@wholekitchensink

RECIPE INDEX

BREAKFAST

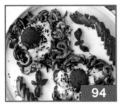
94

Baked Zucchini
Egg Nests

96

Blueberry Maple
Breakfast Sausage

98

Brussels Sprouts
and Bacon Hash

100

Vanilla Maple
Pancakes

102

Taco Scotch Eggs

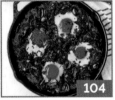
104

Italian Spaghetti
Squash Breakfast
Skillet

106

Sausage and Kale
Egg Muffins

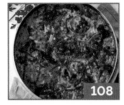
108

Caramelized Onion
and Pancetta
Frittata

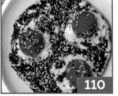
110

Everything
Chimichurri Eggs

112

Fried Radish and
Cauliflower
Hash Browns

114

Green Eggs and
Ham

116

Leftover Breakfast
Bowl

118

Light and Fluffy
Cinnamon Waffles

120

Pesto Baked Eggs

122

Pork Carnitas
Eggs Benedict

124

Chorizo-Spiced
Breakfast Sausage

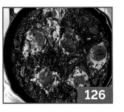
126

Spicy Sausage
Eggs in Purgatory

SNACKS AND STARTERS

Bacon-Wrapped Avocado Fries
130

Charcuterie Board
132

Strawberry Cucumber Mint Salsa
134

Kombucha Gummy Snacks
136

Crispy Baked Barbecue Dijon Wings
138

Cumin-Spiced Pecans
140

Restaurant-Style Salsa
142

Quick and Easy Chunky Guacamole
144

Dinner Rolls
146

Garlic Dill Sauerkraut
148

New Orleans–Style Olive Salad
150

Crispy Oven-Fried Pickles
152

Pickled Asparagus
154

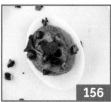
Spicy Fried Ham Deviled Eggs
156

Sugar-Free Dried Cranberries
158

Sweet and Savory Trail Mix
160

SOUPS AND SALADS

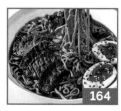
164 Beef Ramen

166 Cabbage Roll Soup

168 Chicken and "Rice" Soup

170 Easy Peasy Wonton-Less Soup

172 Lemony Greek Chicken Soup

174 Spicy Bloody Mary Tomato Soup

176 Supreme Pizza Soup

178 Clam Chowder with Bacon

180 Caesar Salad with Cumin-Spiced Pecans

182 Blackened Chicken Salad

184 Egg Salad Prosciutto Cups

186 Chicago Dog Salad

188 Crab Salad–Stuffed Avocados

190 Cranberry Almond Broccoli Salad

192 Cucumber Dill Broccoli Slaw

194 Kale and Cabbage Chopped Salad

196 Mediterranean Slaw

198 Pork Belly Wedge Salad

200 Ranch Chicken Salad Cups

MAIN DISHES

204

Sesame Chicken Egg Roll in a Bowl

206

Beef Ragout

208

Gingered Pepper Steak Skillet

210

Steak David

212

Sweet and Spicy Barbecue Ribs

214

Jalapeño Popper Chicken Salad

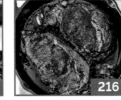
216

Garlic and Herb Skillet Rib-Eyes

218

Chicken Fajita Sheet Pan Meal

220

Beef Pot Roast

222

Easy Cuban Picadillo

224

Balsamic Shallot Pork Chops

226

Barbecue Pulled Pork Sandwiches

228

Beef and Broccoli Stir-Fry

230

Blackened Shrimp Fettuccine Alfredo

232

Braised Bratwurst and Cabbage

234

Chicken Adobo

236

Chili Lime Chicken with Avocado Salsa

238

Chorizo and Chicken Cauliflower Rice Paella

240

Crispy Five-Spice Chicken Thighs

242

Loco Moco

MAIN DISHES *(continued)*

244

Mini Meatloaves with Brussels Sprouts

246

Prosciutto Chicken and Broccoli Sheet Pan Meal

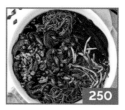
248

Dijon Paprika Pork Tenderloin

250

Garlic Ginger Pork Noodle Bowl

252

Crispy Pork Fried Cauliflower Rice

254

Grilled Steak with Chimichurri

256

Lemon and Herb Chicken Kebabs

258

Meatloaf Burgers

260

Peanut Chicken Zoodle Bowl

262

Puttanesca Pork Chops

264

Quick Braised Sausage and Peppers

266

Slow Cooker Crispy Pork Carnitas

268

Southwestern Pork Skillet

270

Spaghetti Squash with Tomato Meat Sauce

272

Spicy Citrus Meatballs

SIDE DISHES

276

"Cheesy" Herbed Roasted Cauliflower

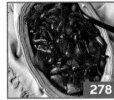
278

Bourbon Onions

280

Cauliflower Rice Pilaf

282

Roasted Mushrooms, Zucchini, and Eggplant

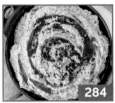
284

Roasted Garlic and Chive Cauliflower Puree

286

Green Beans with Toasted Hazelnuts and Dried Cranberries

288

"Goes with Everything" Garlicky Cauliflower Rice

290

Charred Lemon Pepper Broccolini

292

Oven-Roasted Vegetables

294

Drunken Mushrooms with Caramelized Onions

296

Lemon Pesto Cauliflower Rice with Artichokes

298

Maple Bacon Brussels Sprouts

300

Oven-Roasted Cabbage Steaks

302

Roasted Asparagus with Pancetta

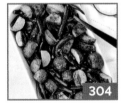
304

Salt and Vinegar Roasted Radishes and Green Beans

SWEET TREATS

308
Fruit and Nut Chocolates

310
Beignets

312
Chocolate Peanut Butter Coconut Fat Bombs

314
Fat-Boosted Chocolate Nut Butter

316
Chewy Double Chocolate Chip Cookies

318
Jumbo Chocolate Peanut Butter Cups

320
Lemon Blueberry Accidents

322
Flourless Chocolate Lava Cakes

324
Salted Caramel Chocolate Chip Cookies

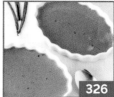
326
Vanilla Bean Custard

328
Mocha Chocolate Chip Muffins

330
Peanut Butter Chocolate Chip No-Bake Granola Squares

332
Pumpkin Spice Chocolate Chip Cookies

334
Snickerdoodles

336
Vanilla Chia Pudding

DRINKS AND COCKTAILS

340
Boosted Keto
Coffee

342
Golden Milk
Two Ways

344
Hot Cocoa

346
Almond Coconut
Milk

348
Cold Brew
Protein Shake

349
Lemon-Lime Soda

350
PB&J Smoothie

351
Shamrock Shake

352
Strawberry Basil
Bourbon Smash

353
Strawberry Mojito

354
Tart Cranberry
Cooler

355
Black Beauty

356
Cucumber Lime
Lavender Spritzer

BASICS

 360

Everything Buns

 362

Garlic and Herb Croutons

 364

Savory Nut-Free Breading Mix

 365

Garlic and Herb–Infused Olive Oil

 366

Whole Roasted Garlic

 367

Coconut Milk Whipped Cream

 368

Pickled Red Onions

 370

Bone Broth

 372

Bacon Fat Hollandaise

 374

Creamy Avocado Dressing

 375

Caesar Dressing

 376

Ranch Dressing

 377

Lemon Basil Vinaigrette

 378

Tomato Meat Sauce

 380

Dairy-Free Alfredo Sauce Two Ways

 384

Classic Marinara Sauce

 385

Ketchup

 386

Mayo Ten Ways

 388

Everything Bagel Aioli

 389

Lime Sriracha Aioli

Roasted Red
Pepper Aioli

Sweet and Spicy
Barbecue Sauce

Balsamic
Horseradish
Chimichurri

Crack Sauce

Peanut Sauce

Pistachio Pesto

Pumpkin Pie Spice

Fajita Seasoning

Blackening
Seasoning

Everything Bagel
Seasoning

Everyday
Seasoning Blend

GENERAL INDEX